"Him on the One Side and Me on the Other"

"HIM ON THE ONE SIDE AND ME ON THE OTHER"

The Civil War Letters of
Alexander Campbell,
79th New York Infantry Regiment
and James Campbell,
1st South Carolina Battalion

Terry A. Johnston, Jr.

University of South Carolina

© 1999 University of South Carolina

Published in Columbia, South Carolina, by the
University of South Carolina Press

Manufactured in the United States of America

03 02 01 00 99   5 4 3 2 1

Library of Congress Cataloging-in-Publication Data

Campbell, Alexander, 1837–1909.
   Him on the one side and me on the other : the Civil War letters of
Alexander Campbell, 79th New York Infantry Regiment and James
Campbell, 1st South Carolina Battalion / [edited by] Terry A. Johnston, Jr.
    p.   cm.
   Includes bibliographical references (p.) and index.
   ISBN 1-57003-265-3 (alk. paper)
   1. United States—History—Civil War, 1861–1865 Personal narratives.
2. Campbell, James, 1835–1905 Correspondence.   3. United States. Army.
New York Infantry Regiment, 79th (1859–1876)   4. New York (State)—
History—Civil War, 1861–1865 Personal narratives.   5. New York
(State)—History—Civil War, 1861–1865 Regimental histories.
6. Soldiers—New York (State) Correspondence.   7. Campbell, Alexander,
1837–1909 Correspondence.   8. Confederate States of America. Army.
South Carolina Infantry Battalion, 1st.   9. South Carolina—History—Civil
War, 1861–1865 Personal narratives.   10. South Carolina—History—Civil
War, 1861–1865 Prisoners and prisons.   11. Prisoners of war—United
States Correspondence.   I. Campbell, James, 1835–1905.   II. Johnston,
Terry A., 1970–   III. Title.
E523.5 79th .C36   1999
973.7'8'0922—dc21   99-6232

CONTENTS

ILLUSTRATIONS

MAPS

PREFACE

The South Carolina Department of Archives and History at Columbia is home to a fascinating collection of personal letters. The seventy-
nine letters of the Campbell Family Papers are the surviving Civil War
correspondence of Alexander and James Campbell, brothers who fought
on opposing sides during our country's greatest conflict. Taken together,
these letters provide an excellent illustration of how the American Civil
War, both figuratively and literally, pitted brother against brother.

Sixty of the letters were written by Alexander Campbell and trace his
wartime service in the 79th New York Infantry Regiment, known as the
Highlanders, from the time of his enlistment at the war's inception to the
resignation of his commission in mid-1863. During his service in the
army, Alexander Campbell experienced both the intensity of battle and
the monotony of camp life; personal accounts of the engagements in
which he participated—Bull Run, Secessionville, and Chantilly—
alternate with tales of picket duty, drill, and the rigors of soldiering.
Campbell's letters to his wife, Jane, at their home in New York City capture these experiences in detail, providing readers with a taste of what it
was like to be a soldier in the Union army during the Civil War.

This is not to say that Alexander Campbell was the typical Union
soldier. There was arguably no such person. A journeyman stonecutter
prior to the war, Alexander Campbell was first and foremost a loving
husband and father. Although he became disheartened and disillusioned
with the Northern war effort, his loyalty to family never faltered. Thus,
these letters not only shed light upon military events that occurred over
130 years ago, but they also remind us of the human element of the Civil
War—fathers and brothers voluntarily leaving their families and coping
with their decisions to do so.

Perhaps the most interesting part of Alexander's correspondence is
his occasional discussion of his brother James. James Campbell, four

years Alexander's senior, lived before the Civil War in Charleston, South Carolina, where he worked as both a drayman and a clerk while serving in the Union Light Infantry, a predominantly Scottish volunteer militia company. As his early letters to Jane express, Alexander Campbell was uncertain of his brother's military status during the early months of the war. He would eventually discover that James had entered into Confederate service—and, ironically, would face him in combat during the June 1862 engagements on James Island, South Carolina.

James Campbell's Civil War experience, as recounted by his nineteen surviving wartime letters, differed significantly from that of his brother Alexander. A soldier in the 1st South Carolina Infantry Battalion (also known as the Charleston Battalion), James Campbell was taken prisoner after the fierce July 1863 engagement at Battery Wagner on Morris Island, South Carolina. From the time of his capture until the end of the conflict in April 1865, James Campbell sat out the war in three different Northern prison camps—Johnson's Island, Point Lookout, and Fort Delaware—where he experienced extreme loneliness, discomfort, and frustration. During his imprisonment, James, a lifelong bachelor, wrote to his brother Alexander, who, by the time of James's imprisonment, had resigned his commission and resumed his life as a civilian in New York City. James's letters from prison, which commence in November 1863, continue through the end of the war and cease in May 1865, when James was released and returned to Charleston.

Compared to the frequent and expressive wartime correspondence of Alexander to his wife, the surviving letters of James Campbell are significantly fewer in number and often lack detail regarding his Civil War experiences—all but two of James's letters were written from Northern prisons, where officials strictly regulated the content and length of prisoners' communications with the outside world. Still, though his correspondence from prison was censored, James Campbell's few surviving Civil War letters are no less fascinating or important than those written by his brother Alexander; in fact, two of James's letters—a prewar letter penned at the time of the 1860 presidential election and a note sent by flag of truce to Alexander after they fought on opposing sides at the June 1862 Battle of Secessionville—are arguably the most substantive missives of the entire Campbell collection. We learn more about James Campbell's commitment to the Southern cause in these two letters than we learn of Alexander's allegiance to the North in his entire body of correspondence.

In the end, the entirety of James Campbell's surviving correspondence to Alexander brings the nature of the brothers' relationship into full view. Although these two men held divergent ideological and political beliefs and soldiered on opposing sides of a vigorously fought struggle, the familial bond that linked Alexander and James Campbell not only survived the Civil War but was apparently strengthened by it.

Much has been written about Civil War soldiers. For years, historians have attempted to reinhabit the soldiers' minds in order to determine their motivations for joining the struggle, the reasons behind their willingness or unwillingness to continue to fight, and their feelings toward and perceptions of the enemy. Thoroughly documented works have been produced explaining the lifestyles and experiences of those who donned either blue or gray between the years 1861–1865; historians Gerald Linderman, James McPherson, Reid Mitchell, James Robertson, Jr., Bell Wiley, and many others have described to the modern reader what it was like for Civil War soldiers to have experienced combat, lived in army camps, eaten military rations, suffered from various sicknesses, been treated by army physicians in army hospitals, and endured life in prison camps.[1] All such credible works rely heavily, if not exclusively, upon the diaries and letters of those who lived and fought during the Civil War.

In addition to these efforts to synthesize surviving wartime writings into comprehensive analyses of the social history of Civil War troops, other Civil War historians and enthusiasts have chosen to edit individual soldiers' letters for publication. The advantage of the latter efforts is twofold. First, the reader is able to follow individual soldiers throughout their service in either the Union or Confederate army, witnessing their triumphs, tragedies, boredoms, and frustrations as relayed in often vivid terms to friends and loved ones. Second, soldiers' letters and diaries, whether written from camp (be it army, hospital, or prison) or at the

---

1. Bell Irvin Wiley, *The Life of Johnny Reb: The Common Soldier of the Confederacy* (Indianapolis: Bobbs-Merrill, 1943) and *The Life of Billy Yank: The Common Soldier of the Union* (Indianapolis: Bobbs-Merrill, 1952); James I. Robertson, Jr., *Soldiers Blue and Gray* (Columbia: University of South Carolina Press, 1988); James M. McPherson, *For Cause and Comrades: Why Men Fought in the Civil War* (New York: Oxford University Press, 1997) and *Battle Cry of Freedom: The Civil War Era* (New York: Oxford University Press, 1988); Gerald Linderman, *Embattled Courage: The Experience of Combat in the American Civil War* (New York: Free Press, 1987); Reid Mitchell, *The Vacant Chair: The Northern Soldier Leaves Home* (New York: Oxford University Press, 1993) and *Civil War Soldiers: Their Expectations and Their Experiences* (New York: Viking, 1988).

front, are generally more reliable historical sources than soldiers' wartime reminiscences, which were often written years later and provided their authors with the opportunity to rewrite history according to their own wishes.

Although a single, edited collection of Civil War letters cannot offer an analysis of the life of the Civil War soldier as comprehensively as do the monographs of Linderman, McPherson, Mitchell, Robertson, and Wiley, some come close.[2] Not all Civil War soldiers spent time in a prison camp, suffered in an army hospital, or even took part in a major military engagement; as a result, no collection of soldiers' letters reflects the entirety of possible experiences encountered by Civil War troops. Even so, edited soldiers' letters are an invaluable resource for the modern historian—the true nature of wartime separation and suffering experienced by Civil War soldiers and their families is almost palpable when viewed through the writings of actual participants. If anything, the absence of certain experiences from various collections of letters reinforces the fact that there was no "average" or "typical" soldier of the Civil War; even men who fought in the same engagement or lived in the same tent or camp had a collective Civil War experience that was necessarily singular. This singularity of experience is best captured through the largely uncensored words of individual soldiers.

The wartime letters of the Campbell brothers are of additional value to the Civil War scholar and enthusiast. Alexander and James Campbell, born and raised in Scotland, were among the substantial body of foreign and foreign-born men who served as soldiers in the American Civil War. Historians estimate that foreigners constituted nearly 25 percent of Union troops and that tens of thousands of foreigners fought for the Confederacy.[3] Surprisingly little has been written to date about the ser-

2. For examples, see the following works: John Michael Priest, ed., *From New Bern to Fredericksburg: Captain James Wren's Diary* (Shippensburg: White Mane Publishing Company, 1990); Robert Hunt Rhodes, ed., *All for the Union: The Civil War Diary and Letters of Elisha Hunt Rhodes* (New York: Orion Books, 1985); Guy R. Everson and Edward W. Simpson, Jr., eds., *Far, Far from Home: The Wartime Letters of Dick and Tally Simpson, Third South Carolina Volunteers* (New York: Oxford University Press, 1994); J. Roderick Heller III and Carolynn Ayres Heller, eds., *The Confederacy Is on Her Way up the Spout: Letters to South Carolina, 1861–1864* (Athens: The University of Georgia Press, 1992).

3. Ella Lonn, *Foreigners in the Union Army and Navy* (Baton Rouge: Louisiana State University Press, 1951), 581–82; McPherson, *Battle Cry of Freedom*, 606; Ella Lonn, *Foreigners in the Confederacy* (Chapel Hill: The University of North Carolina Press, 1940), 218–20.

vice of this nonnative element of citizen-soldiery. Furthermore, what has been written about these men has focused largely upon German and Irish Americans, who together constituted the vast majority of immigrants that donned either the blue or the gray. The letters of Alexander and James Campbell serve to chronicle the participation of Scottish Americans during the war, a role that was as colorful as it was significant.

In the end, however, it is the fraternal story relayed by the letters of Alexander and James Campbell, two brothers separated by war, that makes this collection so noteworthy. In an attempt to describe the widespread and deep-rooted attraction many Americans have to the Civil War, historian James McPherson offered several explanations, the most significant of which was "the poignancy of [the Civil War as] a brothers' war. . . . In hundreds of individual cases," wrote McPherson, "the war did pit brother against brother, cousin against cousin, even father against son. . . . Who can resist the painful human interest of stories like these— particularly when they are recounted in the letters and diaries of Civil War protagonists . . . ?" The wartime letters of Alexander and James Campbell convey one such extraordinary story, "preserved through generations and published for all to read."[4]

---

4. James M. McPherson, "A War That Never Goes Away." *American Heritage* 41 (March 1990): 42.

ACKNOWLEDGMENTS

Many considerate individuals provided me with assistance throughout the course of my work on the Campbell letters. I hope to mention them all here and sincerely apologize if I fail to do so.

My work on the Campbell letters began nearly four years ago, while I was a student in the master's program in history at Clemson University. My thanks to Professor Carol Bleser, who directed my thesis and instructed me on the craft of editing, and to professors William Steirer and Thomas Kuehn, also members of my thesis committee, for their support and contributions.

Patrick McCawley, reference archivist at the South Carolina Department of Archives and History, was an invaluable asset. His availability and knowledge of archival holdings made my many trips to Columbia considerably more productive.

In Connecticut, Dione Longley, director of the Middlesex County Historical Society, and Judith Ellen Johnson, reference librarian and genealogist at the Connecticut Historical Society, spent much time tracking down useful information on the Campbell and Ralston families. I could not have done a better job myself and am grateful for their efforts.

Roger Long, foremost expert on the prison for Confederate officers at Johnson's Island, Ohio, provided me with helpful research leads as well as access to his own personal material and knowledge.

Patrick Brennan, fellow Civil War enthusiast and the leading authority on the June 1862 campaign for James Island, South Carolina, was of great assistance. Thanks to Pat and Jim Coudal for creating the maps.

I am also grateful to the following persons who offered support and/or assistance: William A. Beard, Charlotte Cowe, Roger Duce, George Farr, J. Palmer Gaillard, Dr. Diana Henderson, Lynn and Richard Leveck, Suzanne Linder, Bud Livingston, Greg Macaluso, Michael McAfee, and William Vann.

Acknowledgments

Thanks to the numerous research assistants and reference librarians at the Robert Muldrow Cooper Library and the Strom Thurmond Institute at Clemson University, the U.S. Army Military History Institute, the National Archives, the New York Historical Society, the New York State Archives, the South Carolina Historical Society, the South Carolina Department of Archives and History, the Center for Archival Collections at Bowling Green State University, the Fort Delaware Society, and the Probate Courts of Colleton County, South Carolina, and Cook County, Illinois.

Lastly, thanks to my sister, Jenny, who took the time to read and correct numerous drafts of this work and, along with my parents, graciously endured listening to me talk about "Civil War stuff" for the past four years.

EDITORIAL PRACTICES

Whether composed in pencil or ink, smudged by sweat or seared by flame, written hurriedly or carefully, the original letters of Alexander and James Campbell necessarily remain more powerfully indicative of the nature of the brothers' Civil War experiences than do these published counterparts. For obvious reasons, the following presentation of their letters, edited for clarity and typed out of necessity, cannot capture the essence of their authors as well as the originals.

The first step in the editorial process is transcription. Though partial transcriptions exist alongside several of the original letters in the Campbell Family Papers, I chose to make my own transcriptions of all letters, which I then compared to the originals on three different occasions.

In editing the letters of Alexander and James Campbell, I have sought to make as few editorial interventions as possible. With two exceptions, I chose not to correct the Campbell brothers' frequent misspellings, unless their misspellings were, in my estimation, potentially confusing to the reader. In those cases, I either provided the correction directly after the word in question or introduced the missing letter(s) within the word itself. These and all other editorial intrusions are marked by brackets [ ]. The two misspelled words I chose to silently correct throughout the text were "off" and "too," the former almost always spelled with a single "f," the latter with one "o."

I grouped the letters into chapters, provided introductions and titles for each new chapter, and annotated the letters wherever I thought the reader could use additional information.

I silently introduced the necessary and appropriate punctuation and capitalization to divide the text of the letters into comprehensible sentences. In addition, I introduced paragraphs for easier reading (most of the letters contain page-long paragraphs). I also standardized the position of both the headings and closings of the letters to provide a consistent presentation.

Other minor changes were made. For instance, I eliminated many errant markings, most of which misleadingly resembled commas and, thus, unnecessarily slowed down the reader. Along the same lines, I silently changed the Campbell brothers' occasional use of brackets [ ] to parenthesis ( ) in order to distinguish them from my editorial markings. I eliminated the brothers' sporadic use of superscripts for the sake of consistency. In several places where Alexander Campbell crossed out an insightful word, I restored the word with a slash through it (e.g., ~~word~~); I also removed duplicate words and phrases. I placed words which the Campbell brothers underlined in italics and replaced their hand-written ampersands "+" with "&."

Alexander Campbell's letters were written on stationery that was folded in such a way as to resemble a modern-day greeting card. He began all letters on the outer face, continued on the left inside page, then the right inside page, and, if necessary, concluded on the back (outer) page. Although many of his letters were written on a folded piece of plain paper, several were written on official stationary containing a patriotic print and/or slogan. These patriotic prints were positioned in the upper left corner of the outer face of Campbell's letters. Unfortunately, some, but not all, of these prints were carefully cut out by someone at a later date. As a result, the left inside page of these letters, which contained a full page of writing, now displays a gap the size of the missing print (between one and two inches square). In some such instances, I have attempted to reconstruct the missing words (which, of course, I have placed in brackets); in letters where the gap is too large to reconstruct, I have inserted the words "cut out" in brackets (i.e., [cut out]).

I alone am responsible for any errors in the transcription and/or editing of the following letters.

INTRODUCTION

In the early 1850s, James and Alexander Campbell and their three siblings, John, Peter, and Ann, immigrated to the United States from their native country, Scotland. Whether they immigrated simultaneously is not documented, and their motivations for leaving their homeland are not known. Regardless, the move from Scotland effectively separated the Campbell clan—John and James settled in Georgia and South Carolina, respectively, and Alexander, Peter, and Ann established themselves in New York City and vicinity. For two of the Campbell children, James and Alexander, this separation proved to be ill-fated. Not only did James and Alexander Campbell become soldiers on opposing sides of the Civil War, but, in June 1862, they ironically found themselves "face to face" as "Bitter enemies in the Battle field" at Secessionville, South Carolina.[1]

Little is known about James's and Alexander's life in Scotland. They were the youngest of seven children born to John and Clementina (McLaren) Campbell; both were born in Crieff, Perthshire—a hamlet situated on the "Highland Line," the intangible division between Highland and Lowland Scotland—James on 6 May 1835, Alexander on 20 August

---

1. Pension Case File of Alexander Campbell, wc 686–894, Record Group 15, Records of the Veterans Administration, National Archives, Washington, D.C. (hereafter cited as Pension Case File of Alexander Campbell); James Campbell to Alexander Campbell, June 1862, Campbell Family Papers 1860–1886, Private Papers Collection, South Carolina Department of Archives and History (hereafter cited as CFP-SCDAH).

1837.[2] All of the Campbell children seem to have lived in Crieff until their departure for America.[3] Though no clear records exist, it appears that John and Clementina died in Scotland before 1851, perhaps providing their children reason to relocate to America, a move which nineteen-year-old James and seventeen-year-old Alexander made in 1854.[4]

James Campbell settled in Charleston at a time when the city's immigrant population was burgeoning. Though the population of South Carolina as a whole included less than 2 percent foreign-born residents in 1860, Charleston, like other cities in the Old South, had much higher levels. Foreign-born adult males (age eighteen and older) constituted 45 percent of Charleston's adult, white, male population in 1850; by 1860, the number had risen to 49 percent.[5]

James Campbell, like most immigrants who settled in the urban South, entered the lower ranks of Charleston society. He initially found work in the city as a drayman and was "noted for his rectitude and reliability."[6] Drayage, like other unskilled positions, was increasingly shunned by native-born white Charlestonians as unworthy and degrading and was performed largely by black laborers. In the 1850s, however, blacks in drayage and other unskilled jobs were losing work to new immigrants, mostly Irish and Germans, who were flooding the city's urban workforce.[7]

Despite his meager beginnings, James Campbell rose in status in Charleston, or at least within its Scottish community. He eventually found employment as a clerk, marking his departure from the ranks of the menial laborers and entrance into the growing commercial middle class of the city.[8] He also joined the Union Light Infantry, a largely Scot-

---

2. Old Parish Register Index of Birth/Baptisms for Kilmadock and Crieff Parishes, Pethshire (1839–1830); Pension Case File of Alexander Campbell. Alexander Porteous, *The History of Crieff, from the Earliest Times to the Dawn of the Twentieth Century* (Edinburgh and London: Oliphant, Anderson & Ferrier, 1912), xi.

3. Pension case file of Alexander Campbell.

4. 1900 Federal Population Census for Charleston County, South Carolina, Enumeration District 110, sheet no. 21, line 73; 1900 Federal Population Census for Middlesex County, Connecticut, Enumeration District 284, sheet no. 7, line 4.

5. Jason H. Silverman, "Stars, Bars and Foreigners: The Immigrant and the Making of the Confederacy." *Journal of Confederate History* 1 (Fall 1988): 268; Randall M. Miller, "The Enemy Within: Some Effects of Foreign Immigrants on Antebellum Southern Cities." *Southern Studies* 29 (Spring 1985): 33.

6. *Charleston News and Courier*, 4 March 1907.

7. Ira Berlin and Herbert G. Gutman, "Natives and Immigrants, Free Men and Slaves: Urban Workingmen in the Antebellum American South." *The American Historical Review* 88 (December 1983): 1180–87; Miller, "The Enemy Within," 34.

8. 1860 Federal Population Census, City of Charleston, Ward 3, p. 257b, line 11; Miller, "The Enemy Within," 42–43.

tish volunteer militia company, and by 1861 had risen to the rank of sergeant.[9]

The Union Light Infantry, also referred to as the Scotch Company or the Charleston Highlanders, was one of the oldest militia companies in Charleston, having been formed by the city's Scottish citizens in 1806.[10] Members of the Union Light Infantry were proud of both their Scottish and South Carolinian associations, as reflected in their company banner, which bore the Thistle of Scotland on one side and the Arms of South Carolina on the other.[11]

While James was beginning to establish himself in Charleston, his brother Alexander was in the process of putting down roots in New York City. Shortly after his arrival, Alexander, known as Sandy to family and friends, found employment in stonecutting, an occupation whose largely immigrant workforce earned wages two to three times higher than those offered in Britain.[12] Stonecutting, like many other building trades in 1850s New York City, was predominantly seasonal work. As a journeyman stonecutter, Alexander was able to travel to find employment elsewhere when work was scarce or wages were low, which he did in the late 1850s. Alexander learned his trade well, receiving "a thorough schooling in all branches of stone cutting and building stone work," and would eventually, before the Civil War, cut the first stone laid in the construction of the Terrace Bridge in Central Park.[13]

Sometime before 1856, Alexander Campbell settled as a boarder in the New York City residence of fellow Scots Matthew and Elizabeth Ralston upon the recommendation of one of their sons, James Ralston, with whom Alexander worked.[14] The Ralston family hailed from Wigtown, Scotland, and had arrived in America in 1853. In Wigtown, Matthew and several of his sons had worked as agricultural laborers. In New York, Matthew worked as a cart driver, while three of his sons—James,

---

9. *Charleston Daily Courier*, 28 June 1861.
10. *Charleston Daily Courier*, 15 August 1861.
11. *Charleston Daily Courier*, 3 January 1861.
12. Robert Ernst, *Immigrant Life in New York City, 1825–1863* (New York: King Crown Press, 1949), 215; Kenneth T. Jackson, ed., *The Encyclopedia of New York City* (New Haven: Yale University Press, 1995), 1053.
13. Ernst, *Immigrant Life*, 75; Pension Case File of Alexander Campbell; quote is from H. F. Donlan, ed., *The Middletown Tribune, Souvenir Edition: An Illustrated and Descriptive Exposition of Middletown, Portland, Cromwell, East Berlin, and Higganum* (Middletown, Conn.: E. F. Bigelow, 1896), 29.
14. Pension Case File of Alexander Campbell.

Matthew Jr. and William—found employment as stonecutters.[15] Alexander Campbell's stay with the Ralstons was brief; by 1857, Alexander had traveled southward in search of stonecutting work and, like many New York City immigrants, found it in Charleston, the adopted hometown of his brother James.[16]

In Charleston, Alexander Campbell worked on the construction of the new U.S. Customs House at 200 East Bay Street (which, due to the Civil War, was not completed until 1879).[17] In addition to his work on the Customs House, Alexander, like his older brother James, served in the local militia, probably with the Highland Guard of Charleston, another company of Scots.[18] After two years in Charleston, Alexander Campbell left his job, his new friends, and his brother James and returned to New York City where, on 21 April 1859, he wed Matthew and Elizabeth Ralston's fifteen-year-old daughter, Jane, in the Jane Street Presbyterian Church.[19]

Alexander Campbell and Jane Ralston Campbell, born 1 May 1843 in Wigtown, Scotland, continued to live in New York City after their marriage. Like many immigrants, they were drawn to an area in the city populated by others of the same nationality; in 1860 they shared a seven-family tenement in West Manhattan's Twentieth Ward, which had a substantial Scottish population. Alexander and Jane's first child, John, was born in February 1860.[20] Sometime before the outbreak of the Civil War, Alexander joined the 79th Regiment, New York State Militia

---

15. 1851 census for Sorbie Parish, Wigtownshire, Scotland (1851/Sorbie/897/ED3/Sch27-2 Congleton Cottage), New Register House, Edinburgh, Scotland; 1860 Federal Population Census for New York City, 9th Ward, District 3, p. 1069.

16. Randall M. Miller, "Immigrants in the Old South," in *Dictionary of American Immigration History,* ed. Francesco Cordasco (Metuchen, N.J.: The Scarecrow Press, Inc., 1990), 367; Pension Case File of Alexander Campbell.

17. Pension Case File of Alexander Campbell; Robert P. Stockton, ed., *Information for Guides of Historic Charleston* (Charleston: Arts and History Commission, 1975), 139.

18. The Scottish Guard of Charleston, also known as the Highland Guard, an apparently short-lived Scottish volunteer militia company that, along with the more prominent Union Light Infantry, held its meetings in one of the lower rooms of St. Andrew's Hall, home of the St. Andrew's Society of Charleston. James Campbell to Alexander Campbell, 28 September 1860, CFP-SCDAH; *Scottish American Journal* (New York), 5 February 1859; J. H. Easterby, *History of the St. Andrew's Society of Charleston, South Carolina, 1729–1929* (Charleston: Walker, Evans & Cogswell Company, 1929), 74–75.

19. Pension Case File of Alexander Campbell.

20. 1860 Federal Population Census for New York City, 20th Ward, District 2, p. 323; Ernst, *Immigrant Life,* 40–44, 194. In later years, Alexander and Jane would relocate to lower Manhattan's Greenwich Village (where the Ralston family resided), another area with a large Scottish population.

(N.Y.S.M.).[21] The 79th N.Y.S.M., formed in the early months of 1859, was composed largely of Scots or men of Scottish descent.[22] Like the Union Light Infantry of Charleston, the 79th N.Y.S.M. was more social club than military organization, affording its members the opportunity to meet fellow Scots, display their patriotism and ethnic pride, enjoy various recreational activities, and exhibit their martial skills and colorful uniforms (based on those worn by contemporary British Highland regiments) at numerous balls, parades, and ceremonies.[23] Little could Alexander have known that his service in the 79th N.Y.S.M. would, much like his brother James's involvement in the Union Light Infantry, facilitate, if not ensure, his participation as a soldier in the upcoming conflict.

As the presidential election of 1860 approached, America's sectional hostilities were intensifying at an alarming pace. On 23 April 1860, the Democratic Party formally split along sectional lines over the issue of slavery: Southern Democrats insisted on a platform supporting the protection of slavery in the territories and nominated John C. Breckinridge as their presidential candidate; Northern Democrats, believing that the issue of slavery should be decided by the territories' citizens, selected Illinois senator Stephen A. Douglas, an advocate of popular (or "squatter") sovereignty. Divisiveness within the Democratic Party made the election of Abraham Lincoln, the Republican candidate who opposed the extension of slavery into the territories, a near certainty.

By the time of the election, James Campbell had become "thoroughly identified with the best interests of the home of his adoption and of his choice."[24] His sectional loyalties are made clear in his 28 Septem-

---

21. Although no concrete evidence of this exists, Campbell's history of service in the militia from his days in Charleston, coupled with fact that he went to war in possession of a regimental kilt (which, due to problems of procurement at the outbreak of the war, were possessed mainly by original members of the 79th N.Y.S.M.), suggests that Campbell joined the 79th prior to the outbreak of the Civil War.

22. John P. Severin and Frederick P. Todd, "79th Regiment, New York State Militia, 1860–1861." *Military Collector and Historian* 8 (1956): 20; Michael J. McAfee, "79th Regiment, New York State Militia." *Military Images Magazine* 11 (Sept./Oct. 1989): 28.

23. Several additional advantages to joining the 79th N.Y.S.M. were relayed in a recruitment advertisement in the New York City-based *Scottish American Journal*: members were exempted from jury duty and afforded the opportunity of "manly athletic exercise to develop those peculiarities—the boast of Scotsmen—while it will enable them to distinguish themselves in their adopted country by the exhibition of their ancient military fame for excellence in this chivalrous pastime." *Scottish American Journal*, 23 October 1858.

24. *Charleston News and Courier*, 4 March 1907.

ber letter to Alexander, in which he discussed events in Charleston, family matters, and, as evidenced by the following excerpt, national politics:

> You ask me who our State will go for in the presidental Allection. The Legislature vots for the president in this state but the people send the candidates there who will vote for there party. Breckinbrige will get this state and he will have a magority in all the southern States except Mireland and perhaps Missouri. But unless there will be a understanding between the Dougelas & Breckinbrige parties in your state [and] pensylvina and New Jersia and run a combined ticket Linkin will be our next presidant. If he is defeted & NY & Pa it will go to the house and som of the others may have a chance.
>
> If I had a Million votes at my command Breckinbrige wold have them all for Douglass is getting up some [n]ew scame about Squatter Soveranity that dos not give every State the Same chance. The southe payes her revinew to support the general govermant as well as the North and why not the south have the same prevelages & protection in the Teritorees as the north has. As for Black Republicans they are below scruteny for there platform has not got a single constitunal claus in its whole forse. And my belief goes further for my humble opinion is that Douglas in a mear towel in the hands of the republicans for to plunge our happy country into a sivel war for ther in nothing more certain then that the South will never submit to Abolishion prinsables.[25]

James Campbell's words proved prophetic: Lincoln won the election to become the 16th president of the United States. Six weeks later, on 20 December 1860, the South Carolina legislature unanimously passed an ordinance of secession, refusing to submit to the rule of "Black Republicans."

Eight days after the ordinance was issued, South Carolina commissioners unsuccessfully petitioned outgoing president Buchanan for the removal of United States troops from forts within the state, the most prominent of which were located in Charleston and Charleston Harbor. In the meantime, the 4th Brigade, South Carolina Militia (which included James Campbell's militia company, the Union Light Infantry),

---

25. James Campbell to Alexander Campbell, 28 September 1860, CFP-SCDAH.

"the only considerable body of troops thoroughly organized and disciplined in the State," was called into temporary service to prevent Federal reinforcement of forts in the vicinity of Charleston and to defend Charleston in the event of hostilities. From the time of Lincoln's election to the outbreak of the war, James Campbell and the rest of the 4th Brigade were continuously active in the service of Charleston and vicinity.[26]

During the last week in December 1860, various militia companies of the 4th Brigade, acting under order of the governor, began to seize control of coastal islands and forts in Charleston Harbor. On 30 December, the United States Arsenal in Charleston was surrendered to a detachment from the Union Light Infantry, which, after a two-day siege of the arsenal, marched into the structure in the "most discreet and forbearing manner," demanding its capitulation "in the name of the State of South Carolina."[27] Members of the Union Light Infantry took down the flag at the arsenal and raised the Palmetto flag of South Carolina in its place, marking, in the words of a member of the Charleston Highlanders, their status as "soldiers of a new State."[28]

In the months that followed, South Carolina made further preparations for the expected conflict with the Northern states. Men responded quickly to calls for twelve-month enlistees; by April 1861, approximately 12,000 South Carolinians were "ready to meet hostilities." These new troops were not, however, immediately called to the coast, and militiamen remained the primary defenders of Charleston and Charleston Harbor until the start of the war.[29]

The Civil War commenced in April 1861 with the Confederate attack on Fort Sumter, where Federal troops in Charleston Harbor refused to yield to Southern demands of surrender. After two days of heavy bombardment, the Federal garrison capitulated, and an instantly

---

26. Michael E. Stauffer, *South Carolina's Antebellum Militia* (Columbia: South Carolina Department of Archives and History, 1991), 21.

27. Samuel Wylie Crawford, *The Genesis of the Civil War: The Story of Sumter, 1860–1861* (New York: Charles L. Webster & Company, 1887), 121–22; *War of the Rebellion: Official Records of the Union and Confederate Armies* (Washington: Government Printing Office, 1880–1901), Series 1, vol. 1, 5–9 (hereafter cited as O.R.).

28. *Charleston Daily Courier*, 3 January 1861.

29. William James Rivers, *Rivers' Account of the Raising of Troops in South Carolina for State and Confederate Service, 1861–1865* (Columbia: The Bryan Printing Co., State Printers, 1899), 9–12; John P. Thomas, "The Raising of Troops in South Carolina for State and Confederate Service." *Reports and Resolutions of the General Assembly of the State of South Carolina* 1 (1900): 23.

galvanized North and South mobilized for war. On 29 April, fifteen days after the fall of Fort Sumter, the 4th Brigade, South Carolina Militia, having served four months "in State service, on harbor duty and on Morris, James, Johns and Wadmalaw Islands," was finally relieved and soon after ordered to report to the adjutant general of South Carolina, in Charleston.[30] James Campbell returned to his home in the energized Southern city, where he remained an active member of the Union Light Infantry until he and his company entered Confederate service in March 1862.

In the wake of the Confederate bombardment of Fort Sumter, President Lincoln requested that 75,000 militiamen enter into three-month national service, a call that was eagerly answered by multitudes of Northern men, including Alexander Campbell.[31] On 18 April, three days after Lincoln's appeal, the officers and enlisted men of the 79th N.Y.S.M. unanimously voted to volunteer and stand "ready to march at a moment's warning to defend the flag of the Union."[32] One the first units in the state to offer its services for the war, the 79th N.Y.S.M. was initially undersized and, consequently, unqualified for Federal service—at the time of their vote, the regiment consisted of 300 men in 6 companies (a full-strength regiment was to contain 10 companies and number 1,000 men). The men of the 79th "were doomed to disappointment," as over the next three weeks they watched other militia companies that were accepted in their place depart New York City for the war.[33] Determined to go to war as a unit, the regiment recruited vigorously until roughly 400 men were added to its ranks. On 13 May 1861, the 79th N.Y.S.M., including Alexander Campbell and his brothers-in-law, James and Matthew Ralston, was finally accepted and mustered into Federal service.[34]

The frustrations of the 79th New York did not, however, end on 13 May. President Lincoln's call for 75,000 ninety-day volunteers had been

---

30. Stauffer, *South Carolina's Antebellum Militia*, 22–23; Rivers, *Rivers' Account of the Raising of Troops in South Carolina*, 12–15; O.R., Series 1, vol. 53, 158; Thomas, "Raising of Troops," 69.
31. McPherson, *Battle Cry of Freedom*, 274–75.
32. *Scottish American Journal* (New York), 25 April 1861; *New York Herald*, 18 April 1861.
33. *Scottish American Journal*, 16 May 1861.
34. William Todd, *The Seventy-Ninth Highlanders: New York Volunteers, 1861–1865* (Albany: Press of Brandow, Barton and Co., 1886), 1–3; Joseph G. Bilby, "Blue Bonnets Over the Border: The 79th New York Highlanders in the Civil War." *Military Images Magazine* 3 (July-August 1984): 5.

met before the Highlanders were fully equipped and sufficiently sized to be accepted for service. As a result, the men of the 79th New York entered Federal service under the terms of the president's second call for troops, issued 3 May 1861, in which Lincoln requested an additional 42,000 volunteers to serve for three years—not three months—or the duration of the war. Their services finally accepted, the Highlanders spent another frustrating three weeks in New York City waiting for equipment and going through last minute drills.[35] On 2 June 1861, twenty-three-year-old Alexander Campbell and the 79th New York at last departed for the war.

During his two years of service with the 79th New York, Alexander Campbell participated in more battlefield defeats than victories. Shortly after engaging in the humiliating Union defeat at the First Battle of Bull Run on 21 July 1861, where the Highlanders suffered among the highest number of casualties per regiment on either side, the men of the 79th New York, weary of war and dissatisfied with perceived mistreatment, mutinied at their camp near Washington, D.C. Their insubordination, swiftly quashed by regular army troops, brought opprobrious results— by order of commanding general George B. McClellan, the 79th was ceremoniously stripped of its colors.

After the Highlanders had sufficiently atoned for their insubordination with good behavior and a solid performance during a skirmish with the enemy at Lewinsville, Virginia, in September 1861, their regimental colors were restored, and Alexander Campbell was appointed to color sergeant. In October 1861, the 79th New York, as part of Union general Thomas W. Sherman's expeditionary force, was transported to Port Royal, South Carolina. For the next nine months, the Highlanders remained on the coast of South Carolina, moving steadily closer to Charleston, the cradle city of secession. The Union offensive against Charleston ended in costly defeat at the 16 June 1862 Battle of Secessionville on James Island. The Highlanders were sent back to Virginia in time to participate, as part of the IX Corps of the Army of the Potomac, in Gen. John Pope's failed campaign against Gen. Robert E. Lee's Army of Northern Virginia. After the Union's crushing defeat at the Second Battle of Bull Run on 29–30 August 1862, Alexander Campbell and the 79th New York would play a key role in the rearguard action at the Battle of Chantilly, on 1 September, where Campbell was shot in the left calf while carrying the regimental colors.

---

35. *New York Herald,* 31 May 1861.

Following a brief stay at Emory Hospital in Washington, D.C., Campbell was sent to New York City's Bellevue Hospital, where he remained for three months. In January 1863, Alexander returned to the camp of the 79th New York in Virginia as second lieutenant of Company G, having been promoted to that position in October 1862. Campbell accompanied his regiment in March 1863 on yet another expedition, this time to Kentucky, where the Highlanders were stationed to protect railroad lines against possible attack by Confederate guerrillas. On 29 April 1863, Alexander Campbell, still plagued by his ailing leg, resigned his commission and returned home to New York City to resume his life as a civilian.

Alexander's brother James continued his service in the Union Light Infantry after the bombardment of Fort Sumter in April 1861. The militia companies of Charleston drilled regularly during the summer and fall of 1861. In November 1861, with the Federal expeditionary force stationed off the coast of South Carolina at Port Royal, the 4th Brigade, South Carolina Militia, was ordered into encampment in Charleston.[36] Union forces were slow in coming to Charleston, however, and the men of the 4th Brigade were relieved from active duty in February 1862.[37]

In March 1862, James enlisted as sergeant in the 1st South Carolina Infantry Battalion (Charleston Battalion), which consisted of several former volunteer militia companies from the old 17th Regiment, including the Union Light Infantry. Soon after its formation, the Charleston Battalion was ordered to James Island to help defend Charleston against the slowly advancing Federals of General Sherman's expeditionary force. James was promoted to second lieutenant shortly before the Charleston Battalion participated in the June 1862 Battle of Secessionville, where the Campbell brothers missed a reunion on the battlefield by the slimmest of margins.

After the Battle of Secessionville, James Campbell and the Charleston Battalion returned to Charleston, where they served on provost duty until being called, in the summer of 1863, to the defense of Battery Wagner on Morris Island. During the 18 July 1863 Battle of Battery Wagner, James Campbell was taken prisoner by Federal troops

---

36. Orders No. 93, 9 November 1861, Order Book, 1861–1862, of the South Carolina Militia, 4th Brigade, 2d Division, Wilmot G. DeSaussure Collection, South Carolina Historical Society, Charleston, S.C. (hereafter cited as Order Book).

37. Orders No. 231, 7 February 1862, Order Book, South Carolina Historical Society.

while reconnoitering on the parapet of the fort. From then until the end of the war, James spent his time in three different Northern prison camps: Johnson's Island, Ohio (10 October 1863 to 9 February 1864), Point Lookout, Maryland (10 February to 23 June 1864), and Fort Delaware, Delaware (25 June 1864 to 12 June 1865). After his release from Fort Delaware, James Campbell returned to Charleston to rebuild his life in postwar South Carolina.

Thus were James and Alexander Campbell swept up on opposing sides of the American Civil War. What follows tells the story of the brothers' Civil War experiences from the time of Alexander Campbell's departure with the 79th New York in June 1861 until James Campbell's release from a Northern prison camp at war's end.

Chapter One

"MANY IS THE HOME THAT WAS LEFT FATHERLESS"

4 June 1861 through 28 July 1861

On Sunday, 2 June 1861, after some five weeks of "vexatious delay" and "discouraging uncertainty," the 895 men of the 79th New York Volunteer Infantry Regiment departed New York City for Washington, D.C. Assembled at an early hour, the Highlanders, outfitted in a colorful mixture of state jackets, blue fatigue caps, kilts and tartan pants, were inspected, put through dress parade, and led in prayer by the regimental chaplain before saying their final good-byes to relatives and friends and beginning their march to the Jersey Ferry at 3 P.M. Throngs of patriotic and curious citizens who had gathered to see the colorful 79th go off to war crowded the sidewalks, perched upon piles of brick and the frames of unfinished buildings, and occupied the upper windows of stores along the Highlanders' route of march "as though it were not Sunday."[1]

Escorted to the Ferry by members of the Caledonian Club, the 79th New York embarked for the railroad station in Jersey City, New Jersey, where a crowd of well-wishers, large enough to require police supervision, had gathered. Although delayed by an "accident" with the regi-

---

1. *New York Tribune,* 3 June 1861; Todd, *Highlanders,* 5–6.

*ment's baggage and the well-meaning but disorderly crowd, the High-
landers nevertheless boarded their train, and, sometime after 10 P.M.,
were off for Washington to the "tremendous" cheers of their supporters.
After a stop in Philadelphia, where the Highlanders were lavished with
food and various gifts from a mass of patriotic citizens, the 79th proceeded tensely through Baltimore, where on 19 April secessionist sym-
pathizers had tangled with Union soldiers, before arriving at Washington
in the early morning of 4 June.*[2]

*Alexander Campbell's correspondence home to his wife, Jane, began the
very day of his regiment's arrival in the nation's capital. From his very first
letter, Alexander clearly displays dissatisfaction with his new status, a result
of the frustration and uncertainty of the previous months in New York City,
the discomfort of military life, and the separation from loved ones. Still,
Campbell must have found consolation in the fact that a number of good
friends and familiar faces were nearby, helping to lessen the impact of being
away from home. Two such familiar faces belonged to his brothers-in-law,
James and Matthew Ralston, who served alongside Alexander in Company
F of the 79th New York. Little could Campbell know when he wrote his first
letter home that it would be a long two years before he would be done with
soldiering and could return to his family for good.*

LETTER 1

June 4th, 1861
Georgeton college[3] D.C.

Dear Jane

I take the oppertunity of Letting you know of our arrievel in
wha[shi]ngton Last night or rather this morning entirely wore out &
marshed right into georgeton college the old Quarters of the sixty
ninth.[4] I have given there present encampment a visit this morning

---

2. Todd, *Highlanders*, 6–8; *New York Tribune*, 3 June 1861; *New York Herald*, 3
June 1861.

3. From the time of their arrival in Washington, D.C., the men of the 79th New York
were assigned temporary quarters in the buildings of Georgetown College. Todd, *Highlanders*, 8.

4. The 69th New York State Militia, a predominantly Irish unit from New York City,
had occupied the buildings of Georgetown College immediately before the arrival of the
Highlanders and had been recently moved to nearby Arlington Heights. The 79th and 69th
New York had served together before the war in the 4th Brigade, 1st Division, New York
State Militia. Todd, *Highlanders*, 8; *Military Gazette* (New York), 15 June 1860.

which is right oppisite us. We pased through baltimore Last night & was better received than we expected. We got verry wet. It got dark on us before we got in Line of march.

Jane if i was with you now I woould stay. Shodgering [soldiering] is no better than it is called. I have not slept 2 ours since I Left new york & when I arrived here I was put on gaurd for 2 ours. We got nothing to eat since eather except a Lettle Dry bread & coffie in Philadephia & we [cut out] Dry crackers & coffie [cut out]. We are not sworn in yet [cut out] wont get me to sware in for three years. I will go for three mounths & if that dont sout them I can come home.⁵

Just as I am writing this there is one of the Drumers boys writing along side of me & there wase some of his friengs from new york belonging to some other coumpany & they have been here for forty Days & are sworn in for three years & one of them said if they had to be Sworn in now they wold not get anny of them so you se some of [them i]s Like myself. I dond think our men will not sware fore three years. I cant write at all I so miserable. Little Jonney⁶ has he must me from hom much? I have must him. I am well in Helth hoping to find you & Jonney & all the rest the same.

I will write more of the pirticulars the nixt time. You must write so[on] as thise comes to hand. So good by till nixt time and I remain Your

Afficonate Husband
Alexander Campbell
John stewart⁷ visited here to day. AC

---

5. The vast majority of the Highlanders, including Alexander Campbell, had enlisted on 13 May 1861 to serve for a period of three years. On May 27, 28, and 29, the ceremony of muster-in was performed during which the men of the 79th New York were formally sworn into Federal service. Campbell's misunderstanding of his status on 6 June 1861 may be explained by the utter confusion which characterized the mobilization of troops during April and May 1861. Whereas the 75,000 men who answered Lincoln's first call for troops enlisted for ninety days, the state of New York had also authorized the enlistment of 30,000 men for two-year terms. Although the 79th New York did not enlist under either of these terms, many of its members, including Alexander Campbell, would question their status for the duration of their service. Todd, *Highlanders*, 2–3; New York State Adjutant General's Office, *Annual Report of the Adjutant-General of the State of New York for the Year 1901*, Serial No. 29 (Albany: J. B. Lyon Company, State Printers, 1902), 793–1079 (hereafter cited as *Report of the Adjutant-General*); Allan Nevins, *The War for the Union*, vol. 1, *The Improvised War, 1861–1862* (New York: Charles Scribner's Sons, 1959), 88.

6. John Campbell, thirteen-month-old son of Alexander and Jane Campbell.

Address
Georgeton College D.C
care of Captain Christie[8]
79 Highland gaurd

━━━━━━━◦●◦━━━━━━━

LETTER 2

Georgetown College DC
June 12th 1861

Dear Jane

The Last time I wrote you I felt every thing so odd here that I wished I had wings so as I could frly back but I might have saved my self the trouble for I found that it was no use w[i]shing any such thing. I expected an answer to the Letter I sent you & have been waiting pationtly to here from you & Jonny. I expect he will have forgot me now. Georgetown college where we are Quartered is a cathiloc college & is situated on the banks of the Potimoc. Georgetown is a town by it self right on the oppisite site of the enemys Country.

I was bathing to day in the Potimoc. Matthew[9] & Perison[10] &

---

7. Although the exact origin and nature of their acquaintance is uncertain, Alexander and Jane Campbell apparently knew John Stewart and his wife before the war. The Stewarts resided in Washington, D.C., and, as evidenced by many of Alexander's subsequent letters home, were often visited by many soldier-friends from the 79th New York.

8. Capt. James Christie, Co. F, 79th New York Highlanders. Christie, 40 years old in 1861, remained captain of Co. F. until his discharge from the army on 10 September 1861. Frederick Phisterer, *New York in the War of the Rebellion, 1861 to 1865,* 3d ed. (Albany: J.B. Lyon Company, state printers, 1912), vol. 4, 2849.

9. Matthew Ralston, brother of Jane Ralston Campbell. Matthew Ralston, age 24, enlisted with Alexander Campbell on 13 May 1861 at New York City to serve for three years. He was mustered in as a private in Co. F, 79th New York Highlanders, on 27 May. Compiled Service Record of Matthew Ralston, Co. F, 79th New York Infantry, Records of the Adjutant General's Office, Record Group 94, National Archives, Washington, D.C. (hereafter, all such military service records of members of the 79th New York Infantry Regiment contained in Record Group 94 at the National Archives will be listed as their Compiled Service Record).

10. William Pearson, Co. F, 79th New York Highlanders. Pearson, age 23, enlisted 13 May 1861 at New York City to serve three years and was mustered in as private, Co. F, on 27 May 1861. Promoted to corporal on 15 November 1862, Pearson served with the 79th until mustered out with his company at New York City on 31 May 1864. *Report of the Adjutant-General,* 996.

Brown[11] we all try to keep our selfs clean which is verry neccary here on account of so many sleeping in one room. It is verry Large but non two Large. There is two Companys in it & when they all Ly down at night the froor is all covered. We have nothing to Ly on [but] the bare froor. We generialy spread our glase[12] under us but it is merily to keep the dust off us. Our knapsack is our pillow & who would not be a swad?[13] I was washing yesterday. I washed my canton flanel drawers & my gray & red shirts 1 pair socks 2 hankechiefs. Ther is no tub nor hot water ether.

We had a parade through the city of w[a]shington & old abe & scot revued [u]s as we pased the white house.[14] I was down seeing John Stewart on sunday Jammey[15] was too & they are well. They shoed me a Likeness of yours. It Looks verry Like you only has faded a Lettle.

It is reported here that they have stoped giving any more money to the familys of the voolenteers.[16] If it is so I want you to Let me know for I would not stay if it was to fight for there country. I came here

---

11. James V. Brown, Co. F, 79th New York Highlanders. Brown, age 22, enlisted to serve for three years on 13 May 1861 at New York City and was mustered in as private, Co. F, on 27 May 1861. James Brown served with the 79th until he deserted at Washington, D.C., on 5 September 1862. *Report of the Adjutant-General,* 821.

12. Although glaize (gla[i]ze, gles) is an adjective in the Scottish language meaning "open and coarse in texture, esp. of knitted, woven or plaited work," it appears as though Campbell is using the Scots vernacular here for "clothes." William Grant, ed., *The Scottish National Dictionary* (Edinburgh: Riverside Press Limited, 1941–1976), vol. 4, 315; Dr. Diana Henderson, Edinburgh, Scotland, to Terry A. Johnston, Jr., Clemson, S.C., 12 June 1997, transcript in the hand of Terry A. Johnston, Jr., Clemson, S.C.

13. Swad is a Scottish term for soldier. Grant, *Scottish National Dictionary,* vol. 9, 141.

14. On 9 June the men of the 79th participated in a "grand parade" down Pennsylvania Avenue during which they were reviewed by President Abraham Lincoln, General in Chief of the Union Army Winfield Scott, and other officials. According to one Highlander: "This was the first appearance of the regiment in the streets of Washington, and the kilts attracted a good deal of attention." Todd, *Highlanders,* 13.

15. James Ralston, brother of Jane Ralston Campbell. On 13 May 1861 James Ralston, age 28, enlisted in New York City to serve for three years. On 27 May, he was mustered in as corporal, Co. F, 79th New York Highlanders. Compiled Service Record of James Ralston.

16. Campbell is referring here to the Union Defence Committee of the Citizens of New York. On 20 April 1861, in the wake of President Lincoln's call for troops, a mass meeting of the citizens of New York City convened to address the city's mobilization for war. A Committee of twenty-five (to which six others were eventually added) was there appointed "to represent the citizens [of New York City] in the collection of funds and the transaction of such other business in aid of the movements of the Government as the public interests may require." In short, this Union Defence Committee of the Citizens of New York, with money received from the city council and through various collections and con-

they were to support you & if they dont stand to there promise I dont intend to stand to mine. I suppose they think because they have got us out here they can do any thing they Like.

I must come to a close these time hoping this will find you & Jonney & all the rest well as it Leaves us. When I say us I mean the Boys[17] as you generaly call them. No more this time hoping to here from you soon.

And I Remain Your Afficonate
Husband
A Campbell

Address
6 Co 79 Regiment
Georgetown College
Washington DC

━━━━━➤●◄━━━━━

LETTER 3

Georgeton College
June 22d 1861

Dear Jane

I received your Letter yesterday and was glad to know that you

---

tributions, took on the responsibilities of outfitting, equipping, and transporting to Washington numerous regiments of New York City men to serve in the Union army.

In addition to outfitting soldiers, the Union Defence Committee appointed a Select Committee for the Relief of the Families of Soldiers which was, "for a limited period," to "support . . . the families of those who should go forth in the cause of the country." The "limited" nature of the family relief efforts of the Union Defence Committee was soon evident; the 29 June 1861 report of the Executive Committee of the Union Defence Committee, in reference to the relief of soldiers' families, stated that "this action must speedily cease, the condition of the Fund made applicable to this purpose being nearly exhausted." Between 7 May and 25 July 1861, at which time the relief fund was finally exhausted, the Union Defence Committee distributed over $200,000 to the wives, children, and parents of the soldiers they sponsored. John Austin Stevens, ed., *The Union Defence Committee of the City of New York: Minutes, Reports, and Correspondence* (New York: The Union Defence Committee, 1885), 57, 111–12, 119, 254; Nevins, *The Improvised War*, 88, 174–78.

17. James and Matthew Ralston.

were well & that you got your money of the union Defence
Commitee.[18] I received your Letter of the 11th the day after I wrote.
You menthioned in it that I might have come up before I went away. If
I could have got away I certenaly would. You say Jonney has forgot me
now. Tell me nixt time if he can speek any thing Plain now.

We are expecting to here to Leave here soon for some Place where
we will be of more use. We were all ordered out Last evening with
rashings to goo over into virginia to help the 69th [New York]. It was
romered that they were attacted. It turned out to be fals. The excitement was entence. Some was afraid it was true & some that it was not
true. The 69th was skirmishing & firing blank shot. That was the
whole amount of it.

I wrote a Letter to [Brother] Peter[19] the same Day I wrote you & he
sends me news papers almost every day & they come in verry handey
for pasing the time. I was Down in town. James Ireland[20] & I we called
on John Stewart & Mrs Stewart sends hir respects to you. They treat
us verry Kindely when we call on them. I would have taken my Likeness if I had any money. I had the Kilt on.[21]

---

18. From 7 May until 9 June 1861, the Union Defence Committee distributed funds
in the following amounts: a maximum allowance of $3 a week for the head of the family,
$1 a week for one child, and $.50 a week for each additional child. In reaction to "the
abundance and moderate price of food, together with the unexpectedly large demand upon
the fund," the Union Defence Committee on 10 June permanently lowered the maximum
weekly allowance for the head of the family by $1. Stevens, *Union Defence Committee,*
249–51.

19. Peter Campbell, brother of Alexander Campbell. Peter, born 2 January 1831 in
Kilmadock Parish, Perthshire, Scotland, resided in New York City with his wife, Ann, and
their infant son. Old Parish Register, Perthshire (1839–1830), Kilmadock/362/5, New Register House, Edinburgh, Scotland.

20. James Ireland, Co. F, 79th New York Highlanders. Ireland, age 22, enlisted at
New York City on 13 May 1861 to serve three years and was mustered in as sergeant, Co.
F, on 27 May 1861. Sergeant Ireland did not serve long with the 79th; he was discharged
in August 1861 at Washington, D.C. *Report of the Adjutant-General,* 912.

21. From its inception in 1859, the 79th New York State Militia had adopted the
elaborate dress of contemporary British army Highland regiments. Prior to the war, each
Highlander was issued a glengarry cap, sporran, diced stockings, and a kilt which was usually worn during dress parade in place of the more practical tartan trews (plaid trousers)
of their fatigue uniform. Although the original Highlanders wore their distinctive uniforms
with much pride, the unfeasibility of speedily procuring additional kilts for new members
in April and May 1861 and the impracticalities associated with their traditional garb in the
field led the men of the 79th New York to put away their kilts in favor of either tartan
trews or, in increasing numbers, the standard Union blue uniform pants shortly after their
arrival in Virginia. Michael J. McAfee, "79th Regiment, New York State Militia," 28–29;
William Arley Beard III, *History of the 79th New York Cameron Highlanders, 1859–1876,
with a Treatise on the Uniform and Equipment* (Strawberry Plains, Tenn.: Strawberry

Wee are expecting to get paid to Day but I dout it verry much.[22] Any how I will send you the money as soon as I get it & I hope it will not be Long till we do get it.

We have got a new Colnel Brother to the sectary of ware Cameron.[23] He when elected treate the whole regiment & the officers were mostly all tipsy that night.

I want you to write me as soon is you get this Letter. It is the only Little bit of comfort I have to hear from you for I can assure you there is verry Lettle of it here. James said he will write soon. Mat [&] Brown & c.c[24] is well.

You want to know when I will be home. That I cannot tell. I expect we will have to stay till the ware is over & that might not be Long & it might. I will try & get a pass after a bit to come home & see you but I cannot have the face to ask it yet. John Book the Blacksmith has got his Dicharge & is going hom soon. There is no use of comming home yet for times is not anny better. Yet if you take sick or Jonney that is Dangersly you will send by telegraph & they cannot keep me from going to see you. The Drum mager got a telegraph Despash Last night that his child was Dead & he went away through the night. There was one Drumed out the other Day for bad behaviour. The regiment would be a great deal better wanting a few of such caracters. No more at present but soon again.

> I Remain Your afficonate husband
> Alx Campbell

79 Regiment Highland Guards NY
Write soon a Long Letter.

Plains Press, 1996), 19–23; Clarence Clough Buel and Robert Underwood Johnson, eds., *Battles and Leaders of the Civil War* (New York: The Century Co., 1888; reprint, Harrisburg: The Archive Society, 1991), vol. 1, 185.

22. In June 1861, pay for a private in the Union army was $11 per month. Fred Albert Shannon, *The Organization and Administration of the Union Army, 1861–1865* (Gloucester, Mass.: Peter Smith, 1965), vol. 1, 246.

23. James C. Cameron. The Highlanders had left New York City under the command of Lt. Col. Samuel M. Elliott, the colonelcy of the regiment having been vacated on 29 April 1861 due to the resignation of Col. T. W. McLeay. While the regiment was in Washington, James C. Cameron, brother of Secretary of War Simon Cameron, was offered and accepted the colonelcy of the 79th New York. He was elected to that position on 21 June 1861. Phisterer, *New York in the War of the Rebellion*, vol. 4, 2849; *New York Tribune*, 7 May 1861; Todd, *Highlanders*, 13.

24. Etcetera.

LETTER 4

Georgetown College DC
June 29th 1861

Dear Jane

I received you Letter in Dew time & I was verry happy to here that you was getting along so well & that you feel so pleased of your apartments. I cant say I Like my apartments the best on account of so many in one room but we are going to encampment about a mile & a half up in the country. I was up there this fore noon. James Ireland [and] David Mcfadyen[25] was along with me. It is a fine place for an encampment. All the tents are here & there is about 50 men working at it making roads & taring down fences & cc and we expect to go up there on monday. It is a verry nice place. It stands high. We can see a Long Distance around & away into virginia. The only thing I am afraid water will be scarce. Any how I expect to be a Lettle comfortabler with so many in a tent. I have not found out yet how many there will be.[26]

About the food we get in the morning. About 7:oclock we get Bread & coffie it is not in abundance ethier & at 12 oclock we get some times salt Beef & rice & sometimes Pork & Beens & fresh Beef occasionally & at 6:o clock coffie & Bread. It is not of the Best Quality but I dont grumble for we get as good as anny of the rest of the regiments. Our company the 6th [F] got 2 recruits Last night. There was 4 came & who do you think was one of them but the great Jack Boid. I was coming in Last night when I met him in the hall. I had not any time to talk to him & I have not seen him to Day. Just as I am writing this John Stewart came in & I told him what you told me. I have just got 2 news Papers from [Brother] Peter. I get ether one ore two every day. I was down visiting the Patent office. I got 2 Books & I sent theme on at Le[a]st they sent them on for me to [Brother] Peter. They were Patent office reports.

---

25. David A. Fadyen, sergeant, Co. F, 79th New York Highlanders. David Fadyen, also known as David McFadden, was twenty-six years old when he enlisted at New York City on 13 May 1861 to serve three years; on 27 May 1861 he was mustered in as sergeant, Co. F. Fadyen served with the 79th until his discharge in August 1861 at Washington D.C. *Report of the Adjutant-General*, 866.

26. According to one Highlander, the shelters Campbell and his comrades would soon occupy were "six by eight feet wall tents," into which a regulation eight men were crowded. Todd, *Highlanders*, 14.

Now I must say something in faviour of your Last Letter. It was Long and entresting & I think if you improve in every Letter you send me as much as in your Last you have reason to be proud of your self. I will. I am now.

I must say a few w[o]rds about Jonney. You said the Docter was going to vaxinate. I hope it will take well. Poor Little fellow. He has not sence to Know any thing about whare I am. You say they [the Union Defence Committee] onley give ten Dollars a mounth. Now I would Like you to Let me Know if you are to get money regular of the regimental fund. If not ten Dollars Per mounth wont bee sufficiant. We have got some pay to Day $9=22 cents from the 13th of may till the 31st. I will send hom $5 as soon as I can. I want to keep the rest to by anny Little thing such as a Little milk for my coffie & I want to get my Likeness in the Kilt. We will have another mounths Pay Dew us on monday but I dont think they will give us any more for some time.

I will write no more at Present expecting to here from you soon a Long Letter. Matthew & James is well & has been so all a Long. I am well hopping this will find you & all the rest of your well. I have to go on Dress prade. They are all getting ready. Good night & Joy be with you all.

> I remain your afficontate hosband
> Alexander Campbell

Write soon. Address until I give you another after we move same as before.

⇒➤●◄⇐

LETTER 5

> Camp Lochiel[27]
> Georgetown hights DC
> July 5th 1861

Dear Jane

---

27. On the morning of 2 July, the 79th New York abandoned its quarters in the buildings of Georgetown College and re-encamped a mile north on the heights surrounding the town, naming the location Camp Lochiel after an old Scottish chieftain from whom Colonel Cameron claimed descent. Todd, *Highlanders,* 14.

I received your Letter Last night & was most happy to here that you was well & that Jonney was getting along so well. You will see by the above that we are incamped now. There is nine of us in a tent. James & mat & Brown & my self are in the one tent. The rest are verry aggreable & we get along verry well so farr as that is consarned. We bought planks & floored it & we cut young ceader trees & planted them in front of the tent it shades the sun off & we have seats under them. I am sitting under them whil writing this.

We were out on parade yesterday it being the 4 of July Down in washingtown. All the new york troops was out that is on this side of the Patomac & past in revuew past the Presidant & scot & a host of others. Last night was a great night [cut out]. The regiments encamped aroun[d] [cut out] had great fires burning & rockts flying in the sky. We had a fire Lighted on our hights which I am shure could be seen 50 miles around. We are on verry high ground & can see mostly all the encampments around & a long way into virginia. We got orders Last night that no one was to get a pass to go out for 4 Days is [in] case we might have to march into virginia but I Dont think wee will be out of here for sometime.

I expect before you receive this that you will have got the $5 I sent. James & mat & I sent it along with a great many others to Cristies. I want you to send me word as soon as you get this & Let me know if you have got it. I am not shure when they will give us anny more & I wan[t] to know if it is true that the union Defence Commitee use you Like Dogs when you goo for you money. The Drum Magour has returned & says they use the Wemen verry rude. If it is so tell me.[28]

You want to know when I think we will be home. That is rather a hard Queston to answer. It depends a great deal what congress does. You will see in the news papers how they do & Judge from that. I am shure I wish it was setteled & times good again. The worst thing I Like in the whole thing is our officers. They are so stuck up since they came

---

28. Although it is unclear whether Jane and/or other soldiers' wives were treated "Like Dogs" by the various representatives of the Union Defence Committee, it is certain that the process of drawing upon the relief fund was a tedious one for the applicants. To prevent ineligible persons from receiving funds, the Union Defence Committee conducted "personal examinations of the applicants at their domiciles, for the verifications of their statements as to the number in family, their true relationship to the soldiers, their circumstances and condition, their dependence on the soldier for support, etc." In addition, the sheer number of applicants who applied for relief for their families (estimated at just under 12,000 by the Committee) led to severe overcrowding and lengthy delays at committee offices. Stevens, *Union Defence Committee,* 250–51, 253.

out here. If they were smart I would not say anny thing. Just for instance our wourthy Lutenant mongumary.[29] To be under such as he you Know yourself without me telling you.

I have not got any more time to write more on account of me being on gaurd. I went on this morning at 8:o clock & got off at ten. I have got to go on at 2 o clock again & stand 2 hours more & so on till 8 o clock tomorrow. It comes every 5 days. James got off this morning. Him & Brown went to washington to Day. Mat is Laying in the tent reading. He told me to tell you he was getting on first rate. I will now come to a close hopping this will find you & Jonney & all the rest as it Leaves me & all the rest well. So good Day. Hopping to here from you soon.

I Remain Your afficontate husband
Alex Campbell

Write soon.
Address Camp Lochiel
Georgetown hights DC
In this way
Alexander Campbell
6th Company 79 Rgmt
H[ighland]G[uard] N[ew]y[ork] s[tate]m[ilitia]
Georgetown hights DC

LETTER 6

Virginia
July 11th 1861

Dear Jane

I write you to Let you Know that I am well & I hope that this will find you & Jonney enjoying the same. I was incamped on Georgetown

29. William S. Montgomery, Co. F, 79th New York Highlanders. Montgomery's initial status in the regiment is unclear: he is listed as both second lieutenant and sergeant of Co. F at the time he was mustered into Federal service on 27 May 1861. Either way, he was promoted to first lieutenant, Co. D, on 1 March 1862, and then to captain, Co. F, on 16 October 1862. William Montgomery served with the 79th until mustered out on 31 May 1864 at New York City. *Report of the Adjutant-General,* 977; Phisterer, *New York in the War of the Rebellion,* vol. 4, 2856; *Annual Report of the Adjutant-General of the State of New York for the Year 1861* (Albany: C. Van Benthuysen, Printer, 1862), 606.

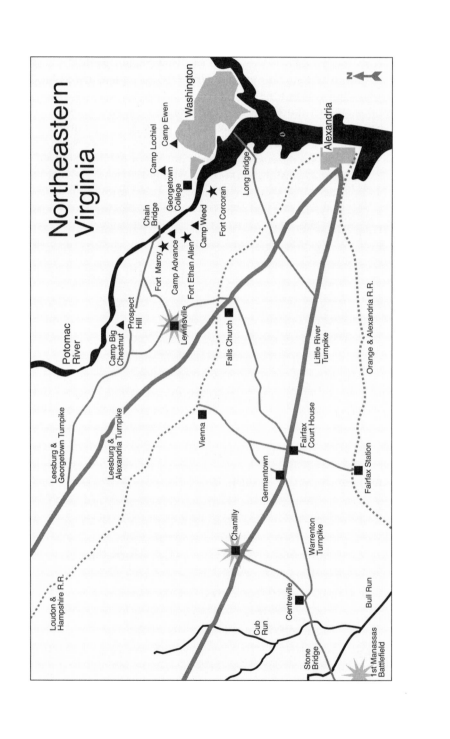

Northeastern Virginia

Washington

Potomac River

Camp Lochiel
Camp Ewen
Camp Big Chestnut
Prospect Hill
Chain Bridge
Georgetown College
Fort Corcoran
Fort Marcy
Camp Advance
Camp Weed
Fort Ethan Allen
Long Bridge
Alexandria

Lewinsville
Falls Church

Leesburg & Georgetown Turnpike
Leesburg & Alexandria Turnpike
Little River Turnpike
Orange & Alexandria R.R.

Vienna
Fairfax Court House
Fairfax Station
Germantown

Loudon & Hampshire R.R.

Chantilly
Warrenton Turnpike

Cub Run
Centreville
Bull Run

Stone Bridge
1st Manassas Battlefield

highs the Last time I wrote you. Now I am in the enemys Country.[30]
We Left & crost in to old virginia on sunday Last & marched right
into the country about 4 miles farther than the 69th [New York] which
is right on the entrance to the state. It was getting Dark when we came
to the place where we were to encamp & our camps was not come up
so we had to unroll our blankets & oil covers & Lay out. It was the
first nights real soagring [soldiering] we have had & we were pretty
well wore out which made us sleep as sound as is if we were on a
feather bed. I did any how. The Dew was verry heavy. Heavyer than I
ever saw it in scotland. We got up in the morning & shook our selfs. I
went out a Lettle way in the country to see what sort of a place it was.
It Looks verry much Diserted Like the people. That is anny that is of
them is verry misirable Looking Creatures. They are not worth saying
anny more about.

I have a verry bad desk to write on my knapsack & I have to
change my self so often the one time on my knees & on every way for
a change it is with candel Light & since I comenced I have thought on
your carisane oil Lamp. I have charge of the tent that I am writing in
and it is after tatoo. They men are all going to bed. We were all out on
a brigade Drill to night. We were Drilled by Col Sherman[31] acting
Brigade General. He is to command us & other 4 Rgmts & we got
orders to be ready at anny moments notice to march so I expect the
nixt time I write you we will be farther into virginia. The Brigade we
are in is expected to do some hard fiting that is if there is to be anny
agoing. There was a General inspecting us yesterday & he said we were
a fine boady of men & that he had work for us soon. The sooner the
better.

Captain Cristie Left here this morning for new york on a four-

---

30. On Sunday, 7 July 1861, the 79th New York was ordered to cross the Potomac
River and enter Virginia. The Highlanders marched past the encampment of the 69th New
York State Militia, whose men had turned out to welcome their fellow New Yorkers to Vir-
ginia, and settled in an area they dubbed Camp Weed. Todd, *Highlanders*, 15–16.

31. William Tecumseh Sherman. Sherman, a graduate of West Point and veteran of
the Mexican War, took command of the 3d Brigade (the 13th, 69th, and 79th New York,
and the 2d Wisconsin), Tyler's division, Army of the Potomac on 30 June 1861. Of his stay
with the 3d Brigade, which came to an end in August 1861, Sherman later wrote: "These
were all good, strong, volunteer regiments, pretty well commanded; and I had reason to
believe that I had one of the best brigades in the whole army." William Tecumseh Sherman, *Memoirs of General William T. Sherman* (New York: D. Appleton & Company,
1875; reprint, Bloomington: Indiana University Press, 1957), 179–80; Mark M. Boatner
III, *The Civil War Dictionary* (New York: David McKay Company, Inc., 1959), 750–51.

lough. I dont think he Likes sogering [soldiering] verry well. He is not fit for a captain now [t]hough he made me a sergant the other Day in place of the ones place I ame in not attending to his duty. I dont Know whether I will be Let Keep it or not.[32] The man hou had it is going around sne[a]king to get back. I will have to come to a close. The Drum is bet to put out the Lights. We have been so much Drilled since come out here that I have not had time to write in day Light. I hop to here from you as soon as this comes to hand. James and mat is well & Brown & the irelands too. No more this time. Hoping to here from you soon. So good night & Plesants Dreams.

> I Remain your afficonate husband
> Alex Campbell

Address to washington DC or elswhere. Be shure & writ soon. Good night.

━━━━━━━⟫●⟪━━━━━━━

LETTER 7

Washington, DC
July 26th 1861

Dear Jane

I expect you will think it strange of me not writing you sooner. I certanely would but they said arround here that no Letters was aloud to Leave here since the Battel of Bulls Runn[33] whether it was true or not. Anny how you must have heard that I was all safe. There was a telagraph Despach came her[e] enquiring if I was all safe & the Magear[34] said to me he answered it so I thought it would ease your mind til I would get a chance to tell you myself. I came out of Battel without a scratch. So Did James & Matthew & Brown. I cant see how we all came off so safe for it was such a tremendous shoure of bullets

---

32. There is no mention of this promotion in the muster rolls for Alexander Campbell, Co. F, 79th New York.
33. The First Battle of Bull Run or Manassas, Sunday, 21 July 1861.
34. Maj. David McClellan, 79th New York Highlanders. McClellan served with the Highlanders from 1 June 1861 to 10 August 1861. Phisterer, *New York in the War of the Rebellion*, vol. 4, 2843.

that god onely knowes how anny of us is Left to tell the tale. I cannot begin to tell you about how the battle begun and how it ended. It would take me a week to write all the sights & seans I seen & came through since I wrote you Last. I wish I could sit in my own house & tell you out of my own mouth all about it.

I was acting as right guid[35] in McFadgan plase. He & Jame & David Ireland was in washington. It was fortunate that she[36] came. It was perhaps the means of saving therr Lives. If you see Daniel gillie[37] or anny of them that worked in McMasters[38] tell them that Daniel Larance[39] is all safe & you are to tell Anney Ireland that her friend walker[40] is safe & that william faset[41] cannot be accounted for. He got wounded in the arm and Left the field & has not been seen since. The

35. "The first sergeant [is positioned] in the rear rank [of the company], touching with the left elbow, and covering the captain. In the manoeuvres he will be denominated *covering sergeant*, or *right guide* of the company." Silas Casey, *Schools of the Soldier and Company*, vol. 1, *Infantry Tactics, for the Instruction, Exercise, and Manoeuvres of the Soldier, a Company, Line of Skirmishers, Battalion, Brigade, or Corps d'Armée* (New York: D. Van Nostrand, 1865), 13.

36. It appears that the wife of 1st Lt. and Adj. David Ireland, 79th New York Highlanders, was in Washington, D.C., to visit her husband on the eve of the battle.

37. Daniel Gillie (or Gilley). A Scottish-born resident of New York City, Gillie, age 29, worked with Alexander Campbell before the war as a stonecutter. 1860 Federal Population Census for New York City, 20th Ward, District 2, p. 322; H. Wilson, *Trow's New York City Directory for the Year Ending May 1, 1859* (New York: John F. Trow, 1859), 306.

38. Either David or James McMaster, owners of stonecutting businesses in New York City. Alexander Campbell and several of his friends in the 79th New York worked for one or both of the McMasters prior to the war. Wilson, *City Directory 1859*, 520.

39. Daniel Lawrence, Co. F, 79th New York Highlanders. Lawrence, age 31, had enlisted at New York City on 13 May 1861 to serve for three years and was mustered in as private, Co. F, on 27 May 1861. On 29 December 1862, Lawrence would be discharged for wounds received during the 16 June 1862 Battle of Secessionville, S.C. *Report of the Adjutant-General*, 930.

40. At the time of the Battle of Bull Run, two men named Walker served in Co. F of the 79th New York. Both shared the same first name, William, enlisted to serve for three years at New York City on 13 May 1861, and were mustered into Co. F on 27 May 1861. The younger William Walker, age 24, was discharged from the regiment in August 1861 at Camp Caustin, Md.; the elder William Walker, age 32, was promoted to corporal on 15 March 1863 and remained with the 79th until mustered out with Co. F on 31 May 1864 at New York City. *Report of the Adjutant-General*, 1061.

41. William Fawcett (or Fausett), Co. F, 79th New York Highlanders. Fawcett, age 24, had enlisted at New York City on 13 May 1861 to serve three years and was mustered in as private, Co. F, on 27 May 1861. Promoted to sergeant sometime before the Battle of Bull Run, Fawcett was captured during the battle and sent to a Richmond prison. *Report of the Adjutant-General*, 867; Alexander Campbell to Jane Campbell, 26 September 1861, CFP-SCDAH; William H. Jeffrey, *Richmond Prisons, 1861–1862* (St. Johnsbury, Vt.: The Republican Press, 1893), 221.

regiment suffered verry severe.[42] Captain Brown[43] was killed by a cannon ball his side was almost carried away & cap shilling[44] was killed by a cannon shot. Manson & farask[45] were taken prisoners & our captan cristie has cleard to new york. He never stoped to se how his men was nor nothing. If anny of you went to enquire after us at him I know the answer you would get.

We are all back in washington & going to encamp in the out skirts of the city & we might not Leave it again till we come home. I am shure I dont want to go into virginia again. We have come trough more hardships since we went over the Potomac than I would Like to go trough again.

I am writing this in John Stewarts. Mrs [David] Ireland was staying here. She has gon out since I came in & she feels quite happy and told

---

42. The 79th New York sustained one of the highest number of casualties among Union regiments engaged during the battle. The Highlanders losses included 32 killed, 51 wounded, and 115 missing (including the captured), for a total of 198 casualties out of an approximate 750 men. O.R., Series 1, vol. 2, 351; William F. Fox, *Regimental Losses in the American Civil War, 1861–1865* (Dayton: Morningside Bookshop, 1974), 426.

43. Capt. David Brown, Co. D, 79th New York Highlanders. While leading a group of Highlanders during the battle, Captain Brown was shot through the neck by a rifle bullet after which a cannon shot entered his side, forcing and pinning him to the ground. Brown, thirty-nine years old at the time of his death at the Battle of Bull Run, had previously expressed, according to one Highlander, "that he might never survive the defeat of the regiment." *New York Tribune*, 29 July 1861; Phisterer, *New York in the War of the Rebellion*, vol. 4, 2849.

44. Capt. Robert T. Shillinglaw, Co. I, 79th New York Highlanders. Although the newspapers listed Shillinglaw as dead from wounds received in both his legs and head, he in fact survived the Battle of Bull Run (albeit severely wounded) only to be taken prisoner by the Confederates. Confined to a prison hospital in Richmond, Captain Shillinglaw was exchanged after roughly five months and returned to New York City on 3 January 1862. On 20 January 1863, Shillinglaw, "still a suffering soldier" due to the severity of his wounds received at Bull Run, was granted his discharge from the service. *New York Tribune*, 29 July 1861; Phisterer, *New York in the War of the Rebellion*, vol. 4, 2858; *Scottish American Journal*, 19, 26 September, 3 October 1861, 9 January 1862.

45. Captains William Manson, Co. A, and James A. Farrish, Co. B, 79th New York Highlanders. Both Farrish (who was wounded during the battle) and Manson were taken prisoner at the Battle of Bull Run and sent to Richmond, where they, along with fifty-six Highlanders and hundreds of other Union prisoners, were held in two adjacent tobacco factories. Whereas Captain Manson remained a prisoner in Richmond, Captain Farrish was moved after two months in the Confederate capital to prisons in Charleston and Columbia, S.C., before being returned to Richmond seven months later and placed in the infamous Libby Prison. Both men were released from captivity in 1862 and received their discharges from the service: Captain Manson on 29 March 1862 and Captain Farrish on 25 September 1862. Todd, *Highlanders*, 50–52; *Report of the Adjutant-General*, 867, 942; *Scottish American Journal*, 26 September 1861, 9 January 1862; Jeffrey, *Richmond Prisons*, 7–11, 220–22.

me to tell anney that she was in for the ware. She says times is verry slack in new york. I dont care how hard they were I would Like to be in it. I think we have dun our share of the fiting & we ought to give them that wants to get out as bad as we did a chance. There is not a man in the regiment but is quite willing to get back.

I suppose you wont have received anny money yet from the union Defence commitee. I Dont see how you are to get along. I dont think that they intend to give us anny. They have got us here & they can do what they Like. It Look like it any how.

I almost forgot to tell you that in passing trough a place called germantown where there had been some of the reabels but had run when they knew that we were comming I found a knapsack Lying in of the road with James Campbell wrote in side of it & I cut the pice out & took it with me. I could almost sware it is my Brothers write & what makes me think so it was south carolina troops that was there.[46] It makes me feel verry bad to think that I was so near my own Brother & him on the one side & me on the other. I might have shot him or he might have shot me & would not have known it.

I cannot say no more this time expecting to here from you soon & Little Jonney. Poor Little fellow. Little did he k[n]ow how his father is or the Danger he was in. Its as well for him. Many is the home that was Left fatherless on that Bloddy 21st of July. It was sunday too—it is always sunday our army makes its grand moves.

---

46. Alexander Campbell's brother James was not among those South Carolinians in Virginia for the Battle of Bull Run; his militia company, the Union Light Infantry, was stationed in Charleston in July 1861 and would not be mustered into Confederate service until 15 March 1862. The knapsack that Alexander Campbell found most likely belonged to a member of the 8th South Carolina Infantry, one of four South Carolina regiments under the command of Confederate General Milledge L. Bonham. Prior to the Battle of Bull Run, on 17 July, Bonham withdrew his troops from their positions northwest of Centreville in the face of the advancing Union troops of Brig. Gen. Irvin McDowell's offensive force. The 8th South Carolina withdrew quickly through Germantown within view of the skirmishers attached to the advancing columns of Gen. Daniel Tyler's 1st Division, which included the 79th New York. Compiled Service Record of James Campbell, 1st (Charleston Battalion) South Carolina Infantry, Compiled Service Records of Confederate Soldiers Who Served in Organizations from the State of South Carolina, War Department Collection of Confederate Records, Record Group 109, National Archives, Washington, D.C., National Archives Microfilm Publication No. 267, Roll 149 (hereafter, all such military service records of members of the 1st South Carolina Battalion contained in Record Group 109 at the National Archives will be listed as their Compiled Service Record); William C. Davis, *Battle at Bull Run: A History of the First Major Campaign of the Civil War* (Baton Rouge: Louisiana State University Press, 1977), 97–99; O.R., Series 1, vol. 2, 454–56.

Address to washington DC. I am & the rest are well hopping this
will find you all the same. Good Day.

I Remain Your Afficonate Husband
Alexander Campbell
Tell [Brother] Peter when you se him that I will write him soon & that
he will Pleas send some Paper.

<hr />

LETTER 8

Washington
Sunday July 28th 1861

Dear Jane

I take the oppartunity of writing you sume more pirticulars about
Last sundays work. We were encamped about 1 mile beyond Centrevell
[Centreville, Va.] which is about 30 miles from washington. We got
orders on saturday [20 July] to march that night & we got our things
packed up & 2 days rashings was served out to us and we were all
formed in Line expecting to proceed but it wa[s] posponed untill nixt
morning. Sunday at two o clock [A.M.] we got ready at the time but did
not get off so soon. Some other regiments went & took there grond in
the woods untill we all got up then our regiment & another one struck
off to the right & scoured the woods to see if there was anny of the
enimy Lurking there. There was sum shots fired but wee saw no one
until we got out of the wood. We could see them away off the hights in
front. We were ordered to sit down but to be ready to spring up in a
moment.[47]

<hr />

47. Alexander Campbell and the Highlanders were waiting for orders to cross Bull
Run and link up with the attacking wing of the Union army, which had crossed Bull Run
earlier in the morning. Union general Irvin McDowell's plan of action was to sweep down
upon the Confederate forces who inhabited the far (southern) side of Bull Run from the
north, turning the Rebel left flank. To help ensure its success, McDowell withheld a portion of his forces, including Tyler's division (to which the Highlanders belonged), on the
northern banks of Bull Run in order to occupy the opposing Confederates while his 13,000
man-strong flanking army crossed the stream at Sudley and Poplar Fords, and moved
southward upon unsuspecting Confederate troops. Tyler's diversionary force would then
cross Bull Run in their front near the stone bridge and link up with the flanking army, com-
pleting the rout. Davis, *Battle at Bull Run,* 69–89; O.R., Series I, vol. 2, 326–327.

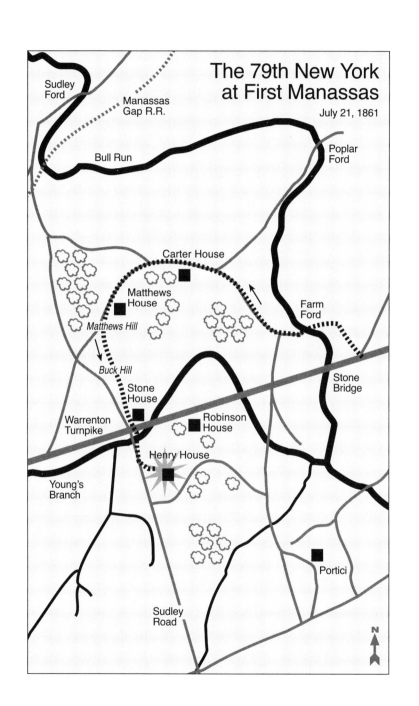

The 79th New York
at First Manassas

July 21, 1861

Sudley
Ford

Manassas
Gap R.R.

Bull Run

Poplar
Ford

Carter House

Matthews
House

Matthews Hill

Farm
Ford

Buck Hill

Stone
House

Stone
Bridge

Warrenton
Turnpike

Robinson
House

Henry House

Young's
Branch

Portici

Sudley
Road

N

There was a battery of artillery on the road a Little below us the battery that acompanied our brigade and it comenced firing shells to find out the enemys position. They knew what they were about and they did not fire a shot from there masked batterys. Then there a company taken from the regiment on our right 13 of new york & they commenced firing with there rifels at the enemys pickets which was returned. Then 4 cannon was brought up and comenced shelling the enemy which could be seen in great numbers running in all directings. Sum of our men went up in trees & got a fine vew of the enemy comming in in great force. We were still Lying in the outskirts of the wood and could see dust rising out among the trees. They when I say they I meen the enemy were comming in from manasses Junchon to reignforce there position away on the right. Hunters Division came on the enemy first & musketry firing commenced in earnest. It was one continual roll of which I niver heard nor can I compare anny thing I ever heard with it.[48]

It was not Long then till we were ordered up in to action. Then Jane I thought I might never see you and Lilttle Jonney again. I thought that James or mat or myself could not all come out clear which thank god we have. There was one of our company william Mitchel[49] [w]ho has a Large family in N Y & when he got shot he Looked up and said my god my family my family. I could tell a thousands Such things only its better not. I would not cared half so much if it was not for the sake of you and Jonney. Poor Little fellow. I am Looking at him while writing. His Likeness is Lying before me. I expect he is changed a Little now.

I was saying we were not Long when we were ordered into action.[50] We had to runn on dubbel quick about a mile till we came to

---

48. Campbell is describing the quickly burgeoning encounter between the Union flanking army and Confederate forces on the far side of Bull Run. Many of the unengaged members of General Tyler's force climbed trees to gain a better view of the fight. In doing so, they were able to witness the Confederate forces of generals P. G. T. Beauregard and Joseph E. Johnston rush toward Matthews Hill to stave the Federal flanking movement of Union brigadier general David Hunter's division. Todd, *Highlanders,* 31–32; Hennessy, *The First Battle of Manassas,* 46–47; Davis, *Battle at Bull Run,* 166–172.

49. William Mitchell, Co. F, 79th New York Highlanders. Mitchell, age 35, enlisted at New York City on 13 May 1861 to serve three years and was mustered in as private, Co. F, on 27 May 1861. Mitchell survived the wounds he received at Bull Run and served with the 79th until 7 April 1862, when he was discharged at Beaufort, S.C. *Report of the Adjutant-General,* 976.

50. Sometime between 11 A.M. and noon, Sherman's brigade of Tyler's division, 3,400 men strong, crossed Bull Run and rushed to join the fight. One Highlander described their

where the fiting was going on and the enemy was running up the [Henry] hill in great haste scattered in all directions & we thought the battle was all over but it was not right begun.[51] There masked battries opened on us and such cannonnading. We were ordered down the [Buck] hill right in front of there firing & when we got down a Little out of the way of our own artirlere commenced firing over our heads & they were firing in among us and when we got down in [t]he hollow we Lay down so as to avoid getting struck as much as possable and when Lying there I came verry near being shot from our own side. A grapeshot struck the ground about 2 inches from my hip so you can amigon [imagine] the crictal place we were in.[52]

The amineshan of our artirally run out and we were ordered up the [Henry] hill to take it and such a shaturing I cannot begin to write about. A man that is in the battle cannot tell much about it. Annyhow we had them entirely Licked. You could not se anny of them then. We came down and the generals were forming the regiments in squares to receive calvelry. Us and [the] 69[th New York] formed together but it was no use. General Jonston had arrived with his whole army of fresh troops and we had non[e] so we had to retreat and such a retreat. The most of the regiments was without officers and the generals rode off on

---

advance: "We sprung from the earth like the armed men of Cadmus. On we rushed by the flank, over fields, through woods, down into ravines, plunging into streams, up again onto rising meadows, eager, excited, thrilled with hot desire to bear our share in routing the enemy." Todd, *Highlanders*, 33; Davis, *Battle at Bull Run*, 185; William C. Lusk, ed., *War Letters of William Thompson Lusk* (New York: William Crittenden Lusk, 1911), 57.

51. Upon their arrival, Sherman's brigade augmented the Union forces at the point of battle to roughly 18,000 men; Confederate colonel Nathan "Shanks" Evans, although having received reinforcements, still had only 3,000 men with which to face the oncoming Federals. Shortly after noon, the severely outnumbered Confederates appeared to be routed as they beat a hasty retreat southward from Matthews Hill, around which the initial fighting had occurred, and regrouped upon the heights and far (southeastern) slope of nearby Henry Hill. With apparent victory in his sights, commanding general Irvin McDowell inexplicably delayed his pursuit of the broken Rebels for nearly two hours, giving the Confederates on Henry Hill time to receive reinforcements and prepare for the renewed Federal advance. It was in defense of this hill that Confederate general Thomas Jonathan Jackson, in successfully rallying the Confederates, earned his name and reputation as "Stonewall." Hennessy, *The First Battle of Manassas*, 62–63, 72–73; Davis, *Battle at Bull Run*, 193–203.

52. At about 2:30 P.M., McDowell ordered Sherman's brigade to enter the recently renewed fight for Henry Hill. Sherman's four regiments (13th, 69th, and 79th New York, and the 2d Wisconsin) descended the slope of Buck Hill, crossed the Warrenton Turnpike and Young's Branch, and paused to reform at the foot of Henry Hill in the relative safety of the depressed Sudley Road. Hennessy, *The First Battle of Manassas*, 102.

horseback telling the men to hurry up or the enemy would be on them so they did come on us.[53] The calvelry came upon us on the road. I wa[s] comming along myself the onely one I mean of our regiment to the road when bang went a volley from the enemys calvelry which had come up on us. I runn right into the woods and came up with another of our regiment. Then we came across a field running as fast as we could. We tried to get into another wood. I was not able to go anny farther so I Lay down and gave up all hops. There was 2 more of us and we Lay in sight of the road. We could see our army retreating and the men cutting there horses Loose from the wagons and monting there backs and galloping off as fast as they could. We Lay a Long while then we started for the woods and kept in them till we came in sight of the ground we started from in the morning. But there was no 79th there so we cept well up of

53. General Sherman, like other Union commanders throughout the day's battle, sent the regiments of his brigade piecemeal up the slope of Henry Hill into the fire of its Rebel defenders. As a result, the Confederates on Henry Hill, steadily growing in number as fresh reinforcements reached their position, did not face the full force of Sherman's brigade at once; attacking virtually unsupported, the regiments of Sherman's command had little chance to succeed in their individual assaults.

Shortly after 2:30 P.M., Sherman sent the 2d Wisconsin up the hill, which was repulsed and sent back down the slope bloodied and disorganized. As the remnants of the 2d Wisconsin rushed back down the hill, the men of the 79th New York were ordered up the slope. In the words of one Highlander: "Soon it came our turn to charge. As we rose to our feet and advanced, a long cheer went up from the men, which could be heard above the boom of the cannon and the roar of musketry. We moved slowly and steady at first, for the way was extremely uneven, and it was difficult to preserve the regularity of the line. . . . Numbers of our men went down as the hurricane of Iron [from Confederate artillery] swept by us, and it was with no little difficulty that we could close up the line so as to charge effectively. . . . The Confederates waited until we appeared above the brow of the hill, and then poured such a volley upon us as decimated the regiment in an instant. Scores of men fell forward on their faces with a peculiar supine motion, as a wave falls forward on a beach."

As the men of the 79th clung to the slope of Henry Hill, "still obstinately firing," their colonel, James Cameron, was fatally shot in the chest. Then from among the Highlanders rang out the cry "Cease firing! You're shooting your own men!" (Confusion had reigned on the battlefield as several Federal units, like the 2d Wisconsin, were dressed in gray, while Confederates rallied around the Stars and Bars, a flag which closely resembled the Federal Stars and Stripes.) For the 79th New York on the slope of Henry Hill, the momentary hesitation which the confused call produced proved deadly; seeing what appeared to be a Union flag among the troops in their front, the Highlanders held their fire long enough for their Confederate opponents to pour two more volleys into their ranks. Disorganized and beaten, the Highlanders fell back to the base of Henry Hill and deployed into squares to defend against an expected cavalry attack. Todd, *Highlanders*, 37–43; *New York Tribune*, 29 July 1861; Hennessy, *The First Battle of Manassas*, 102–8; O.R., Series 1, vol. 2, 368–371.

the road till we came into centervall and the regiments that was at the fight tryed to get themselvs together but it was impossable. Sume of our regiment was scatterered all around among the regiments. I tryed to find out if mat or James was there. I could not get anny word of them so I gave them up for Lost then started with a small party for arlington hights. Sometimes I would be along with one or two of our own men other times I would be [by] myself. I traveled till I was sleeping wa[l]king along. I Lay Down in some cut wheat that was near the road side and slept 2 hours or about that. Then I started on the road again and I met in with one of our hand men. He was as bad as myself in reguard to knowing anything about them.

So I marched on passing men on the way without shoes or stokings and the most of them Lame. On I went till I came to the place where we Left our tents & knapsacks and when I arrived there the most of them wa[s] taken Down. So I took my knapsack and started for fort corcran 4 miles more. It was rainning verry hard too and when I arrived at the fort the first thing I asked for matthew & James & I was told that they were all safe. I did no[t] se them for some time after that. Each one was stowed away the best way he could from the rain. There was nothing for us to eat. We were all entirely wore out.

I met in with David Mcfadgan and he gave me Jonneys Likeness and I was glad to se it. My space wont admit of finishing it as I would Like to. Any how we are encamped in a verry nice place not verry far from where John stuart Lives.[54] Its not in the city and its not out of it. Thats as near as I can give. The place is verry nice but I am sick of sogren [soldiering] and I cannot feel satisfied no where but home and if I can get away at all I will come. Mat & James is well. J is to write soon. So Jane this is a rough sketch of the battle & retreat of Bulls Runn.

No more this time But Remains
Your afficonate husband.
Alexander Campbell

I sent the piece I cut out of the k[n]apsack with Jamess name on it with one of our Company that has got his Discharge.

---

54. As of 26 July, the Highlanders were encamped at Camp Ewen, "on the east end of the range called Meridian Hill, at the head of Tenth street" in Washington, D.C. Todd, *Highlanders,* 54.

Chapter Two

"THERE IS A GREAT CHANGE IN THINGS HERE NOW"

September 1861 through 18 October 1861

Alexander Campbell was not the only one tired of soldiering after the Battle of Bull Run, which served as a humiliating and costly wake-up call to most Northern soldiers and civilians. Forced to acknowledge that their Confederate opponents were both able and willing to fight, previously confident Union soldiers had to swallow the bitter pill of defeat and recognize that the war might not soon be over.

The exhaustion, frustration, and humiliation within the Union army produced by the defeat at Bull Run soon turned to hostility among the men of the 79th New York. Increasingly disgruntled with their brigade commander, Colonel Sherman, who on a rainy and cold 22 July had ejected a group of weary Highlanders from a barn so as to shelter horses within the structure, the men of the 79th New York successfully petitioned the secretary of war, Simon Cameron, for a transfer from Sherman's command. This did not significantly improve the sagging morale of the Highlanders, however, who were falling prey to illness in increasing numbers. To add to their woes, many of the regiment's officers, weary of war and yearning to be reunited with their families, resigned their commissions and returned home, leaving a significant void in the unit's command structure. Additionally, scores of dissatisfied enlisted men began to desert, further weakening the strength and morale of the regiment.[1]

The 79th's spirit lifted in late July, when it appeared the regiment would be sent to New York to refill its depleted ranks via recruitment and to elect a new colonel. This would have provided the Highlanders with their first opportunity to visit friends and loved ones since their departure. On 10 August, however, the Highlanders were suddenly presented with their new colonel, Isaac Ingalls Stevens, a West Point graduate and former governor of the Washington Territory, who, unbeknownst to the members of the 79th, had been appointed their commanding officer by the War Department on 30 July 1861.[2] Shock soon turned to anger as the Highlanders not only realized that their right as a militia unit to elect their commanding officer had been denied, but that their much anticipated return to New York was highly unlikely.[3]

The doubts of the Highlanders were confirmed on 13 August 1861, when Colonel Stevens issued orders at dress parade that the 79th would strike camp the following morning and relocate to Maryland—not New York. When company officers ordered the Highlanders to strike their tents and prepare to move on 14 August, only two companies (I and K) obeyed. Many officers, while attempting to enforce Stevens's orders "amid the jeers, the taunts, and the insults of an infuriated mob" of Highlanders, were treated roughly by their men. Upon learning of the open and hostile insubordination of his troops, Colonel Stevens solicited the assistance of his superior, who in turn informed commanding general McClellan of the situation.[4]

McClellan acted quickly, sending an intimidating detachment of regular infantry, artillery, and cavalry to suppress the Highlanders' insurgence. Authorized by McClellan to use force if necessary, the troops approached and surrounded the mutinous Highlanders, effectively quashing the mass insubordination.[5] The Highlanders were then

---

1. Jeffry D. Wert, "Mutiny in the Army." *Civil War Times Illustrated* 24 (April 1985): 13–14; Todd, *Highlanders,* 52–55; Lusk, *War Letters,* 67–68; *New York Herald,* 17 August 1861; Lonn, *Foreigners in the Union Army and Navy,* 131.

2. Todd, *Highlanders,* 58–60; Wert, "Mutiny in the Army," 15.

3. *New York Herald,* 17 August 1861.

4. Lusk, *War Letters,* 74; Todd, *Highlanders,* 61–62.

5. Hazard Stevens, *The Life of Isaac Ingalls Stevens* (Boston and New York: Houghton, Mifflin and Company, 1900), vol. 2, 325.

marched under armed guard to Fourteenth Street in Washington, where thirty-five ringleaders of the uprising were placed under arrest. More insulting, however, were the words of General McClellan, whose Special Order No. 27 was read aloud to the men of the 79th. McClellan ordered the regiment's colors taken away, not to be returned "until its members have shown by their conduct in camp, that they have learned the first duty of soldiers—obedience—and have proven on the field of battle that they are not wanting in courage." With these words, the colors of the 79th were surrendered. "Not till then," remarked one Highlander, "did many of the men realize to what an extent their insubordination had led them."⁶

No letters from Alexander to Jane Campbell between 28 July and 3 September 1861 are extant. Although no known records survive to document the role Alexander Campbell played in the mutiny or to trace his exact whereabouts throughout the month of August, it is certain that he did return home to New York City during this period.⁷ Whether or not Campbell's visit home was authorized (roughly 140 Highlanders deserted during the period of the mutiny) remains unclear. Regardless, Campbell stayed away from the 79th New York longer than permitted and was listed as absent without leave after 15 August. Muster rolls show that Alexander Campbell returned to the regiment on 2 September, an event which, as evidenced by his next letter to Jane, took a good bit of planning.⁸

LETTER 9

[Sept. 3d 1861]

Dear Jane

I arrieved here in dew time and went right to John Stewarts. By good Luck Jammey was there he having got a pass till 4 o clock and he was verry glad of what your mother sent. He had to go way to the camp so as he would be ther at the time on his pass for they are verry strick now. He said it would be better for me to stay away from camp

---

6. Todd, *Highlanders*, 63, 66.

7. Confirmation of Alexander Campbell's visit home is found in several of his subsequent letters to his wife Jane. See Alexander Campbell to Jane Campbell, 3 September 1861 and 29 July 1862, CFP-SCDAH.

8. Compiled Service Record of Alexander Campbell.

to night and he would tell Mcnie[9] that I was come back and he would k[n]ow what would be the best way to do. Jammey thinks it will be all right. David Ireland told Jammey two o 3 times to write for me to come back. He said how he wanted me to come back. Any how James Brown is in John Stewarts yet he is waiting for money from his folks in Cunnicut. I got my carpet Bag that time when I went to see [Brother] Peter. It was all right. I will write you as soon as I get all right again which I expect will be tomorrow.

> So dont worry. I think it will be all
>   right.
> Your husband
> A Campbell

⟶➤●≪⟵

LETTER 10

> The bivoc of the Center Divison of
>   the grand army of the Potomac
>   near Chain b[r]idge virginie[10]
> Sept 6t[h] 1861

Dear Jane

I wrote you a Letter on the 3d. I had not time to get it posted for we Left in such heast none of us knew anything about it unill we were on the road. We marched up and croast the chain Bridge and have bivoced here. It has been wet and dissegreable weather. Our reighment

---

9. 1st Lt. Robert McNie, Co. F, 79th New York Highlanders. McNie, age 40, enrolled to serve three years in New York City and was mustered in as first lieutenant of Co. F on 27 May 1861. McNie was promoted (no date) to the captaincy of Co. F after the resignation of Captain Christie on 10 September 1861, and would remain with the regiment until his own discharge on 18 May 1862. Phisterer, *New York in the War of the Rebellion,* vol. 4, 2855.

10. Early in the morning of 4 September 1861, the 79th New York Highlanders, now attached to Stevens's brigade (consisting of the 2d and 3d Vermont, the 79th New York, and the 6th Maine) of Gen. W. F. "Baldy" Smith's division, Army of the Potomac, crossed the Potomac River via the Chain Bridge and entered Virginia. The camp established there was named Camp Advance. Todd, *Highlanders,* 71–72; Stevens, *The Life of Isaac Ingalls Stevens,* vol. 2, 328.

worked in the trenches yerterday making a fort. The woods is getting cut down all arround.[11]

Since I commenced writing we have got orders to go a on a scouting expidion for twenty four hours. Things is conducted in a differant way on this expidison. Its reported that the enemy is on the advance. We are going out to see any how.

I dont know how I am to get this sent. I will have it ready for the first chance. I have not had time to write to Brother Peter since I came out. I hope he will not be angry about it for reighments is moved about so often that when we holt and fix a place for ourselves we have to mouve.

Sunday Sept 8th

I have got back from the scouting expedision Last night. I am writing this on my catridge Box beside a corn field with our miskets [muskets] is stalked in line before us. We are expecting to mak[e] a foreward movement every movement. Jane I have not had time to get this posted this morning and I have not got a in[v]elope and I dont know how I am to get one. The Letter I wrote you before Leaving camp I gave to one of our company that was Left behind. I had no stamp. I told him to give it to John stwart. I expected him to stamp it for me. I had no Idea that we would have to start so soon. We have all got 48 hours rashions with us. God knows where we are going. No one knows anything about movements Know. I canot write with this pincle. I dont know how you are to read it for I cannot read it myself but I cannot do any better. I will come to a close this time hoping this will find you and Jonney and the babby[12] well as it Leaves me. James and matthew is well. I hope to hear from you soon. Good day.

---

11. In the wake of the Union defeat at Bull Run, apprehensive Northern military leaders sought a more formal and elaborate system of protection for the nation's capital. Gen. George B. McClellan, who had replaced Gen. Irvin McDowell as commander of the Army of the Potomac, enthusiastically endorsed such a plan; in August 1861, construction was begun on a series of forty-eight forts and other defenses around Washington on which the men of many regiments stationed nearby, like the 79th New York, were used as laborers. The Highlanders were employed on the construction of Fort Marcy, located south of the Potomac River, which guarded the approaches to the Chain Bridge. Upon completion, Fort Marcy had a total perimeter of 338 yards with emplacements for eighteen guns. Benjamin Franklin Cooling III and Walton H. Owen II, *Mr. Lincoln's Forts: A Guide to the Civil War Defenses of Washington* (Shippensburg, Pa.: White Mane Publishing Company, 1988), x, 1–6, 30, 112; Todd, *Highlanders,* 72.

12. Alexander Campbell, Jr., apparently born the previous month.

I Remain Your Afficonate Husband
Alexander Campbell

━━━━►>●<━━━━

LETTER 11

Camp Advanced Virginia
Sept 9th 1861

Dear Jane

I received your Letter Last night and was happy to hear you was
well and the baby and Jonney was getting along so well. I wrote you a
Letter and sent it off the other day. It was wrote with pincel I not having any ink. I know you wont feel satisfied with it. I could not do any
better.

We have to worke in the trenches so many hours in the day. They
are making this place verry strong. It comands the chain bridge. Theres
one fort made and another on the way.[13]

There was a soldier going to be shot here to Day. There was 5 of
our reighment Detailed to do it but he got pardoned. It was for sleeping on his post that is when on sentry.

I have just returned from Dress prade. I cannot get time to finish a
Letter when I com[cut out] is such activity among t[ime we] thing is don
up to [cut out] if we be forst to retreat this [cut out] will have sumthing
to fall beh[ind. I] think that Mclellan intends [cut out] up entrenshments
everry 5 mil[es in] advance. We are ready all the [time to] march. We
have crackers and salt horse that is the soldiers name for beef for 48
hours. This place is about 4 miles from Georgetown on the Potomac.

There was a number of recruits came in here to night. The reighment is getting up verry well. I have got to be a sergant again.[14] You
know I always told you they Could not get allong without me. I dont
meen that you know. As I am writing this Matthew is sin[g]ing Roys

---

13. In addition to Fort Marcy, another fort, Fort Ethan Allen, was constructed during September 1861 to protect the Virginia approaches to the Chain Bridge. Larger than
Fort Marcy, Fort Ethan Allen was 736 yards in perimeter and was designed to contain
thirty-six guns. Cooling and Owen, *Mr. Lincoln's Forts*, 30, 118.
14. This promotion is not recorded in the Compiled Service Record of Alexander
Campbell.

Wife a val the valloch.[15] He is a pet in the company. He keeps them all Lauphing speekin broad scotch.

I am glad you got the money from the union defence commitee. I dont know now how about our pay on account of being sent out here. I here its treasury noats they pay with so the brokers will have a discount on them.

Its reported here to night that Jonston is crost in to mariland with 50000 men and they seem to think here that is just what they want. They have to keep there men moving to keep them from getting disheartened.[16] Mclelland is allways around inspecting everry thing with his own eye and setting everry to rights.

I will have to come to a close this time. The candle is getting dun. I [had a] hard job getting it. There is non allowed here to us. James and mat is well. I am in verry good helth myself and I hope this will fiend you the same. Write soon. Good night.

Your afficonate husband
Alex Campbell

Write soon.

LETTER 12

Camp Advance
Sept 13th 1861

Dear Jane

I have just received your Letter and have Lost no time to answer it. Its Late to night and I have not had your Letter over 20 minits. We have just got in from the trenshes after being in them from 8 o clock.

---

15. "Roy's Wife of Aldivalloch," an 18th century Scottish song in which a husband laments the loss of his cheating wife. George Farquhar Graham, *The Popular Songs of Scotland, With Their Appropriate Melodies* (Glasgow: J. Muir Wood and Co., 1887), 138–39.

16. No such movement was made by General Johnston, head of the Confederate Department of the Potomac, who remained stationed with his army at Manassas. E. B. Long, *The Civil War Day by Day: An Almanac, 1861–1865* (New York: Da Capo Press, Inc., 1971),116; Boatner, *Dictionary*, 441.

We worked our regular Days work but had to got to work with the moon on account of the enemy advancing [and] the country folks having come in to our camps to get out of the way. Things is in a great state here to night. All the reighments was called out on account of some cannonading that was heard in the direction of the enemys Lines. We expect a fight tomorrow and I think if they attack us we feel confident that they will be driven back never to rally again. There was great fires seen all along the enemys Lines to night. I think its a signal for there advance.

You will have seen by the news that we had a but brush with the [enemy] the other day. I have not time to g[o into] the pirticulars about it but it was [a sh]arp brush.[17] There was one of our compan[y woun]ded. Its verry slight. It was a shell that burst right over our heads. One of the other that was wounded died since. Our company was detailed to go a scouting. There was a man with us Leading us all through the places that there was a suspision of them being. I have not time to say any more about it but the 79th has to go every where. There is no rest for them. The other reighments think the highlanders is great fellows.

I wrote you a Letter stating that I was a sergant and I sent a Letter to [Brother] Peter. I had no stamps so I had to write soilders Letter.[18] The 4 stamps you sent will come in virry handy.

We had a great time here one night since we came over here. We were revuied [on 10 September] by General Mclelland and the presi-

---

17. On 11 September 1861, a force of approximately 1,800 men under the command of Colonel Stevens was ordered to "cover and protect a reconnaissance [by Lt. O. M. Poe's U.S. Topographical Engineers] of the village of Lewisville and vicinity to determine all the facts that would be required for its permanent occupation and defense."

As the 79th approached Lewinsville, two of its companies were deployed in front as skirmishers. One of these was Co. F, to which Alexander Campbell and James and Matthew Ralston belonged. Once the reconnaissance was completed, the skirmishers, having yet to encounter any of the enemy, were recalled. As they began to withdraw, hidden Confederate infantry and artillery fired into their ranks. Although the enemy, according to Capt. David Ireland, "could not have been more than fifteen yards from them [the skirmishers] at the time they opened fire," casualties among the Highlanders were slight (varying reports record their casualties from one to three men). Their mission accomplished, Stevens's force retired in order back to Camp Advance. O.R., Series 1, vol. 5, 168–76; Todd, *Highlanders*, 76–79.

18. On 3 August 1861, Congress approved an act which allowed Union soldiers to send letters without prepayment. The postage for these "soldier's letters" was paid by the recipient. John D. Billings, *Hard Tack and Coffee* (Boston: George M. Smith and Co., 1887), 63–64; O.R., Series 3, vol. 1, 383.

dant [and the] sectuary of war and a great many prominent men. Mclelland spoke verry good of us and told us we would have our colours back and sai[d] we never disgreasest them. And Cameron said his house would be a home for any of the 79th.

Jane you will have to excuse me to night for this scribling. I worked too hard with the pike and showvel and my hand [is] shaking and another thing I have to hurry. We dont know the moment we w[ill be] called out. We have to sleep with our catrich box on and 40 rounds in it. I can assure you time is verry pracious with us at present. There is other reighments working in the trenches and will be all night. There was a balloon on the other side of the river asending and desending all day to day watching the enemys movements.[19] I have not time to say any more this time. Hoping this will find you all well as it Leaves us. Mat told me to tell you that we were to give them blases tomorrow. So good night. If god spares us I expect we will soon have the ware all over and peace and happyness in the country soon again. So once more good night again. They are all mostly asleep around me. I hope to here from you soon

and I Remain your ever Afficonate
Husband
Alexander Campbell

We expect to get payed soon. I will send you the money as soon as I get it.

A Campbell

LETTER 13

Camp Advance Virginia
Sept 21st 1861

---

19. Balloons were used by both Union and Confederate armies during the Civil War for aerial reconnaissance. Early in the war, aeronaut Thaddeus C. Lowe convinced the United States government of the advantages of aerial reconnaissance as performed by observation balloons; Lowe was attached to the Army of the Potomac in August 1861 and awarded a contract to deliver seven such balloons by June 1862. Although a hazardous and imperfect means of reconnaissance, observation balloons could nevertheless provide invaluable military information to those who used them. Patricia L. Faust, ed., *Historical Times Illustrated Encyclopedia of the Civil War* (New York: Harper & Row, 1986), 35–36.

Dear Jane

I received your Letter of 17th in dew time and was most happy to here that you Jonney & the baby was well. The Last time I wrote you there was great excitement here. We were expecting to be attacked every day and we had to be always on the alert but now its Quite different. All the expecting of an attack has died away becaus we are ready for them now. We have got this place well nigh finished and if they show there nose in this direction it will be verry apt to get smashed.

You ask if I have got a blanket. I have and we have all got nise over coats so th[at] we are well clade and we have got our tents now we were without the first week.

You will have seen by the newspapers that we have got our Colours back.[20] I am appointed to carry one of them yesterday afternoon.[21]

General Mclelland & staff accomp[anie]d with the Prince De Join-

---

20. On 14 September 1861, Major General McClellan issued the following order to General Smith: "The colors of the New York Seventy-ninth will be sent to you tomorrow. Please return them to the regiment, with the remark that they have shown by their conduct in the reconnaissance of the 11th instant [at Lewinsville, Va.] that they are worthy to carry the banner into action, and the commanding general is confident they will always in future sustain and confirm him in the favorable opinion he has formed of them."

Two days later, the men of the 79th New York assembled on the parade-ground of the brigade to receive their colors, which were escorted there by the 3d Vermont and General Smith, who briefly addressed the Highlanders: "Soldiers of the Seventy-Ninth: By direction of the Major-General commanding [McClellan], I restore to your custody the banners of the regiment. Since you have been under my command you have earned them. I hope that when an opportunity offers you will prove yourselves worthy of them." Although the brief ceremony was not, according to one Highlander, "quite so stupendous and imposing as the *taking-away* process," it nevertheless brought an official and lasting end to their past period of insubordination. O.R., Series 1, vol. 5, 168; Todd, *Highlanders,* 80; *Scottish American Journal,* 19, 26 September 1861.

21. As a newly selected color-bearer, Alexander Campbell played a prominent role during the ceremony of 16 September: "The ceremony of giving back the colors commenced by General Smith advancing, and, after a few appropriate remarks common on such occasions, the vouchers of our former services to the country were placed in the hands of our color-bearers, John R. Hunter (1st company) and Alexander Campbell (6th company), the two best-looking soldiers, doubtless, in the estimation of the adjutant."

Appointment to the regimental color guard was widely considered to be an honor; as such, the men of the color guard were carefully chosen: "The corporals for the color-guard will be selected from those most distinguished for regularity and precision, as well in their positions under arms as in their marching. The latter advantage, and a just carriage of the person, are to be more particularly sought for in the selection of the color-bearer." *Scottish American Journal,* 26 September 1861; Casey, *Schools of the Soldier and Company,* 16.

vell[22] came [cut out]. Of corse stevens and his Highlanders had to turn out. We were the only reighment that was called on. We were drawen up in Line awating his arrival which we were to know by a salvo of artirallie. He [McClellan] revuied us. He came along our Line till he came to the center where the colnel was. I was right behind him. The other colour bearer too. He holted and shook hands with our colnel & said he was glad to see us with our colours back and he seemed to think a great deal of us. He think the world of our colnel. He interduced him to the Prince.

The reason why I did not send a Line for you to get money out of the bank I thought we were to get payed in a day or so from that time but we havent got it yet. I will send a Line so as you can get money. Its verry hard to think that you cannot get it without a Line from me.

You say your mother wants to know if I am in the tent with mat. James & mat is together and Brown too. I am not in the same tent. I dont belong to no company now since I got to carry the colours. I am staying in the 6th [F] Companys tents yet till we get one for ourselvs.

You said in one of your Letters it was getting cold nigts now. Its getting cold here too nights. I think if Mclelland Lets the Southerners alone a Little Longer the cold will chase them away. The reighment has to work in the trenches from 1 PM untill 5 1/2 PM every day except sunday. I have just received 4 newspers from [Brother] Peter and they come in verry good. I get one mostly everry day. I would Like to know if [Brother] Peter got an answer from the South about [Brother] James

---

22. François-Ferdinand-Philippe-Louis-Marie d'Orléans, the Prince de Joinville (1818–1900). The third son of King Louis-Philippe of France, de Joinville, a vice-admiral in the French navy, was exiled along with other members of the Orléans family following the Revolution of 1848. In early 1861, de Joinville traveled the United States to place his sixteen-year-old son in the Naval School at Newport, Rhode Island. When war broke out in April 1861, de Joinville and the two nephews who had accompanied him on his journey took advantage of the opportunity to experience a military campaign. The trio was received by President Lincoln and assigned to the staff of General McClellan as aides-de-camp. The prince and his nephews served with McClellan from 20 September 1861 through the end of the Peninsular Campaign in July 1862.

Writing of de Joinville and his nephews, General McClellan praised the foreigners, stating that his "personal experience with the three members of the family who served with me was such that there could be no doubt as to their courage, energy, and military spirit." Edgar Leon Newman, ed., *Historical Dictionary of France from the 1815 Restoration to the Second Empire* (New York: Greenwood Press, Inc., 1987), vol. 1, 532; Lonn, *Foreigners in the Union Army and Navy,* 277–79; Jay Monaghan, *Diplomat in Carpet Slippers: Abraham Lincoln Deals with Foreign Affairs* (New York: The Bobbs-Merrill Company, Inc., 1945), 139–41; George B. McClellan, *McClellan's Own Story* (New York: Charles L. Webster and Company, 1887), 144–45.

or if he has wrote to Brother John.[23] I have not got any more news this time. Hoping this will find you & your care as it Leaves me. Please write as soon as you receive this and I remain your ever afficonate Husband.

Alexander Campbell

LETTER 14

Camp Advance
Sept 26th 1861

Dear Jane

Your Letter of the 23d was in my tent Last night when we arrieved home and I was happy to heare from you. You say the baby has the hooping coph. Poor Little fellow as you say. It must be soor on him. I hope it will soon be better. Im glad to here that Jonney is getting along so well. I know you must be wore out with them but it cannot be helped.

Our reighment was out yesterday from erly morning till after dark. There was other reighments two 5000 men besides a great amount of arterily. It was to get hay and corn that was at Luinsville and se and find out the enemys posihon. If corse the 79th had to go first and scour all the woods that Lay in the direction of the enemy. They drove in there pickets all along and captured one. He was one of Stewarts calvery he did not [cut out] idea of being taken a bit. There w[ere] [cut out] detailed to take him to general smiths head Quarters. I asked one of them if he said anything about the south. They told me he was Quite stiff and he said the northe never would subdue the south. There was some exchanges of shells but it did not amount to much. One of

---

23. John Campbell, brother of Alexander Campbell. Born 26 February 1824 in Kilmadock Parish, Perthshire, Scotland, John, an unmarried farmer, lived in Georgia and South Carolina before 1861. His whereabouts during the war are uncertain. James Campbell to Alexander Campbell, 28 September 1860, June 1862, CFP-SCDAH; Alexander Campbell to Jane Campbell, 31 July 1862, CFP-SCDAH; Old Parish Register, Perthshire (1839–1830), Kilmadock/362/5, New Register House, Edinburgh, Scotland.

our men was struck on the shoulder with a shell. It was slightly. They would not come out of the woods so as they would be seen.[24] One of the sergants of the 6th [F] comp[any] escaped from richmond william paccet.[25] He was ten days on the road. He had some verry narrow excapes on the road. He is in camp now. He sayes there men are in a sad state for shoues and clothing and food and they have verry few tents which accoints for having such sickness among them. I dont know what they are to do in winter if it does not be setteled before that. They cannot stand it no how. I dont know in fact what we are to do ourselvs for its getting cold enuph now nights. I hope it will soon be over and Let us to our homes in winter.

You say David Ireland is in new york. He was glad to Leave here I think so.[26] The colnel I dont think Liked him much. I undirstand he was always snaping him. I tell you the Little colnel makes our officers fly round. David or rather Captain Ireland did all he could for me to get me back without any trouble.

Pearson is back and nothing said to him. You said you would have

---

24. On 25 September 1861, General Smith sent 5,100 infantry, 16 pieces of artillery, 150 cavalry and some 90 empty wagons on an expedition to acquire grain and forage in Lewinsville. As Campbell accurately describes, six companies of the 79th were sent ahead of the main force as skirmishers. Much like their previous experience at Lewinsville on 11 September, Union troops saw little of the enemy until, their mission complete, they began to withdraw. As the skirmishers of the 79th were returning to the main force, they captured a Rebel trooper who claimed to be an aide to the flamboyant Confederate cavalry commander Col. J. E. B. Stuart. Stuart's horsemen were quickly approaching the Union position at Lewinsville, and, although both sides exchanged fire briefly upon their arrival, the Federals were able to withdraw with their newly acquired supplies virtually unmolested. O.R., Series 1, vol. 5, 215–17; Todd, *Highlanders,* 82–83.

25. Campbell is referring here to William Fawcett, Co. F, 79th New York Highlanders. Wounded at the Battle of Bull Run and taken prisoner afterwards, Sergeant Fawcett was among those who made their escape from captivity in Richmond in September 1861. Capt. William Manson, Co. A, 79th New York Highlanders, a prisoner at the facility which had held William Fawcett, penned the following lines in a 15 September 1861 letter to the *Scottish American Journal* which helps illuminate the incident: "We have not been allowed out to market in some time. I think it is on account of some of the prisoners making their escape from here, and putting the authorities to considerable trouble, and at the same time it makes them more stringent with us." Fawcett remained with the 79th New York after his escape but was absent in arrest at Fort Columbus, New York Harbor, at the muster out of his company on 31 May 1864. *Scottish American Journal,* 26 September 1861; *Report of the Adjutant-General,* 867.

26. Captain Ireland had served as adjutant of the 79th New York since 1 June 1861. He was discharged from the Highlanders on 12 September 1861 so that he could accept a position in the Regular Army (137th Infantry). According to one member of the 79th, "Captain Ireland was much thought of by the Highlanders, not alone on account of his ability as an officer, but for his personal and social qualities as well." Todd, *Highlanders,* 80; Phisterer, *New York in the War of the Rebellion,* vol. 4, 2853.

sent some gin. James and mat was expecting some. He said only for Daniel Mcglachlan[27] he would have taken it. He told him he would be searched and it taken from him. A Little would go verry good here now. There is plenty men feels worse for the want of it than me. There is no getting Liquour of any kind here.[28]

This is thanks giving day and it is respected as such with the exception of some men thats working in the fort.[29] Our Pay master was here to day but I dont know when we are to get payed.[30] I think it wont be Long and as soon as I get it I will send it you the first chance. You must want money now. You ought to draw the money out of the bank.

I will now come to a close hoping this will find you well (& Little Alexander. I suppose you have him named him that. You said that was to be his name). I hope he will soon be better & Jonney too. He says I am gon to fight for the union. Poor Little fellow. I am shure I wish it was over till I would be home and going to my days work again. Good afternoon and I hope you will answer this one as Quick as you did the Last one and oblige you ever afficonate husband

Alexander Campbell

27. Daniel McLauglin, Co. F, 79th New York Highlanders. McLauglin, age 22, enlisted on 13 May 1861 at New York City to serve for three years and was mustered in as private, Co. F, on 27 May 1861. He was promoted to corporal on 6 April 1863, returned to ranks, and then promoted to corporal again on 1 April 1864. McLauglin retained this rank until he was mustered out at New York City on 31 May 1864. *Report of the Adjutant-General*, 966.

28. Restrictions on liquor in the Union army varied from unit to unit. Although the presence of liquor among enlisted men was not necessarily disdained by their officers—the Federal Government itself occasionally distributed liquor to Union troops in the form of whiskey rations—drunkenness was. Officers employed various measures to curb excessive drinking among soldiers and the undisciplined behavior it often produced, including the inspection of incoming boxes from home for alcohol, which, if found, was subject to confiscation. Wiley, *Billy Yank*, 198, 252–54; Billings, *Hard Tack and Coffee*, 139–42, 219.

29. By order of President Lincoln, Thursday, 26 September 1861 was designated as a day of "humiliation, prayer, and fasting" in the North. Long, *Civil War Day by Day*, 121; Todd, *Highlanders*, 83.

30. Union soldiers were supposed to be paid every two months. The military system of payment, however, was tedious and often inefficient. Every other month, soldiers were inspected and "mustered for payment" by a designated mustering officer who compiled rolls of all men present. The muster officer then sent copies of the muster rolls to both the adjutant general in Washington and the paymaster general. Only when the paymaster, whose job it was to calculate the amount owed to each soldier, received the necessary funds did he travel to various camps and distribute pay to anxiously awaiting soldiers. Not surprisingly, soldiers' pay was often months late in arriving. O.R., Series 3, 1:421; Wiley, *Billy Yank*, 48–49; Shannon, *The Organization and Administration of the Union Army*, vol. 1, 244–45.

LETTER 15

Camp Advance Va
October 4th 1861

Dear Jane

I received your Letter this evening. I thought there was sumthing
rong or you would have wrote sooner and it made me feel all the more
anxiouser to hear from you. I hope the poor Little baby is over the
worst of it now. It must be hard on so young a thing as him and the
weather comming on too makes it worse. You had no word in your
Letter whether you got the $20 twenty dollars I sent the same day I
sent the Letter. I have just been Looking at the receite. You could not
have got neither the Letter or money for I only sent it on the 1st and
your Letter is dated 2d so I made a mistake above. I am sorry to hear
such news about W. Guthrie[31] and his children sick too.

Our camp is shifted back a Little more in the shelter and things
Looks as if we were going to stay here sumetime. Its Late to night and
the Bugle has sounded sumetime ago to put out Lights but I must finish
this Letter to be ready to send with the post man in the moarning and
if it should not be a Long one you know the reason. Jammey was over
seeing me to night. I told him what you told me to tell him. You dout
that I am farr away from the rest because I say he was over seeing me
only the camp is Laid out on a Large scale and the tents is spread over
a considerable pice of ground and the tent I am in is away back a good
ways from the companys tents.

Theres no word about the enemy here now at all since they fell
back. Every one seems to think they have retired Back on Manasses
only a few Left in the vicinity of farfax.[32] I would Like verry much to

---

31. William Guthrie, 31, a Scottish-born resident of New York City. Before the war
Guthrie apparently worked with Alexander Campbell as a stonecutter and lived for a time
in the house next to that of Jane Ralston Campbell's parents. Alexander Campbell to Jane
Campbell, 10 October, 4 December 1861, CFP-SCDAH; 1860 Federal Population Census
for New York City, 9th Ward, District 3, p. 1068.
32. On 1 October 1861, President Jefferson Davis and generals Beauregard and Johnston, among others, held a conference on grand strategy at Centreville, Va. It was there
decided that the Confederate army in Virginia, located, as Alexander Campbell correctly
believed, near Manassas, was not yet strong enough to launch an invasion of the North,
and thus would maintain a defensive position. Long, *Civil War Day by Day*, 123; O.R.,
Series 1, vol. 5, 884–87.

know if [Brother] Peter has received anny word about Brother James yet. I see by the news papers that a great many of our Reigement that was Prisoners is sent to south Carolina and that there was a frindly feeling among the Irish of Charleston towards Colnel Corchran of the 69th.[33] There is a great many Irish there and the Cathloc Church is verry strong so that if they rise to free him Charleston would be in a bad fix. I would Like to pass the winter there. I would rather be home of corse.

I must come to a close this time hopping this will fiend you and Jonney & Alexander well as it Leaves me and you must write a Long Letter with all the news. Its Late. My tent mates is gon to sleep so I will bid you good night and may god watch over you all.

> I remain you ever Afficonate Husband
> Alexander Campbell

Be sure and write soon.

LETTER 16

> Camp Advance Va 79th NYsm
> October 7t[h] 1861

Dear Jane

33. On 10 September 1861, 156 Union prisoners of war, including several men from the 79th New York, were relocated from the tobacco warehouses in Richmond to Castle Pinckney in Charleston Harbor. Among those men sent south was Col. Michael Corcoran of the 69th New York State Militia. Corcoran, a native of Ireland, had been captured at the Battle of Bull Run and, refusing to sign a parole, remained a prisoner of war until his exchange on 15 August 1862.

In his reminiscences of his captivity, written shortly after his release, Colonel Corcoran discussed in depth his journey from Richmond to Castle Pinckney. About his transfer to Charleston, "that fountain city of secession," he wrote: "We got in during the afternoon, and I must acknowledge that I was much surprised, and equally pleased with the reception we received. From the time I had been captured up to the moment I set foot in Charleston, there was no place where I had been so well, or, rather, considerably treated as in that city." Promoted to brigadier general after his release, Corcoran continued to serve in the Union army until his accidental death on 22 December 1863 when the horse he was riding fell on him. *Scottish American Journal*, 26 September 1861; Boatner, *Dictionary*, 175–76; Jeffrey, *Richmond Prisons*, 17–18; Michael Corcoran, *The Captivity of General Corcoran* (Philadelphia: Barclay & Co., 1865), 39, 45.

I take this oppertunity of writing you a few Lines to Let you know that I send you $20 by adams express[34] this morning by one Going to washington on pass. I got payed Last night only privets pay.[35] Its too bad. It was all Mcnies falt. He is such a selfish being. He does not care about any one but himself. I out to got $34 but only got $23. I cannot give Mrs [John] st[e]wart anny this time for I know you must want it worse.

There is a great change in things here now. The rebels has retired back and we have got 3 days rashions in our haversacks ready to march to any point that they may try to cross the Potomac. Its only in case they try. Its best to be ready. I have not got time to write you much on accoint of the post man going away soon. Only I am in good helth. James & Mat is well. James said that Jonney and the baby had the hooping coff. I thought they were getting better. Send word as soon as you get this how they are.

Its getting Quite cold nights here now. Our colnel is made a Brigadear General.[36] [The] 79th is in his Brigade. His son is our Adjudant.[37] The Father will Look after us on that account. [Secretary of War] Cameron was up seeing us on sunday [29 September] and made a

---

34. The Adams Express Company. "In 1839 Alvin Adams, a produce merchant ruined by the panic of 1837, began carrying letters, small packages and valuables for patrons between Boston and Worcester. . . . By 1847 he had penetrated deeply into the South, and by 1850 he was shipping by rail and stagecoach to St. Louis. In 1854 his company was reorganized as the Adams Express Company. . . . The South was almost entirely covered by the Adams express service in 1861, when the Civil War necessitated the splitting off of another company, which, for politic reasons, was given the name of Southern. There was a mysterious kinship between the two ever afterward, they having joint offices at common points." James Trunslow Adams, ed., *Dictionary of American History* (New York: Charles Scribner's Sons, 1940), vol. 1, 9.

35. By Act of Congress on 6 August 1861, the pay of privates in the Union army was raised from $11 to $13 per month. At the time of Campbell's letter, a Union sergeant was to receive $17 per month. O.R., Series 3, vol. 1, 402; War Department, *Revised Regulations for the Army of the United States, 1861* (Philadelphia: J. B. Lippincott & Co., Publishers, 1862), 351.

36. On 28 September 1861, the Highlanders' Col. Isaac Ingalls Stevens was promoted to brigadier general; the following day, Stevens was formally assigned to the command of a brigade in Smith's division, which consisted of the 33d, 49th and 79th New York, and the 47th Pennsylvania. Despite his promotion, Stevens still retained immediate command of the 79th New York. Todd, *Highlanders,* 83–84; Stevens, *The Life of Isaac Ingalls Stevens,* vol. 2, 335–36.

37. 1st Lt. Hazard Stevens, son of Brig. Gen. Stevens. The younger Stevens, who had been performing the duties of adjutant since the departure of David Ireland, was formally appointed to that position by his father on 26 September 1861. Todd, *Highlanders,* 80–81; Stevens, *The Life of Isaac Ingalls Stevens,* vol. 2, 335.

speech & called us his Country men and his children and as Long as he was head of the war department he would see to us.

I am verry comfortable now in the tent I am in. There is only 3 of us and we have our place fixt nice. I have a nise bed fixt up for myself and we have a nice table which I am writing on now and shelfs and racks to hang our things on. We draw our own rashions and cook for ourselves. You would Like to see our shantie. If they would only Let us stay but we dont know the moment we will be called away. A soldier cannot call a moment his own. I will hav to come to a close this time hopping to hear from you soon and

> I Remain Your ever Afficonat Hus-
> band
> Alexander Campbell

Write soon a Long Letter.

⟶⟫●⟨⟵

LETTER 17

> Camp advance Va
> octr 10th 1861

Dear Jane

I received your Letter of the 8th this morning and was most happy to hear you and children was getting along so well. Since I wrote you Last we have had a forward movement and it came so sudden that no one even dreamt of it.[38] Orders came to our tent to be ready to start at 4 oclock in the moarning with 24 hours rashions and mind you that was between 12 & one oclock so I got up and got a fire Lighted [and] onother went for the meat and I got it cooked and got sun coffie made and tooke it. We had to pack up our knapsacks and Leave them so as they could be took after us. We got to gether the best way we could in the dark. Our rigement had to hurry most for as is always the case we have always to take the Lead. We advanced Casiously untill we came

---

38. It appears that Campbell misdated this letter. On 11 October 1861, Smith's division, with the Highlanders deployed in front as skirmishers, left Camp Advance and proceeded to and beyond Lewinsville, Va. Todd, *Highlanders,* 84.

to a place I dont know the name of it. Any how we were twise there before I need not mention all the minouvers only there was skirmishers throwen out to se if there was any sesshers Lurking in the woods. There happened to be non. Then the rest of the regiment advanced on to Luinsville. Then they were all throwen out about 2 miles beyond that as a picket so we were ordered back to head Quarters with the colors. Thats one advantage I have got now not having to be on picket.

Our tents is to be shifted to morrow. Its not farr from where we were before.[39] I am writing this in our old camp. I came back to get paper and ink. The regiment is all Lying where we are to camp. Our pickets is advanced 4 miles and connect with them from falls church and all this was dun without a shot being fired. Jammie and mat was out on picket. I was asking if they say the enemy. They saw sume of there calvery. We only avance slolely but I think surely. I wish it was over which I hope will be before the cold weather or us in good Quarters.

I had a Letter from [Brother] Peter. He told me he saw [Sister] ann that she was Living out in christoper St and about her having wourd from Brother James and that he was in the army. I was almost shure of it. Its getting dark and I have no Light so I must come to a close this time hopping that this will fiend you well. I hope the baby is all right now. I am glad that Jonney is getting such a fine boy. Now you must write right away after you get this for I always think Long for a Letter from you. I canot see whether I am on the Line or not so good nigt.

and I Remain Your ever Afficonate
husband
Alexander Campbell

I have just raised a Light and contented to stay in camp to night rather than go where the regiment is for its raining a Little and as I said befor have no tents and I have taken possession of one of the officers tents. It will be more comfortable for to night for me to stay where I am. You say you wished it was me that had the job in stead of W. Guthrie. I would stay better at it. I dont think he will ever get wise for

---

39. As a result of the movement of 11 October, the Highlanders' base was in the process of being shifted approximately five miles west of Camp Advance to Prospect Hill, where their new quarters were dubbed the Camp of the Big Chestnut. Todd, *Highlanders,* 84–85.

himself. I think if he was out here for a while he would Like stone cutting for eighteen shillings a day well enuph. I suppose he dont Like to work hard now. I guss Bet[40] is heart broke between one thing and another. Everry one has their own troubles in this world and I think you have as much at present as the nixt one. So I will come to a close wishing your troubles soon over that is me soon home. Good night.

your husband
Alex Campbell

$$\text{━━━⇒⧫⧫⧫⇐━━━}$$

LETTER 18

Camp of the 79th Va
octr 13th 1861

Dear Jane

This beng sunday night and having a few spare moments I take the oppertunity of writing you a few Lines to Let you know how I am getting along. As I mentioned to you in my Last Letter that we were moving a Lettel farther ahead. Well we have got all fixed again in a verry nise Little field about 2 miles farther ahead. We had verry wet weather the time of moving and of corse we were out in the wet without tents. But now thank god we have our tents and the weather clear and dry. Its a butiful moonlight night as I am writing and the air is could but the wind ha[s] calmd it being verry windy all day. The regiment is out on picket to day again. They went out at 3 oclock this morning.

Jane its verry cold here nights now espessally getting up in the moarning and I woul[d] Like if you would send me a Little brandy or gin or sume of both. You can send it by adams express and if your mother wanted to send any thing to the boys it could all be sent together. If you had seen Jammy to night you would been sorry for him. His company in on gaurd at head Quarters and when I went there he came to me and asked if I knew where he could get a smell as he calls it. Theres no such a thing to be got. His face was blue with the

40. Most likely Elizabeth Guthrie, age 29, wife of William Guthrie. 1860 Federal Population Census for New York City, 9th Ward, District 3, p. 1068.

could. I never hear him complain of being sick or sore now at all. Mat is standing it Like a brick always joking a merry [and] seems Quite content. I am Quite well myself only at present I have a slight cold and sume nights cofh a good deal but it dont amount to much. You must not think I send this for the Likour alon and if it puts you to a Little trouble as I have no dowt it will do you Know its for a poor soger that has no other way of getting it. I would give sumthing for a good drink of gin & molasses at present to stop the cofh. It always commences at this time of night.

I have no more to say to night only I hope this will fiend you and the children well and I think there wont be much fighting in Virginia. The rebels is all clearing away from here which meens that they are afraid to meet us on an open fight. They are falling back on bull run again so as they can get behind there fortifications but they wont Lead us into no trap this time and I begin to think that they are getting tierd of it now. I hope so. They cannot be too soon tierd of it for me. No more to night for its time to be in bed. So good night and I Remain your ever Afficonate husband

Alexander Campbell

Write soon.

———⊰●⊱———

LETTER 19

Camp of the big chesnut Va
october 16th 1861

Dear Jane

I have just received your Letter of the 14th and am most happy to hear you and the children is so well. You see I Loss no time in answering it. I know you feel anxious to hear from me all the time but you cannot fee[l] more anxious to hear from me than I feel to hear from you. When I think its about time that I should have a Letter from you I watch the comming of the post man verry anxiously. You must bear in mind that a Letter from home is thought a great deal of out here. Just consider yourself away in the wilds of Virginia and Living the way I am or I may say we are here. I know you would feel happy when you would hear from them you Loved. So you see its the only thing that makes me feel real happy when I hear good news from home and I trust in god I shall always here good news from home and you from me.

Theres a great change taken plase in the 79th this afternoon. You know steavens was made a Brigdeer General sumetime ago but he still acted as our colnel and he Kept us allways beside him in his brigade and he made his son our Augutant and in fact the men had such confidence in him that they would go anny where with him. Well he was called away by the war department this afternoon and of corse his son went with him.[41] He Knew nothing about it until a dispatch came for him to report in washington right away. The regiment turnd out so as he would take farewell of the 79th. He roade along the Line biding us all farewell. He mad[e] a speach his country called him and he must obey. He seemd to fee[l] sorry for Leaving. The men cried out for to take us with him.[42] It has ca[u]sed Quite a gloom amongst the men. So the 79th is Left with out a colnel or I may say officer at all. It seems verry unfortunate for officers.

There was an alarm Last night. The regiment thats on picket commenced firing all along there Line. Well the Long roll beat and all the regiments got under arms thinking it was the enemy and sume 2 companyes of the 79th went out to se what was up. And to there astonish-

---

41. On 16 October 1861, Stevens received orders to relinquish command of his brigade and to report to Gen. Thomas W. Sherman at Annapolis, Md., the following morning. Accompanied by his son Hazard, who had received a promotion to captain and assistant adjutant general of U.S. Volunteers, the elder Stevens was placed in command of a brigade in Sherman's Expeditionary Corps set to depart for operations on the coast of South Carolina. Stevens, *The Life of Isaac Ingalls Stevens*, vol. 2, 338; Phisterer, *New York in the War of the Rebellion*, vol. 4, 2858; Todd, *Highlanders*, 85–86; O.R., Series 1, vol. 6, 179–80, 185.

42. Upon learning of Stevens's sudden orders to leave the 79th, senior officer Capt. David Morrison asked the general before he departed to address the Highlanders, who had formed to see him leave. One Highlander remembered the scene: "As he [General Stevens] spoke to us, and recalled the events of the past two months, his voice faltered, and it was quite evident that he regretted the parting as much as we did. Just as he turned to ride off, one of our number, stepping a pace or two in front of the line, shouted: 'For God's sake, General, *tak' us wi' ye!'* This touched a responsive chord in every breast, and the cry was at once taken up by the whole line: 'Take us with you!' The General stopped his horse, turned towards the line and looked a moment at us, as with outstretched arms we repeated the request. This appeal was more than the General expected. Recovering himself after a moment, he found voice to say: 'I will if I can;' and then, putting spurs to his horse, galloped off." Todd, *Highlanders*, 86.

ment it happened to be a bull that was wa[l]king about in the woods. So the regiment that raised the fals alarm has to stay 24 hours Longer for it. Thats the way they punnish them for rasing fals alarms.

I have no more news Jane this time hopping to hear from you soon. I am well and the boys is well so good night and I Remain Your ever afficonate Husband

Alexander Campbell

Write soon.

LETTER 20

Camp of the big chesnut Va
october 18th 1861

Dear Jane

I have Just received your Letter this moment and I send you a few Lines to tell you not to send anything for the regiment is going away to anaplis right away. Stevens you Know Left us 3 days ago. He was called away verry suddenly so we are called off to Join him so we have to Leave at eight oclock to night and its now 6 1/2 so you see I have not got much time to write.[43] I have all my things to pack up yet. You dont write any more till I write for I dont Know where we will be. I will rite you as soon as we get to our new place. The regiment has just

---

43. General Stevens kept his departing promise to the men of the 79th; proceeding directly to the War Department on 17 October, Stevens requested, through Assistant Secretary of War Thomas A. Scott, that the Highlanders be attached to General Sherman's Port Royal expeditionary force. Although General Sherman quickly consented ("I want the Highlanders (Seventy-Ninth), and I have transportation. Send them immediately"), Commanding-General McClellan refused ("I gave General Sherman all the regiments he asked for. . . . I will not consent to one other man being detached from this army for that expedition. I need far more than I have to save this country, and cannot spare any disciplined regiment"). Rebuffed but not defeated, General Sherman telegraphed Lincoln regarding his wish to have the 79th New York attached to his expeditionary force. Although initially conceding to the wishes of General McClellan ("I have promised not to break his army here without his consent"), President Lincoln soon after allowed for the reunion of Stevens and the Highlanders, who learned of their new assignment on the afternoon of 18 October. O.R., Series 1, vol. 6, 179, 181; Stevens, *The Life of Isaac Ingalls Stevens,* vol. 2, 340; Todd, *Highlanders,* 86–87.

come in from picket. This has come so suddenly that every one is in a regular flurry. They are all Quite proud about going with steavens. So the nixt time I write it wont be from virginia I guss.

I am glad to hear that you and the children is well. I am in verry good helth and my cold has Left me altogether. This is about swiftest wrote Letter ever I wrote. I hope i will have more time the nixt one. We pass through washington tonight. It will be Late but the moon is up and its a beutiful night. No more s[o] good night and I remain your ever Afficonate

Alexander Campbell

Annapolis is the way to spell it. Mat and Jammey is well.

Chapter Three

"I WOULD LIKE TO BE AT THE TAKING OF CHARLESTON"

23 October 1861 through 31 May 1862

On 18 October 1861, Alexander Campbell and the 79th New York arrived in Annapolis, where they were reunited with their former colonel, Isaac Stevens, now a general. Stevens had been given command of the second brigade (consisting of the 79th New York, the 50th and 100th Pennsylvania "Roundheads," and the 8th Michigan) of Brig. Gen. Thomas W. Sherman's 12,653-man-strong expeditionary force. Although the Highlanders were not certain of their destination—the nature and logistics of the expedition had remained largely secret—many guessed correctly that they were headed for South Carolina, considered by most Northerners to be the state responsible for the outbreak of the Civil War.

General Sherman's expeditionary force was headed for Port Royal, a strategically important harbor on the coast of South Carolina. Port Royal Sound and its surrounding islands, situated between Charleston and Savannah, formed the ideal base for sustaining the Union's naval

60

blockade of the Southern coast and launching operations against the Confederacy's interior.[1] Many Union political and military leaders considered the Federal occupation of Port Royal the key to the eventual taking of Charleston, the birthplace of secession.

On 19 October, the Highlanders were loaded onto the steamship Vanderbilt, one of thirty-six transports used to carry the men of Sherman's expedition southward. The transport fleet departed the next day for Fort Monroe, located on Old Point Comfort at the tip of the Virginia Peninsula, where, on 21 October, they rendezvoused with the fifteen war vessels of their naval escort commanded by Flag Officer Samuel Francis Du Pont.[2] For Alexander Campbell, the departure from Virginia carried him closer to his brother James, whose militia unit, the Union Light Infantry, would soon be employed in the defense of Charleston.

LETTER 21

on Board the steamship Vanderbelt
at fortress monroe
october 23d 1861

Dear Jane

I have just arrived at the above namd place. You would Know by the Letter I wrote that night we Left virginia that we were off for annapolis. Well we got there sunday [19 October] and embarked without delay and started nixt morning that was monday. We arrived here this morning tusday and are Lying at ankor right in front of fort monroe. Its verry wet and nasty weather so I dont enjoy it verry much and there is another regiment on Board and its verry crowded on board.[3] I

---

1. E. Milby Burton, *The Siege of Charleston, 1861–1865* (Columbia: University of South Carolina Press, 1970), 66–69.

2. Todd, *Highlanders*, 89–90; Burton, *Siege of Charleston*, 69.

3. The 79th New York was crowded on board the steamship *Vanderbilt* with the 8th Michigan and five companies of the 50th Pennsylvania. While on board the *Vanderbilt*, the men of the 8th Michigan, who had just recently been mustered into Federal service (on 23 September 1861), were apparently less than thrilled with their Highlander comrades. According to one Michigander: "The men of the Eighth Michigan and Seventy-ninth New York looked distrustfully on each other. The ship was rather uncomfortably crowded, having eighteen hundred persons on board, and every effort to obtain better storage by one party was jealously watched by the other. The Eighth regarded the Seventy-ninth as a set of foreigners and sots, and the latter regarded our men as a lot of undrilled bush-whackers tinged with verdancy." One Highlander noted a possible reason for the friction: "They [the

dont Know where we are going nixt. There is a great number of vessels Loaded with soilders at this place. They are going on sum secret expidssion down south. I have no idea what part but you will hear of it in the news papers when we Land where ever it is. I am shure I wish it was over for I think this will be the finish of it. At Lest I hope so and I am shure you do. I am afraid I cannot write to you so often that is there wont be mail communication so often but Jane Let us hope it will only be for a short time for mind you I am still of the opinion that I will be with you in new york on new years yet I dont Know how this Letter is to go but I see the rest writing so I write too and as soon as I get the nixt chance I write again.

Jane you must excuse th[e] pincle fo[cut out] I cannot get any ink. Ther is no [cut out] accomidation on bord at all so I dont ca[cut out] how soon we get on Land again. There [cut out] a good manny sick on board they [cut out] say its the measels. I think its a [cut out] verry rong thing to ship sick men [cut out] south. There is non of the 79th sick. Them that was sick was Left in georgetown. There was only a few. This regiment [8th Michigan] that is on board along with us is only a short time out there from michigan and they fetched the measels along with them. I had them when I was young so I am not a subsitute for them now.

James & Matthew is well. Matthew was here once before that time in the great Eastern.[4] Theres a great Quantity of soilders in the ships here. You would think that the ships and men thats here would carry everry thing before them and then they ant all arrived here yet. This is the head Quarters for them all to meet before Leaving for there desti-

---

Highlanders] . . . arrive on shipboard in a horrible state of intoxication, with bloody faces and soiled clothes. The Chaplain of the 8th Michigan Regiment is horrified. He preaches to his men, and says: 'I wish to make no invidious comparisons, but after what I've seen of late, I'm proud of you for your excellent conduct!'" Despite initial animosity between the two regiments, the men of the 79th New York and 8th Michigan, serving together for the rest of the war, would form a strong and lasting mutual respect and friendship. Edwin O. Wood, *History of Genesee County, Michigan: Her People, Industries, and Institutions* (Indianapolis: Federal Publishing Company, 1916), vol. 1, 355–56; Lusk, *War Letters*, 91–92; Todd, *Highlanders*, 89.

4. The steamer *Great Eastern*. The *Great Eastern*, constructed in England, was "expressly built to be one of several vessels to trade between England and India, by way of the Cape of Good Hope." The massive steamer could accommodate over 800 passengers, and made numerous trips between England and the United States after her initial voyage in September 1859. *Scottish American Journal,* 1 August 1861.

nation and where that is remains a secret. I beleive the rebels is getting greatly alarmd about it. They dont Know where its going you see.[5] General steavens is on board this ship. He has taken command of us again. I beleive he had hard work getting us along with him. He telegrapht to General Mclellend and he would not Let us go and cameron sectary of warr I beleive did not want to Let us goo then stevens telegrapht to the President and he Let us goo. He told them that there was no use of him going without his Highlanders. He said there was only five hundred of them but they were worth a hole Brigade. What do you think of that? I am afraid he thinks too much and he might get deceived. There is too many Irish in the regiment and they are regular skeamers.[6]

I must come to a close this time and I will write you again the first oppertunity. I would Like to hear from you but I must content miself for a while and I will give you the address when there is any chance of us being Long enuph in one place. This Leaves me in good helth and I hope it will find you and the chidren enjoying the same.

So Good day and I am your ever

afficonate Husband

Alexander Campbell

---

5. Knowledge of the "secret" Federal expedition to Port Royal had previously reached South Carolinians via the Yankee press, when, in early October, Northern newspaper correspondents had learned of and published the plan; confirmation of the departure and approach of the combined forces of General Sherman and Flag Officer Du Pont did not reach the *Charleston Daily Courier* until 4 November, the day that the Union fleet arrived and anchored in sight of Port Royal. Subsequent issues of the *Daily Courier* kept local citizens closely informed as to the progress of the Federal expeditionary force, which was characterized in turn as "the Hessian fleet," "Lincoln's Armada," and, in sarcastic jest, the "*Invincible Armada.*" William M. Fowler, Jr., *Under Two Flags: The American Navy in the Civil War* (New York: Avon Books, 1990), 70–73; *Charleston Daily Courier*, 4, 6 November 1861.

6. Although the original six companies (roughly 300 men) of the 79th New York State Militia were comprised largely of Scots or descendants of Scots, the regiment, desperate for recruits after the outbreak of the war, began admitting non-Scots into their ranks. Many of these new recruits were Irish. In her monumental work on foreigners in the Union armed forces, Ella Lonn noted the resulting reduction in the percentage of Scots in several companies (which, under Federal guidelines, were to contain 101 men each at full strength) of the "Highland" regiment: "In Company A there were forty-five Irish-born, thirty-two Scotch-born, and thirty Americans (Only if every one of the thirty Americans had been of Scotch descent would the two groups together have outnumbered the Irish). In Company B there were thirty-four Irishmen, only nineteen Scotchmen, and twenty Americans. . . . In Company C there were thirty-four Irish and only five Scots. In Company D there were twenty-five Irish and one Scotchman, as compared with thirty-four Germans. In Company F [to

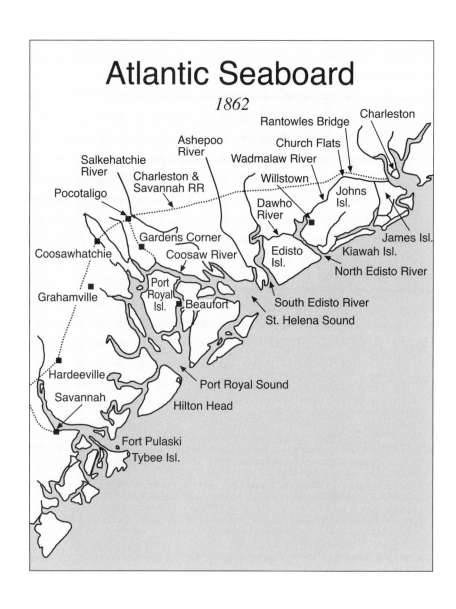

Atlantic Seaboard
1862

LETTER 22

Port Royal entrence Bay Point SC
November 13th 1861

Dear Jane

You will I have no dowt think I ought to have wrote you before this time. I certenly would only I could not see any chance of sending it away. I heard to day that a steamer Leaves tomorrow and that she is to take the mails. I hope you will take the above as an excuse.

Well Jane I have had both good & bad times since I wrote you Last when on board the vanderbilt. It was verry crowded and there was no regularity at all and we was Long enuph on board to have went to California. We Left fortress monroe october 29th and arrived in sight of this place Nov 2d and ankerd out of range of there guns. 3 days gave them plenty time to prepare for us.[7]

It was a grand sight to see the bombardment. The ships that carried the soldiers were all Kept out of the way so that we could see better than if we had been engaged. Never shall I forget that moarning when the ships of war & gun boats heaved anker and got in position the [U.S.S.] wabash taking the Lead & the rest all following. They had (rebels) 6 or 8 s[t]eamers Lying close in shore under cover of there battries and you ought to see them cleare when the wabash came in front of there battries. They fierd at her from this fort that we have now but she never payed and head to them and every eye was on her for she was to open fire first. It was evident that she wanted to get a shot at there steamers but they were making traks as fast as ever they did for the creeks that Lead away from here. Everry one was saying why dont

---

which Alexander Campbell belonged with James and Matthew Ralston before his promotion to color sergeant], there were eighty-nine Irish, sixty-two Scotchmen, and eighty Americans. In this last company the record obviously includes replacements." Lonn, *Foreigners in the Union Army and Navy*, 130.

7. The Confederate defenses of Port Royal consisted of two dirt forts, one on each of the islands (Hilton Head and Bay Point) bordering the entrance of the Sound, and Commodore Josiah Tatnall's "mosquito fleet," comprised of three small river steamers and a tug. Unfortunately for the Confederates, both Hilton Head's Fort Walker and Bay Point's Fort Beauregard, separated by close to three miles of sea, were insufficiently armed and manned to successfully deter the Federal advance. Burton, *Siege of Charleston*, 67–68.

the wabash open fire on that steamer that she is chasing. It seemd that they were within shot of each other to us.[8]

Well we was gratified at Last for there goes smoke from the wabash both at the rebel steamer and fort. All follow suit and it became general all over. All the ships steamd around in a circle. It was one of the grandest sights that one can see in a Lifetime each ship vomiting shuch smoke there was sumetimes they could not be seen with smok. The enemy returned the fire with eaquial vigour for sume time but it was impossibal for them to stand under such a fire. The shells that burst among them was fearful and when the ships got the right rang of the enemy you could see the dust rising all around the fort. The bombardment Lasted 4 hours. There was one gun from there fort that Kept firing away for sumetime but it was soon silenced. Then there was no reply.[9]

A boat was sent ashore from the fleet and the stares & stripes runn up on the fort [Walker] and then came the chearing from every ship on the expedition and soldiers were Landed as fast as possible. We were not Landed that night. This was only on one side [Hilton Head] that the troops Landed. On the other side [Bay Point] it was not Knowing if the enemy had Left or not till nixt moarning when a small boat was sent ashore to see. They found it entirely diserted. We thought that we would go ashore along with the rest of the troops but it seemd not. Steavens and his Highlanders took possession of bay point island themselves so that if we were not the first Landed on the one side we were first on the other.[10]

---

8. On the morning of 7 November 1861, after two days of minor skirmishing with Confederate commodore Tatnall's fleet and the guns of Forts Walker and Beauregard, Flag Officer Du Pont sent his fleet up Port Royal Sound in two parallel columns. While the right column, consisting of six gunboats, was to prevent Tatnall's force from getting to the troop transports anchored out of range of the forts, the left column, consisting of heavily gunned men-of-war and led by the flagship *Wabash*, was to break to port and engage Fort Walker. Burton, *Siege of Charleston*, 70–71.

9. The *Wabash* and other ships of the left column pounded Fort Walker for roughly four hours before the Confederate defenders, having received some 880 rounds from the guns of the *Wabash* alone, withdrew under fire and hastily retreated inland. Upon the evacuation of Fort Walker, the Confederates at Fort Beauregard, fearful of being cut off and surrounded by the quick-moving Federals, similarly withdrew. *Charleston Daily Courier*, 9, 11 November 1861; Burton, *Siege of Charleston*, 72–74.

10. Uncertain on 7 November whether the garrison of Fort Beauregard had been evacuated, Union commanders did not land troops on Bay Point until the next morning (8 November), when Stevens's brigade was loaded onto small boats and sent to secure the island. Todd, *Highlanders*, 97–98.

They Left all behind them. There is 24 cannon mounted on this island & and there is over 300 tents and any Quantity of provisions. The soilders that has been here Lived high I can tele you. They Left clothing of everry Kind. I have got one pair of pants & a shirt & socks and a great many other things. Matthew & Jammey has got any Quantity of sessesh [secessionist] trophes. Any thing thas sessesh goes high. They must have been affully scared. You cannot form any idea of what they have Left. Sume Left there watches pocket books & sume even there sweet hearts Likeness. What dou you think of that?

I was out on another island on a scouting expidision and everry house is diserted. Nothing but negroes. All white has runn & Left there houses & everry thing thats in them. They told the negroes to runn for we would Kill them. They are comming in to the fort every day. We will soon have a rigement of them.[11]

I think that south carolinans would rather have peace now its getting too near there owne door. Its all verry good to do all the fiting in virginia but if they dont come to terms soon this state will have to suffer. I think charleston will soon be in our hands.

I would Like to see a news paper about this. You must send or tell [Brother] Peter to send me sum. I got a Letter yesterday from you addressed to the camp of the big chesnut Va dated october 19th and I was glad to hear that you was all well. I wrote you a Letter that night we Left Va and another from fortress monroe. I hope you got them. Let me Know if you did. We Live high here at present. Turkies & chickens is all the goo. It wont Last Long. This is a sea bathing place in summer and they have been building new houses for the soldiers and it comes in verry good for us. I have got a coat to sleep on and a matress

---

11. On 10 November, the 79th New York began exploring Bay Point and nearby St. Helena Island, where they encountered many abandoned slaves. In the face of the advancing Federals, the white inhabitants of the coastal islands had hastily fled inland, leaving behind many valuable possessions, including slaves. The fate of the abandoned slaves was open to interpretation. Whereas the Charleston papers stated that the occupying Federals were "seiz[ing] all of the able bodied men on the plantations and carr[ying] them on board the[ir] fleet," Flag Officer Du Pont issued orders to suppress "any excesses on the part of the negroes, and . . . to assure the white inhabitants that there is no intention to disturb them in the exercise of their private rights or in the enjoyment of their private property." In all, some 10,000 slaves, or 'contrabands,' were left behind by fleeing white owners, many of whom would become part of the upcoming abolitionist experiment at Port Royal. *Charleston Daily Courier*, 15 November 1861; *Official Records of the Union and Confederate Navies in the War of the Rebellion* (Washington: Government Printing Office, 1894–1922), Series 1, vol. 12, 338 (hereafter cited as O.R. Navy); McPherson, *Battle Cry of Freedom*, 371.

& pillow filld with cotten and it feels nise and soft. This paper that I write on is sessesh and ink too. I will send an envilope that I got in a house here stampt. I only wish I could send you sumething better. The regiment has got payed for the Last 2 months. I ha[v]e not got mine yet but as soon as I get it I will send it to you. Jane I think the ware will soon come to an end now and then we shall be home. When you write you must write a Long Letter for I am entirely Lost for not hearing from home for so Long a time.

I must come to a close this time hopping to hear from you by return of post. I hope this will fiend you all well. I am in as good helth as ever I was in my Life. Mat & Jammie is first rate and in fact the whole 79th is well. The weather is fien and warm here and theres a fine beach to beath on. The water is non of the best. Its so close on the sea. Theres holes dug about 4 feet deep and a barrel with both ends out put down and that is what they call a well & cc.[12] No more this time so good day.

Be shure and write soon and oblige
your ever afficonate Husband
Alexander Campbell

Address
79th Highlanders Bay Point
Port Royal entrance South Carolina
Now be shure and write soon.

———➤●◄———

LETTER 23

Bay Point S.C.
December 4th 1861

Dear Jane

I got your Letter day before yesterday. I would have answerd it

---

12. Another Highlander concurred: "We . . . were obliged to content ourselves with the brackish water obtained by sinking a barrel three or four feet below the surface of the ground; into this receptacle the water would settle to the depth of three or four inches; but even this supply was at times quite limited, and we often wished for a drink of good, clear, sparkling water." Todd, *Highlanders,* 99.

right away but I wanted to get my pay so as I could send it to you by this Letter but I have not got it yet but I expect to get it soon. Its all the falt of the smart officers that we have got. Theres only a few of us that has not got payed and the pay master stays on the other side and he wont come over here to pay so few and them that has the power to get it for us does not seem to care whether we get it or not. You must be in want of it now.

The times in new york must be hard this winter but its nothing to compare with the south. I was out on Port royal Island a few days ago and the negroes told me that the white people stripted the negroes any of them that good cloths and [cut out] them on themselves. They Left here in suc[h a hu]rry that they had not time to t[ake the]re cloths.

The regiment is all toge[ther] in. The compnies that was sent on the other islands to see if the enemy was on any of them has returned. They got 3 two ritch planters that had come in to take off the negroes but they got catched. The enemy has retreated away back on the main Land about 25 or 30 miles from here. Theres 3 compnies of our regiment on the big guns. James & matthew is drilling on them everry day.[13] They are getting along first rate. The weather is a Little cold here at present. There was a Little ise on a pail of water that I went to take a drink out of this morning but sun is out and it is plesent now.

I am sorry to here of the Death Little william guthrie. Its too bad. You must have had a hard time with Alexander but as you say he is well now. I Know its not without a great deal of care on yor part. I am most happy to hear that you and th[e] Children has got along so well as you have and its all my thoughts about you and the children and when I here from you and that you are well I feel Quite happy.

I have not much Knews to tell you about what is going on here. I heard Last night that the fleet was going to bombard savanah to day but I dont se any sign of it to day. You have no idea how Lies gets up here. Theres one thing certain the goverment must go ahead and get through before summer or the men cannot stand the summer sickness in south carolina. We could get along here first rate in summer for this is a summer sea bathing place for the people of buefort. Its a fine beach.

I no more news of any amportance and when ever I get money I will

---

13. Companies E and F of the 79th New York drilled daily on the big guns in Fort Seward, the former Confederate Fort Beauregard. *Scottish American Journal*, 26 December 1861.

send it right off. I hope you and the children will enjoy good helth. I am well myself. No more. Good day and I Remain Your Afficonate husband

Alexander Campbell

P.S. You must write when you get this. I have a Little bottle to send to you that I got on an island above here but I dont see how I am to send it and I have got a bible too and a good many other things. I have them in my Knapsack and I hope I will bring them hom on my own back.

Ever yours
A Campbell

LETTER 24

Port Royal Ferry S.C.
December 16th 1861

Dear Jane

I received your Letter of the 30th two days ago and was sorry to hear that you and the children was so bad with the cold. I hope you will all soon be well again.

As you see by the above we have Left bay point.[14] We got on board the steemer Deleware which took us to Buefort and reported to general steavens then wend to a suitable place and pitched tents and before dark all was pitched. I had a fine room in one of the houses that was to be Head Quarters. You Know the colors is alway Kept there and them that carries them has to be as convenient to them as possible so we had a room up stairs. There was a fine Large bedstead in the room and a chist of drawers and o wasnt there a hansome Cradle. It was one of that Kind that swings clear of the floor. The same as them that winds up Like a clock only it went by hand. I thought of Little Alexander how nice he would go to sleep in it and I wished I could send it home but we did not get Long to enjoy our nice room. I went to bed

---

14. On 11 December, a portion of the 79th New York, including Alexander Campbell, occupied Beaufort; on 15 December, they were joined by the remainder of the regiment. Todd, *Highlanders,* 107–8.

expecting a good nights sleep. I had no more than got a sleep when I woke up with one calling out my name and shaking me. I asked what was the matter (it was the othe[r] color beare[r]). He said we had orders to proceed at once to port royal ferry[15] in Light marching order so up I had to get and get ready.

The bugle sounded [and] the regiment got in Line. Off we started for the ferry. Its a splendid road. All along on each side is Large trees and it has a verry anchient Look. It was a butiful moon Light night and we marched verry Quick only resting for a few minuts on the way. The distance is 10 miles between buefort & port royal ferry. We got there or here I should say before morning and turned in off the road where there some neagro shanties in one of them which I am writing this.[16] We have now been 5 days here and we expect to be releived soon and goo back to buefort. There is 5 companies of another regiment here along with us & 2 guns of shearmans battry.

The first morning I went to see the ferry which is a Little over a mile farther. Our men is on picket in a Loag house on this side of the ferry. Its Quite narrow and there was a house on the other side but our men swame over and destroyed it and took away there flat boats that was used for crossing. I dont mean the 79th when I say our men for all was don before we came. The 2 guns commenced shellng them [Confederate soldiers] for they are making breast works and planting guns to Keep us from crossing. They work always at night. Our pickets on the ferry can hear them working Quite plain. The fools. If they only Knew it we dont want to cross. We are to keep them from crossing or sinking any thing in the ferry. If they could get over on this island again they would burn up everry thing so we are mearly here to prevent them if possible from doing that. As I was up taking a Look over at them they a party of them got up on the breast work and waved there flag and cheared but our 2 cannon sent a few well directed shots which mead them dissepear verry soon.

Buefort is a hansom town. Its inhabitants has mostly all been r[i]ch

---

15. Port Royal Ferry connected Beaufort Island with the mainland. Ibid.

16. Another Highlander remembered the move as follows: "On the 11th the brigade, with a part of our regiment, occupied Beaufort. . . . We got our tents up about three o'clock in the afternoon but had little time to look about us before dark; we retired early, but about eleven o'clock were turned out and ordered to fall in, in light marching order. We were soon on the road, but the night was so dark we could not tell the direction of the march. About three o'clock the next morning we reached a point near Port Royal Ferry." Ibid., 107–9.

planters and they had to Leave everry thing and the negroes when ever
the whites Left plundered every house and broke all the firnature. The
people has Lived Like princes but everry house has been ransacked
before the soldiers came.[17]

The weather here is Quite warm. Its always cool at night but when
the sun gets up it gets warm. We are verry Lucky thats out of Virginia
for I know it must be verry Cold.

Theres more troops I here comming out here. They ought to send
plenty and march right through south carolina for she deserves it more
than any of the rest. I fully beleive they think we are to show no Quarters but they ar mistaken.

You say the union devence committee has stopt payment. I think
its only for a short time. At Least I hope so. If I had got my money
when the rest got it you would have had it before now but I have got it
now and I am wating till adams express starts as I hear its going to
have its Head Quarters in buefort. So as soon as its ready I shall send it
for its not safe to send it in a Letter. I would Like you to have it as
soon as possable for its only a nusance to me but I know it wont to
you. There will soon be 2 more mounths dew to us so that if they pay
us rigular I think I can send enuph to keep the house if you dont get no
more from the union defence committee. I am almost sure we wont
have many more pays to get from uncle sam for as I ust to say I expect
all hands to get the sack. I dont think you will be sorry for me getting
sacked from this job.

Well Jane its shure to come and the way things is Looking I think
it wont be verry Long for I cant see how the south can Keep up much
Longer. There was a family of negroes escaped from the main Land
and came in here the night before Last. They say that the white folks is
fighting among themselves in charleston and that on the other side of
the ferry they are ready to runn when ever we commence to cross and
the negroes Laughs hertly and says that there officers cannot Keep
them from running. Theres one thing certain that the officers could not
Keep them at there gunns on Hilton head. But I dont wounder at that
for the firing from the fleet was terrable. There was a flag of truce

---

17. After securing Beaufort Island, General Stevens "at once cleared the blacks out of
town, and established a camp in the suburbs for the temporary reception of refugees and
vagrant negroes. He placed the troops under canvas in the outskirts, and prohibited their
entering the town without a permit, and strictly forbade all plundering, or even entering
the empty houses. . . . Patrols were kept scouring the streets, and the strictest order and discipline were enforced." Stevens, *The Life of Isaac Ingalls Stevens,* vol. 2, 356.

came in at the ferry 2 days before we came up here. They wanted to know how many troop we had here and what we were going to do and some more such foolish Questains. He was told to tell his comanding officer that we were going to hold this place for the present and the future would tell for its self and further that we were going to make good citizens of them so that they would behave themselves for the future.

Thats all the news I have to tell you at present only that Mat & James [are] well and I never was better in my Life as at present. I hope by the time this reaches you you will all be well again. You must excuse the pincle for I could not get anything else up here our things being in buefort and when I get there I will write again soon. You must write as often as you can for I am always anxious to hear from you so good day and

I Remain Your ever Afficonate
Husband
Alexander Campbell

Now will you write so[o]n.
Address to Buefort S.C.
I got 2 packages of news papers from [Brother] Peter that night I got your Letter. Write when ever this comes to Hand.

A Campbell

LETTER 25

Port Royal Ferry S.C.
December 21st 1861

Dear Jane

I recived your Letter Last night. I am surprised that you have not got my Letter that I sent before I Left bay point. It must have went astray sum how. I wrote one on the 16th with pincle. You cannot have got it yet. I hope you wont think its neglect of mine for I know how you must feel when you dont here from me. I hope before this reaches you you will have got the other Letters I sent so you will see that I have wrote. I would have sent the money in a Letter only I was afraid it would goo astray. The vanderbilt was gon before I got payed or I would sent it along with the rest. I am going to buefort twomorrw and if adams express is started I will send with it $35 thirty five dollars. Its more than I got. I only get $17 per mounth which makes 34 in two mounths. I made 5 dollars at bay point which I am going to send to you for I know you have use for it. I only wish I could send you twice as much.

You speek of feeling Lonly. You must not beleive what [Brother] Peter sayes about it being three years before I bee back. You Know I wont stay so Long as that but theres no use thinking such a thing as that. I am of opinion that its diying of its self so Jane you must keep up your spirits. I know how you must feel when any of them comes to see you. By the time this reaches you it will be getting on for new years. I hope you will enjoy it. I only wish I was home to enjoy it with you.

I will come to a close this time hopping to hear from you soon. I am happy to hear you and the children is so well in helth. I am Quite well. James & mat is well too. Mat got a Letter Last night. James has wrote to day. I am going to take my coffie now or I wont get any. I will write more the nixt time. I havent got any more news of importance so good night.

> And I remain your ever Afficonate
> Husband
> Alexander Campbell

⸻⸻⸻

LETTER 26

> Port Royal Ferry S.C.
> December 31st 1861

Dear Jane

I received your Letter Dated 16th inst and was glad to hear that you and the children was so well. I wrote you a Letter sume time ago. I guss you have got it before thise. I sent $35 by adams express the same day which I menthioned in the Letter. I hope you have got it all right. I went to buefort myself with it. Adams express was shut on accoint of it being sunday so I gave it to our clerk whou has charge of such things and he sent it and has got the receits which I will get the first time I see him.

I thought you drew the mouney out the bank Long ago before I Left virginia. You must draw it and get what things you want. I am shure you must want a good many things for the winter and when you get the money I sent you must send me something for my new years. In the first place I want some under clothing for I have got nothing but what is on my back. I gave all the rest out to be washed d[o]wn in buefort and I got word Last night its all been stolen. So I would Like you to make me 2 gray flanel shurts with colors and sume sort of a neck tye. Thats all the cloathing but y[o]u must not forget sumething to drink. James & mat wants sum sent in the same box. You can send it by adams express for it has an office in buefort now.

I met with an axident the day I went to buefort to send the money. I was on horse back and comming ~~home~~ back to camp. I was going along pretty fast when all at wonce the horse turned off the road and it was so sudden that I was throwen clean off and fell on a stump of a tree which I struck right of the small of my back. It took the wind from me. For sumetime I neither could sit nor Lay. The only way I could ease it was standing. But its almost well again. Its got better faster than I thought it would.

The weather is plesent here. Theres a slight frost at night but when the sun rises it feels Like may in the north. This is the Last day of 61 and many is the change that will take place before the Last of 62.

Since I sat down to write this there is a regiment came up from buefort and by what I cane hear we are going over on the main.[18] The enemy is throwing up breast works on the other side of the ferry so as to Keep us from Landing but our gun boats can shell them out. And I hear that theres some of them comming up to day. They mean to keep us from getting a fast hold on the main if possible. The negroes is stealing away from the other side and coming over to us every chance they can get. I was talking to three that came over 2 nights ago. One of

---

18. On 30 December 1861, General Stevens received the following orders from Sherman: "Agreeably to the conversation already had with you, it is designed to cross a force over the Coosaw River on the morning of the 1st, and seize upon the enemy's batteries at the ferry and other points on that river. According to our understanding, you will be able to land from 1,500 to 2,000 men suddenly from the means of transportation at your disposal. . . . It must be understood, however, general, that the object of this dash is simply the destruction of the enemy's batteries, and no advance must be made beyond what is necessary to effect that object." O.R., Series 1, vol. 6, 45–46.

them was a woman. She had a young child in her arms. The poor thing had got its arm broken sumetime ago an never got it fixed. They said that all the white people except the soilders was going away back in the country and that they were carrying the cotton with them.

I will now come to a close hopping to hear from you soon. We are going off from here this after noon. I dont Know where its for but direct your Letter to Buefort S.C. and dont fail to write as soon as this comes to hand. Now Jane Good day and I wish you a happy new Year.

I hope this will find you in good helth as it Leaves me.

I remain Your ever Afficonate Hus-band
Alexander Campbell

I will sign the drapht and send it in this Letter.

A Campbell

LETTER 27

Buefort S.C.
Sunday January 5th 1862

Dear Jane

[In] the Last Letter I wrote you dated December 31st I said we were going to march that afternoon. I scarley got finished writing when the bugle sounded to get ready. We thought there was going to be a fight. We marched that afternoon about five miles. It was dark before we halted. We Lay down and slept until three ocklock nixt morning when general steavens came and roused us up. Then we embarked on board the flat boats that was sent up to take us on the main Land. It was day Light before all was ready to start. It was a grand sight to see three regiments all in small boats. The order was given to start and of corse the 79th took the Lead.[19] I have not got enouph of paper to give

---

19. General Stevens launched, and personally led, a three-pronged attack of the mainland; the right wing of the attacking force consisted of the 8th Michigan, the 50th Pennsylvania, the 47th and 48th New York, and seven companies of the 79th New York (including Alexander Campbell). Ibid., 47–48.

you the full acount of the our days work (you can see it in the papers).

We Landed on the main Land under cover of a gun boat an four Launches with one gun on each. The boat I was in was the first to Land except general steavens hou was first on shore. You Know we was bound to have the 79th colors first on the main and so we did for when ever our boat touched the shore general steavens asked for one of the flaggs and I handed mine to him which he stuck in the ground and Looked his watch and it was exactly 8 oclock. There was not a rebel to be seen. It was a flank movement we was making.

We was not Long on shore till the gun boats commenced shelling them [the Confederate soldiers] at the ferry where they had a fort. We advanced towards the ferry and when near to it they opened on our skirmishers shelling them and as is always the case with them they Kept in the woods. We payed no heed to there shells. You have no Idea how cool all hands Kept. They expected to through us into confusion but w[e] marched along as if nothing had happened.[20]

The 8th mishigan was most behind us and they got orders to send skirmishers in to the wood where the firing came from and to find if there was a Large forse of them there. W[e] got orders to halt and we Lay down to hear what would be the result. We had not Long to wait till bang bang goes t[w]o cannon then a volly of mouktry [musketry]. I was Laying thinking many a one was killed with that volly but it turned out otherwise. On our side there was only one killed an four wounded. The skirmishers came in and reported the enemy having 4 cannon and a Large body of infantry and our 79th skirmishers reported the fort at the ferry in our possission so g[eneral] steavens gave us orders to occupy it. They had Left it with firing a shot and Left one Large cannon.[21]

They sent in a flag of truce that night before dark to ask pirmission to take off there dead. They got an hour nixt morning. We took away the gun they Left and destroyed the fort and set fire to two houses that

---

20. In his report of the day's events, Major Morrison, commanding those Highlanders involved in the right wing of the attack, stated: "The men were eager to tackle the enemy, and it was with difficulty I could restrain them from pushing forward [towards the enemy's fort at Port Royal Ferry]. Having advanced about the distance of 1 mile the enemy opened fire upon us from a battery in the woods on our right flank, some of the shells falling in our midst, but happily without doing any injury, my men remarking that 'their shells were warranted not to kill.'" Ibid., 56.

21. By 4:30 P.M., Stevens's force had taken the abandoned Confederate fort at Port Royal Ferry, in which remained a lone spiked cannon. Ibid., 50, 56.

they stayed in. That was what we went over to do and when it was don we was to come back.[22] I dont think they will come back to make a fort there again. The gun boats gave them a tremendes shelling over our heads that morning before w[e] came back. There must have been a number of them killed. The 79th came off verry safe.[23] Non of us got touched and now we are all back in buefort and I am well in helth hopping this will find you and the children enjoying the same. James & mat is first rate. I will come to a close this time hopping to hear from you soon so good day.

> And I Remain Your ever Afficonate
> Husband
> Alexander Campbell

Please send the 2 shirts that I spoke of Last Letter as soon as you can. I signed the check and sent it in the Letter of the 31 December. Write soon and Let me know if you got the money I sent.

⟶➤●◀⟵

LETTER 28

Buefort S.C.
March 10th 1[8]62[24]

Dear Jane

I received your Letter that you sent in the box that James got and was glad to hear you and the boys was getting along so well. I also

---

22. On the morning of 2 January, Stevens's force finished its work of leveling the former Rebel fort and then destroyed several buildings in the vicinity, including two large mansions, before withdrawing back to Beaufort Island. O.R. Series 1, vol. 6, 51; Todd, *Highlanders,* 112.

23. Union losses for the day totaled 2 killed, 12 wounded, and 1 missing, while the Confederates—whose forces consisted of the 12th and 14th South Carolina, Captain Leake's Virginia Battery, and some 40 cavalry—suffered 8 killed and 24 wounded. The 79th New York sustained no losses. O.R., Series 1, vol. 6, 66, 67, 75.

24. There is a two-month gap in Campbell's correspondence home for which later letters offer no concrete explanation. Although letters written during this period may have been lost, there appear to be more fitting reasons for the break. First, for a period in late January, the Highlanders were prevented from sending letters home by order of Sherman, who, according to one Highlander, had been scheduling a secret expedition against Fort Pulaski near Savannah and did not wish his plans to be revealed. Second, the Highlanders' ability to correspond while at Beaufort was dependent upon the arrival and departure of

received t[h]e other things that was in the box and I drunk [to] your helth with all the honours and that the war would soon be over and us all home and I think it will come to pass one of these days if they only keep on as they have been dooing in the west. Thats been a gloryies number of victories for the union.[25] If they only were driven out of Virginia now it would be all over with them. The nixt news from the north I expect to hear of Mclellan giving them what they got at fort Donolson.[26] We expect Savannah will soon be taken. Our forses has got forts built on both sides of the river between the city and fort pulaskie & cut off all communication between the city and the fort so that it must surrender before verry Long.[27] So you see the work goes gloriesly on. There was an expedition went from hilton head a few days ago to the cost of florida and one of the steamers came back to

---

less-than-timely steamships. Thus, it is entirely possible that Campbell did not write at all during this time, a theory which seems to be supported by the lengthy distances between subsequent letters written by Alexander that spring.

The reminiscences of other members of the 79th New York illuminate the nature of life for Alexander Campbell and his comrades during this period. One Highlander remembered the early months of 1862 as "a season of almost uninterrupted repose" which "was utilized to improve the troops in drill and discipline." Capt. and Asst. Adj. Gen. Hazard Stevens similarly recalled the period in question: "Thus well occupied with drills, dress parades, guard-mounting, picketing, and study, in that beautiful region and delightful winter climate, profusely supplied with fresh beef, poultry, and sweet potatoes, in addition to the ample regular ration, the troops greatly enjoyed their sojourn at Beaufort, while they rapidly gained soldierly discipline and efficiency." Lusk, *War Letters,* 119; Todd, *Highlanders,* 115–17; Stevens, *The Life of Isaac Ingalls Stevens,* vol. 2, 372.

25. Fueled by recent military successes, spirits were generally high among Union soldiers in March 1862. In the West, troops under Gen. Ulysses Simpson Grant forced the surrender of Forts Henry (6 February) and Donelson (16 February) in Tennessee, compelling Confederates to abandon their foothold in parts of that state as well as in Kentucky, while providing Union forces with control of the strategically vital Tennessee and Cumberland Rivers. In addition, Federal forces occupied Nashville on 25 February, and a Union victory at the Battle of Pea Ridge (7 to 8 March) in Arkansas effectively quashed Confederate hopes to control Missouri and hampered their efforts to maintain the Mississippi River. Long, *Civil War Day by Day,* 167, 169–72, 175, 179–80; Boatner, *Dictionary,* 352, 394–97.

26. On 10 March 1861, McClellan's mammoth Army of the Potomac was slowly making its way southward through northern Virginia, forcing General Johnston's opposing Confederates back toward Richmond. McClellan was maneuvering to launch his Peninsular Campaign, in which he planned to transport his army via coastal waterways to the Virginia Peninsula and take the Rebel capital from the southeast. Long, *Civil War Day by Day,* 181–83; Boatner, *Dictionary,* 632–33.

27. Fort Pulaski, which guarded the sea approach to Savannah, was surrendered by its Confederate defenders on 11 April 1862 after a heavy two-day bombardment. Boatner, *Dictionary,* 296.

day with the news that they had taken farnindeniad (its in florida) with all the guns and every thing holes poles.[28]

The weather took a change and snowed a Little the other day but it was so Little it melted as it fell and to day it was so warm that the white wemen that has come here to teach the darky children was using umbrallows to shed the sun off them. Theres a great many men and wemen come out with the Last steamer.[29]

I was sorry to hear about henrys Little boy being so bad and you say Little Alexander has been sick too. Poor Little boy. I would Like to see him now. I am glad to hear Jonney is getting on so well. He must be getting [to be] a big fellow now.

You want to know if I can give you any idea when we will be home. That is rather a hard question to answer but its belevied that it cant stand Long I think. I will come to a close this time hopping this will find you in good helth as it Leaves me. James & mat is well. I will write soon again. I will come to a close hopping to hear from you soon and I Remain Your ever Afficonate Husband

Alexander Campbell

LETTER 29

Beaufort S.C
Aprile 2d 1862

Dear Jane

I received your Letter of the 24th in dew time. You say Little

---

28. On 3 March 1862, Federal forces commanded by Flag Officer Du Pont occupied Fernandina, a town on the Atlantic coast of Florida. By the time of Du Pont's attack, the Confederates had virtually abandoned their positions there. Fowler, *Under Two Flags*, 54, 77.

29. In the wake of the Federal occupation of Port Royal (and simultaneous evacuation of its white inhabitants), fifty-three Northern missionaries arrived at Beaufort in early March 1862 and began what was to be known as the Port Royal Experiment. The missionaries, mostly young anti-slavery men and women from Boston and New York, came to construct, assist, and educate a community of abandoned ("contraband") slaves while indoctrinating them with the Northern ethic of free labor, all in a general effort to demonstrate both the worth (i.e., intelligence, capability for self-reliance, etc.) of the ex-slaves and the superiority of the Northern economic system. Willie Lee Rose, *Rehearsal for Reconstruction: The Port Royal Experiment* (New York: Oxford University Press, 1964), 37–63.

Alexander isnt verry well and that you dont feel well yourself which I
am sorry to hear. I hope you ar better by this tim[e]. You worry yourself too much. You must Keep up your spirits a Little while Longer for
I think it wont bee great while till we be home. The rebels is getting
beat in everry fight that takes place and if Mclellan captuers all them
thats in Virginia and I think he intends to then its all over with them.
We cant do anything out here for we hav not got enuph of [a] force. I
hear that theres to be a Large army sent out here so that we can go
right on to charleston. Theres another general come to take command
of this department[30] and all we want is more troops and march right
through south Carolina for as I have always said it deserves punish-
ment more than all the rest.

I hope the war will be over before the verry warm weather comes.
I think the goverment is Looking to that and hurring it up. Its getting

---

30. On 31 March 1861, Maj. Gen. David Hunter replaced Sherman as commander of
the Federal Department of the South at Hilton Head, S.C. Hunter ordered the siege of Fort
Pulaski near Savannah, and it fell to Union forces on 11 April. In a controversial move,
Hunter declared free all slaves in his army's hands (12 April) and subsequently abolished
slavery throughout the entire Department of the South (9 May); both declarations were
countermanded by Lincoln, who perceived Hunter's proclamations as falling outside the
purview of his military powers. Hunter did, however, receive governmental approval when
he sanctioned the formation of the first Negro regiment (1st South Carolina) for service in
the Union army.

Few white Union soldiers applauded the idea of arming former slaves; while at Port
Royal, one member of the 8th Michigan wrote: "The measure proposed . . . that it might
be expedient to arm the Negroes, I am afraid will engender strife & divide the Councils of
the nation & may embitter the minds of many who are really Union Men. I have seen none
of these *Colored Gemmen* as yet who would be capable of fighting & will venture the
assertion, such is their servility, that fifty of their Masters would put to flight a Reg. of
them."

The regimental historian of the 79th recorded the Highlanders' reaction to their first
sighting of black soldiers in early July 1862: "Candor compels us to place on record of fact,
that at this time the Highlanders, with possibly a few exceptions, were bitterly opposed to
raising the negro to the military level of the Union soldiers. When we saw the negroes, uni-
formed and equipped like ourselves—except that their clothing and accouterments were
new and clean, while ours were almost worn out in active service—parading up and down
the wharf [at Hilton Head], doing guard duty, it was more than some of our hot-headed
pro-slavery comrades could witness in silence. For a while the air was filled with the vile
epithets hurled at the poor darkies, and overt acts against their persons were only prevented by the interference of our officers." Although the historian admitted that "a short
time after, when the colored troops became a part of the Union army in the field, they were
welcomed by us all as brothers in arms," the initial hostility exhibited towards Negro
troops was clearly as deep-rooted among many in the 79th as it was among the rest of the
Union armies. Boatner, *Dictionary*, 778; George M. Blackburn, ed., "The Negro as Viewed
by a Michigan Civil War Soldier: Letters of John C. Buchanan." *Michigan History* 47
(March 1963): 81; Todd, *Highlanders*, 170.

Quite warm here now. Its our regiments turn to go up to the ferry on picket monday first and we will be there two weeks. Theres not many of the enemy to be seen on the other side now. Its supposed they have went towards savannah for our forces is building battrys in other words beseaging that city. We can hear firing in that direction occasionally. Theres a great time here about the ~~missonaries~~ abolutionsts thats come down here to teach the neagroes. There finding it rather a hard Job. The female part of them is rather a hard Looking croud. Our men calls them the skirimishers. It will take a Long time to make negroes doe anything unless som one stands watching them. The small pox is verry bad among them at present and theres gards stationed to Keep them by themselves so that the soldiers wont take them. It would a bad thing if it was to break out among the soldiers.

This place is consideried verry healthy. Theres Quite a number of stores opened here now and theres a Likeness establishment started here now too.[31] I would have mine taken and send it to you only there too dear and not good at that. I would Like you would get yours taken and Jonnies and send them out to me. Dont get them taken verry Large and you can send them by mail the same as a Letter. Alxander is too young or I would Like to have his Likeness too. You be shure and send them. Now I must come to a close. Mat & James is well & I am well and its my most earnest wish that this will find you all in good helth and I will expect an answer on recept of this so good night and plesant Dreams.

And I Remain Your ever Afficonate
Husband
Alexander Campbell

My love to you all. Now be shure and write soon and send yours & Jonnies Likeness.

A.C.

---

31. According to one Highlander: "An enterprising photographer had established himself in town, and scarcely a soldier, or darky either, but had his or her picture 'took,' fifty cents being the price. Quite a number of stores had also been opened, generally by regimental sutlers, who did thriving business with the colored people as well as the soldiers." Todd, *Highlanders*, 126.

Unidentified corporal, 79th Regiment, New York State Militia, circa 1861. This man dons the full Highland dress uniform worn by the pre–Civil War 79th New York, including glengarry cap, sporran, diced stockings, doublet, and kilt (tartan trews, or plaid pants, were also worn). For a variety of reasons, the soldiers of the 79th New York put away their Highland garb in exchange for the standard blue uniform of Union troops soon after their departure for the front in June 1861. Collection of Michael J. McAfee

The 79th New York State Militia on parade in Tyron Row, New York City, 4 July 1860. This was one of the earliest parades of the Highlanders, who wore their kilts for the occasion. The regiment looked largely the same when it departed for the war in June 1861, though its ranks had been significantly increased. Collection of Michael J. McAfee

Sergeant James Cambell, Co. F, First South Carolina (Charleston) Battalion, circa 1862. James was promoted to second lieutentant in May 1862, a rank he held for the remainder of the war. Campbell Family Papers and Photographs 1860–1886, Private Papers Collection, South Carolina Department of Archives and History

James Campbell, post–Civil War. Campbell Family Papers and Photographs 1860–1886, Private Papers Collection, South Carolina Department of Archives and History

Alexander "Sandy" Campbell. Alexander, shown here in his midfifties, was by the time of this photo an established and successful stonecutter in Middletown, Connecticut. *Middletown Tribune*—Souvenir Edition

Alexander Campbell's Rapello Avenue stone yard, Middletown, Connecticut. Alexander is standing second to left. *Middletown Tribune—* Souvenir Edition

LETTER 30

Beaufort S.C.

May 12th 1862

My Dear Wife

I am most happy now because I have heard from you. I thought you had forgot to write me altogether. I received your Letter of the 2d in dew time and was glad to hear you and the two boys was in such good health for thats the greatest blessing we can have. I only wish I was home so that I could feel happy. I know you would. But I am mostly shure it wont be a great while now. Thats the general opinion here and I trust in god that it will be so.

Jane its 12 mounths tomorrow since we swore in to go to the war. If I had thought then it would Last the one half of that time there would have been no swearing in of me. You may bet your Life it will be the Last war that I will go to. Its not because I am afraid but its because I have too good a wife to Leave and two nise Little boys also.

I got the Letter you sent in the box to [da]y. Jammey brought it over. It was sent to him and he is over on Ladyes island³² with his company. They are over there on picket so him and mat was over in beuafort to day. He says that all the writing paper and invelops was spoiled with the mustard. The bottles had got broke. The envelope of my Letter was all covered with it. James said it Looked (well I wont say). You can guss what he would say it Looked Like. I only wish you had sent your Likeness out. I will only Look the more anxious for it nixt time. I know you must be scarce of money (its too bad). I have no idea when we will get our nixt pay. I hope it will be soon.

You say that [Brother] Peter seen Mcnie that ust to board with me in charleston. I would Like verry much to see him. He knows Brothers John & James verry well. He says [Brother] James is in the 15th infantry of S.C.³³ I think I heard something of that regiment being over

---

32. Ladies Island, one of the many coastal islands in the vicinity of Beaufort, S.C.

33. James Campbell was not a member of the 15th South Carolina Infantry. In March 1862, Campbell enlisted as sergeant in Company F of the newly formed 1st South Carolina ("Charleston") Battalion, which was sent to James Island, S.C., shortly after its creation. The 15th South Carolina Volunteer Infantry, 813 men strong, was formed in response to Governor Francis Pickens's call for 3,000 troops (then the quota for the state) after the First Battle of Bull Run, and mustered into service for the war in September 1861. The 15th South Carolina had seen its first action during the 7 November 1861 engagement at Port

on the main but they are all gon from there now to strenthion some other place. I think he must be wishing he was out of it now. I wonder if he Knowes that I am here. I would Like to hear from Mcnie. Please tell [Brother] Peter the nixt time he sees hin to write to me and Let me Know how things is in charleston and about my old aquanteces.

It is my opinion our forces are preparing to attack charleston so our regiment might have a chance to go there. There was a flag of truse sent to savannah the other day asking them to surrender the city so I hear. They are willing to do so on conditions. I dont know what the conditions are. The southren people ought to see by this time that there case is hopeless and they s[h]ould surrender all and become good citizens of threre united states and Let us get home to our wives and families. We expect the nixt mail to hear of Mclellan being in Richmond.[34] If he only could get hold of Jeff Davis[35] and some more of the ring Leaders. They told the flag of truse that went to savannah that there was a fight going on at corinth for three days and it was still going on when the flag of truse Left there.[36] All this might be false for there is all sorts of false reports out here. Its one of the greatest victories yet the taking of new orleans.[37] I hope they will follow it up. I would Like to get some news papers. Tell [Brother] Peter I have not received any from him in some tim and I would Like him to send me some.

Royal and would continue to serve in the Confederate Department of the South until transferred to the Army of Northern Virginia in the summer of 1862. Rivers, *Rivers' Account of the Raising of Troops in South Carolina*, 18–20, 25; Stewart Sifakis, *Compendium of the Confederate Armies: South Carolina and Georgia* (New York: Facts on File, Inc., 1995), 88–89.

34. On 3 May, after a month of resistance, Johnston's army evacuated Yorktown, Va., retreating toward Richmond in the face of McClellan's massive Army of the Potomac. On 9 May, Norfolk fell into Union hands as McClellan's forces slowly moved up the Peninsula toward the Confederate capital. Long, *Civil War Day by Day*, 206, 209.

35. Jefferson Davis, president of the Confederate States of America. A graduate of West Point and veteran of the Mexican War, Davis had been a U.S. senator and President Franklin Pierce's secretary of war prior to the outbreak of the Civil War. Boatner, *Dictionary*, 225.

36. In late April and early May 1862, a 100,000-man Federal force under the overall command of Gen. Henry Halleck moved slowly toward Corinth, Miss. Opposing Halleck was General Beauregard, who possessed an army roughly two-thirds the size of the advancing Union force. Between 1 and 12 May, several skirmishes were fought near Corinth between the two forces. Long, *Civil War Day by Day*, 205–11.

37. On 29 April, the city of New Orleans was surrendered to the joint Federal forces of Adm. David Glasgow Farragut and politician-turned-general Benjamin Franklin Butler, who had initiated the attack on the city and its defenses on 18 April. The capture of New Orleans was a key first step toward Union control of the Mississippi River. Boatner, *Dictionary*, 591–92.

Jane I sent a Bible and a rattle for Little alexander. The Bible I got in one of the tents when we Landed on bay point. Lewis web[38] the agutants clerk is gon on furlow. I sent them with him. I will come to a close this time hopping to hear from you soon. I am in good helth and I hope this will find you the same. Tell Jonney his papa will soon be home to take him out a walking. No more this time. Write soon.

I Remain Your ever afficonate Husband
Alexander Campbell

LETTER 31

Beuafort S.C.
May 22d 1862

Dear Brother [Peter]

I received your Letter of the 12th in dew time. I was sorry when I heard of the Death of your boy. Jane sent word about it shortly after it happened and I saw it in the scottich american you sent me.[39] I got the three papers you sent along with the Letter and I see by them that Mclellan is going ahead in the east and the army and navy of the west is performing wondiers. The southe must give up and the sooner the better for themselves. The only militry Department thats Laying idle is this of ours but it wont be so Long.

We are on the eave of some important movement. We have been practising in camp movement this two days to see how Quick we could be ready for to move when the order comes which we expect every day. I think Charleston is the place of our destination. I hope so. I

---

38. Louis Webb, Co. F, 79th New York Highlanders. On 13 May 1861, Louis Webb, then age 26, enlisted at New York City to serve for three years and was mustered in on 27 May as private, Co. F. Webb served with the 79th until 13 May 1864, when he was discharged from an Alexandria, Va., hospital. *Report of the Adjutant-General,* 1065.

39. The *Scottish American Journal,* a weekly New York newspaper "with the aim of representing efficiently, effectively, and without fear or favor, the Scottish people on the American Continent," reported the following on 3 April 1862: "On Thursday, March 27, Stanley, the beloved and only son of Peter and Anne Campbell, aged 1 year, 2 months, and 22 days [died]." *Scottish American Journal,* 19 April 1861, 3 April 1862.

want to be at the taking of that city for its got to be taken and that verry soon. I wonder how Brother James feels now about the southe. You Know when he wrote to me the time of the charleston convention he said he was going to fight for his Little state. Mcnie took the best plan to get out of the southe altogether. The rigement Brother [James] is in is a Militia rigement and the compny I was in belonged to the same.[40] I suppose it is bursted up Long ago.[41]

Theres no rebel troops on the main oppisite here now. They have all been taken away to some other point. You have heard by this time of a party of negroes running out of charleston with a steamer and 6 guns and surrendering to our blocade.[42] It came down this way and Lay in beuafort here for a few days. I was aboard and had a talk with the hands and one of them said he recollects of seeing me in charleston. He told me the boat belonged to a scotch man named ferguson. I Know him verry well. The state had hired it from him for taking amonition and such from the city to the batteries along the creeks. The negroes says that things such as provisions is verry dear and that a great manny

---

40. Alexander Campbell is referring to his pre-war service in the South Carolina militia. Campbell's company, the Highland (or Scottish) Guard, had belonged with the Union Light Infantry to the Charleston-based 17th regiment, 4th brigade, 2d division, South Carolina Militia before the war. Stauffer, *South Carolina's Antebellum Militia,* 19. For more on the organization of the South Carolina militia before the war, see pp. 16–20.

41. The status of the Highland Guard at the time of Campbell's 22 May 1862 letter is uncertain, though it appears that the company folded just prior to the secession of South Carolina. In his September 1860 letter to Alexander, James Campbell indicated that his brother's "old company H. G.s has caved in," not an uncommon occurrence among the less-established volunteer militia companies of Charleston. James Campbell to Alexander Campbell, 28 September 1860, CFP-SCDAH; Stauffer, *South Carolina's Antebellum Militia,* 11.

42. Early in the morning of 13 May, the Confederate steamship *Planter,* used to run ordnance to and from various posts in Charleston Harbor, was stolen by the slaves on her crew. Robert Smalls, a slave and the *Planter's* pilot, led the coup. While the vessel's white officers were on shore, Smalls and his tiny band sailed the *Planter,* with Confederate flag flying, away from the wharf. As they passed successive Confederate forts in Charleston Harbor, Smalls and his crew issued the usual salute by blowing the *Planter's* steam whistle; Confederate sentinels in the Harbor, believing her to be pursuing her normal business, failed to stop the *Planter* as she sailed by. As soon as the *Planter* cleared the guns of the last Rebel fort, Smalls hauled down the Confederate flag and replaced it with a white one. From there, the *Planter* sailed toward Port Royal, where Smalls turned the vessel over to the U.S. ship *Onward* of the Federal blockading force. After the war, Robert Smalls, who settled in Beaufort, S.C., and became a local leader of its black community, was elected to the state legislature and ultimately the U.S. Congress. O.R., Series 1, vol. 14, 13–15; Department of the Navy, Naval History Division, *Civil War Naval Chronology, 1861–1865* (Washington: U.S. Government Printing Office, 1971), VI, 286; Todd, *Highlanders,* 128–29.

of the wemen had Left and went up the country and they expect we will attack charleston soon.

We have got L.C. Morrison back again.[43] Theres been some trouble in the regiment Latly about a Major. You know the one morgan[44] sent us was no use and he had to resign and the officers I mean the majority of them wanted cap[tain] Manson[45] to be major and they had a meeting and elected him subject to the aprovel of governer Morgan and sent word to that effect to manson. The General wanted Cap Ellot[46] son of L.C. Ellot that commanded us when we Left new york[47] so that there was Quite a muss about it and the result was that five of our gallant officer resigned and Mcnie is one of them and they are going home the first steamer.[48] The general steavens is getting verry unpopilar in the 79th. We all subcribed to give him a sword and there [is] a general opinion that he wont get it now.[49]

---

43. Lieutenant Colonel Morrison had traveled to New York on 27 April to bring back recently paroled Highlanders who were taken prisoner at the Battle of Bull Run. Upon his return to the regiment around 1 May, Morrison assumed command of the 79th New York due to the absence of Col. Addison Farnsworth (promoted to that position on 28 December 1861), who had recently returned to New York on sick leave and would not rejoin the regiment until early June. Todd, *Highlanders,* 120, 125; Phisterer, *New York in the War of the Rebellion,* vol. 4, 2851, 2856.

44. Edwin Denison Morgan, governor of New York and Union general. Boatner, *Dictionary,* 565.

45. Capt. William Manson, Co. A, 79th New York Highlanders.

46. William St. George Elliott, captain, Co. E, 79th New York Highlanders. At the age of 23, William Elliott had enrolled in New York City to serve for three years and was mustered into service as first lieutenant, Co. I, 79th New York on 27 May 1861. Promoted to the captaincy of Co. E on 19 January 1862, Elliott was promoted to major of the 79th New York on 12 May 1862. Phisterer, *New York in the War of the Rebellion,* vol. 4, 2850.

47. Samuel McKenzie Elliott had served as lieutenant colonel of the 79th New York from 1 June 1861 until 10 August 1861, when he was discharged in the wake of the mutiny. Phisterer, *New York in the War of the Rebellion,* vol. 4, 2843.

48. Between 12 and 22 May 1862, six officers of the 79th were discharged from the service: 1st Lt. and Adj. Lawrence Beattie, 2d Lt. Gerritt S. Conover (Co. D), Maj. Francis L. Hagadorn, 1st Lt. Gavin Hamilton (Co. E), 2d Lt. John R. Hunter (Co. K), and Capt. Robert McNie (Co. F). On 27 May, another officer of the 79th, 2d Lt. Robert Marshall (Co. H), was discharged. Although Alexander Campbell attributes the loss of most of these officers to the supposed controversy surrounding the appointment of a new major, another Highlander offered an alternative explanation: "Between the 15th and 28th of the month considerable excitement was manifested in camp. Several officers who had been summoned to appear before a board of examiners, failed to pass and were allowed to resign." Phisterer, *New York in the War of the Rebellion,* vol. 4, 2848–59; Todd, *Highlanders,* 129.

49. General Stevens would receive the $550 sword, along with dress and service scab-

I hant got any thing else to say this time only when you get this Letter Let Jane know that I am well & James & mat is well too. You say you have taken a store. I hope you will do well. I will now come to a holt as they say in military hopping to hear from you soon. I hope this will find you & your wife enjoying good helth.

I Remain Your Brother
A Campbell

LETTER 32

Beuafort S.C.
May 31st 1862

Dear wife

I take this oppertunity to write you a few Lines to Let you Know that we are going away from here tomorrow morning. We are going on board a steamer. We think its charleston we are going to or as near to it as we can get. Theres two more regiments going from here. We dont Know whether we will be back here again or not. We have been under orders this some time and we were beginning to think we were not going at all. But I think its shure now for the steam boats came up from Hilton Head to night thats to take us.[50] I only wish it was to take us to New York. I hope that that time will soon come.

Jane I have not had a Letter from you in some time. I had one from [Brother] Peter Latly. He says my two Boys is getting along well

---

bards, at a ceremony on 22 June 1862. The sword was "the gift of the non-commissioned officers and privates exclusively, for they had refused to permit the officers to contribute a cent towards or bear any part in the testimonial." Todd, *Highlanders*, 165; Stevens, *The Life of Isaac Ingalls Stevens*, vol. 2, 416. For details on the ceremony, see Stevens, vol. 2, 416–19.

50. On the evening of 31 May 1862, the 79th New York, 688 men and 26 officers strong, received orders to be ready to move out the following morning. At daylight on 1 June, the Highlanders, accompanied by the 100th Pennsylvania "Roundheads," boarded steamships and joined the previously departed 8th Michigan at Hilton Head Island later that afternoon. The 79th New York was destined for James Island, one of several coastal islands near Charleston, as part of Gen. Henry Washington Benham's force designed to take the prized city. Todd, *Highlanders*, 132–38; Stevens, *The Life of Isaac Ingalls Stevens*, vol. 2, 387–90.

and that Jonney is getting so big I wont Know him when I come home. I hope the nixt Letter I write will be from Charleston. Brother James is there for they have all Left from oppisite here except a few calvery.[51] When the boat that the negroes stole away from chareston [the steamship *Planter*] came here I was asking one of them if there was many troops around the city. They said there was verry few but that they were expecting more soon. I ust to wish when we were in Virginia how I would Like to be at the taking of charleston. I have every chance to be gratified altho I had no expectations of it then.

Jane I have not much time to write more tonight. Its Late and every thing has to be packt to start early in the moarning. The weather is getting verry warm here now. Our regiment is verry healthy at present.[52] Jammie & Matthew is Quite well & I am Quite well myself & my most earnest wish is that this will find you and the two Boys enjoying good helth. We ought to get payed soon. I cant see how you get along with all I send but I cant help it. Jane I wish I could send more. Now Jane I will wish you a verry good night.

> And I Remain Your ever Afficonate
> Husband
> Alexander Campbell

Write soon.
I sent a map with captain Mcnie. He is going hom. I told him to give it to [Brother] Peter and he wood take it up to you. Its a verry Large one and tell [Brother] Peter to Look after it for you.

> A.C.

This is the letter I got from Sandy. I got one to day and I thought I would send them down to you would se them. You must bring them back.[53]

---

51. James Campbell and the Charleston Battalion were situated near the town of Secessionville, on James Island. O.R., Series 1, vol. 14, 30–31.

52. Alexander Campbell's reference to the good health of the Highlanders was corroborated by one of his comrades who, as special correspondent of the *Scottish American Journal*, wrote the following on 5 May 1861: "It is a common remark that in war more men die of disease than by the sword and bullet. This has not been the case with the Seventy-Ninth. Since the regiment left New York there have been only three deaths from disease. The extraordinary good health of the regiment was the cause of a special investigation by a medical officer from Hilton Head, who, at the conclusion of his inquiries, stated that he had been twenty-five years in the service, and never saw such a healthy regiment." *Scottish American Journal*, 15 May 1862.

53. These final lines, which appear on the back of the last page of Campbell's letter, were most likely written by Jane Ralston Campbell and meant for Peter Campbell.

Chapter Four

"I HAVE DONE MY LAST SOLDIRING"

10 June 1862 through 9 September 1862

On 1 June 1862, the Highlanders found themselves on board a steamship headed for James Island, South Carolina, as part of Union general Henry Washington Benham's planned offensive against Charleston. With the combined force of Stevens's and Gen. Horatio G. Wright's divisions, roughly 11,500 men, and the support of Federal gunboats, Benham hoped to overpower the Confederate defenders of James Island, at its closest point located only one mile from Charleston, and open a direct route to the "arch Rebel city."[1]

The 79th New York arrived in the waters surrounding James Island (the Stono Inlet and River) on 2 June, disembarking on Battery Island that day and the following day. Battery Island, its earthworks abandoned by its Confederate defenders, lay adjacent to the southwest corner of James Island and was separated from it by a small marshy creek.[2]

The excitement that accompanied their movement toward Charles-

---

1. Stevens, *The Life of Isaac Ingalls Stevens*, vol. 2, 387–88; Burton, *Siege of Charleston*, 98–103; *New York Tribune*, 28 June 1862.

2. Stevens, *The Life of Isaac Ingalls Stevens*, vol. 2, 390–91; Todd, *Highlanders*, 138.

ton was not long lived among the men of the 79th New York. Unbe-
knownst to Alexander Campbell, the next three months would be the
busiest and most violent of his wartime service. During this period,
Campbell and the Highlanders participated in two bloody engage-
ments—the 16 June Battle of Secessionville, South Carolina, and the 1
September Battle of Chantilly, Virginia—and saw their ranks drop from
474 to 208 men.[3] And, most painfully, it was during this period that
Alexander Campbell and his brother James faced each other on the bat-
tlefield.

LETTER 33

Jameses island near charleston S.C.
June 10th 1862

Dear wife

The Last time I wrote you I menthioned that we were under orders
to Leave Beuafort. I had an idea it was charleston we were going to.
We Landed on this island a week ago yeasterday and are campt on a
small Knoll of Land all surrounded with swamps. Theres a breast work
on the creek but they abandonded it sometime ago. Our regiment was
the first to Land and a part was sent out to feel for the enemy. They
drove in there pickets and nixt morning our men went still farther out
and met the enemy in considerable forse and the result was a brisk
skirmish. Our men stood Like bricks. There was part of another regiment out with our men and they were taken prisoners.[4] All our regiment was ordered out and and the enemy fell back and there was
parties sent out from different regiments and took three of there cannon. We have one in our camp. There was one of our regiment

---

3. O.R., Series 1, vol. 14, 62; Todd, *Highlanders*, 225.

4. On 3 June, following up a brief reconnaissance the previous day, General Stevens
led a force (consisting of parts of the 28th Massachusetts, the 100th Pennsylvania Roundheads, and the 79th New York Highlanders) up James Island; they encountered the enemy
near the slave quarters, cotton fields, and woods of an abandoned residence ("Legare's
place"). A brisk skirmish resulted, during which the Charleston Battalion, including James
Campbell, was brought up to reinforce the already engaged Confederates. The Rebels were
finally repelled, in part due to a bayonet charge by the Highlanders, but not before the
Charleston Battalion had captured twenty-two men of the 100th Pennsylvania. Stevens,
The Life of Isaac Ingalls Stevens, vol. 2, 390–92; O.R., Series 1, vol. 14, 28–31.

wounded and he died that night after he was taken into camp. There was 2 killed of another regt & 3 or 4 wounded.

The 79th took one of the rebels. He was shot in the Leg a slight flesh wound. He was a Luetenant and belonged to the same company that Brother James is in.[5] I had a Long talk with him. He said he would have Knowen me by my Brother. He says [Brother] James was made a Luetenant about a week ago.[6] He says he is thought a great deal of in the company. Theres six companies of them and its called the Charleston Battillion.[7] So you see we are not farr from each other now. This man that was telling me about him said that [Brother] James talked often about me. He heard that I was wounded and taken prisoner at manasses and he wrote to Richmont to find out if it was true and it was a Long time before he got any word and at Last he found out it was not me and he did not Know whither I was in the northern army or not. He told me that uncle James Died Last January and he told me about a great many of my aquantence and they are all in the southren army. This is a warr that there never was the Like of before Brother against Brother.[8] Jane all I wish is that it wont Last much Longer and that god will spare us all to return to our homes in safty.

The rebels has got this island strongly fortified and as I am writing they are shelling our advance. Our gun Boats isnt taking the Least

---

5. During the day's fighting, the 79th captured 2d Lt. Henry Walker, adjutant of the Charleston Battalion. Walker belonged, with James Campbell, to Co. F; he had enlisted as second lieutenant on 15 March 1862, at age 21. According to the regimental historian of the 79th New York, Lieutenant Walker, himself a Scotsman, had upon his capture "seemed quite relieved when he found himself in the hands of some of his countrymen, and remarked: 'Had I known I was to have been taken prisoner, I would have worn my kilts.'" Compiled Service Record of Henry Walker; O.R. Series 1, 14:30–31; *Charleston Daily Courier,* 4 June 1862; Todd, *Highlanders,* 142.

6. James Campbell had been elected and appointed to second lieutenant of Co. F, Charleston Battalion, the previous month. Compiled Service Record of James Campbell.

7. The Charleston Battalion consisted of six companies, which were formed from the following South Carolina militia units: the Sumter Guards, the Charleston Riflemen, the Calhoun Guard, the Irish Volunteers, the Charleston Light Infantry, the German Fusiliers and the Union Light Infantry. Stauffer, *South Carolina's Antebellum Militia,* 23–25.

8. The irony of the Campbell brothers' situation was not lost on the regimental historian of the 79th New York, who, in discussing Alexander's conversation with the captured Lieutenant Walker on 3 June, wrote: "Quite an interesting conversation took place between him [Walker] and Sergeant Campbell, one of our color bearers, who had a brother in the Charleston Highlanders . . . and of whom he now enquired; he was told that Lieutenant [James] Campbell was then on the island, and had been engaged with his company against us in the morning. Truly this was a fratricidal strife." Todd, *Highlanders,* 142.

notice of them. We have got a strong force here and when we make the grand advance on charleston the fire from our gunn Boats and field Battries will teach them a Lesson that they wont be apt to forget in sometime. The weather has bee[n] verry wet. Since we came here [its been] raining everry day. This is the first dry day we have had since we Landed here.

I will come to a close this time. You must excuse this writing for I have to sit Like a tailor with piece of board on my Knee and write. I hope I will have better accomadation the nixt one that is that we may be in charleston. Mat and James is well & I am in first rate helth and I hope this will find you all the same. Now Jane good by until I write again.

I Remain Your ever Afficonate
Husband
Alexander Campbell

You will have the map I sent by this time.

⋙●⋘

LETTER 34

Jameses Island near Charleston S.C.
June 13th 1862

Dear Wife

I am going to write you a few more Lines because I Know you will be anxious to hear from me thinking that we have had a fight. Well we havent had one yet and things Looks at present as we was not going to have one for sometime unless the enemy attacks us which I hardly think they will. They got enouph of that the other night. There was two regiments of georgia troops came from Savannah and they were going to drive us all off the island but they got ratherly taken down. They attacked general Wrights Brigade at night thinking to take them by surprise but they were taken by surprise themselves. One of our battries opened on them with grape and canister and cut them up terrebly and they had to be[a]t a heasty retreat Leaving a great part of there Killed and wounded in the woods which our men went out nixt day and Burried. I hear our men Burried over one hundred of them. They were just newly arrived on the island. Some of the wounded said so.[9]

We are getting Large guns here and are making Battries to place them in to shell them out of there Breast works. I think we are going to have a Large fleet sent here to attack them in front so that they will have too much to attend to all at once and I would not be a bit surprised if I was to hear of them surrendering or avaquating Charleston and all I hope is that they will see to either in time and save any more Blood shed.

We had a mail Latly with papers of the 7th inst[ant] and I see that Mclelland has had a verry severe fight near Richmond which drove his advance back.[10] I heard Last night that Mclelland had taken Richmond and ten thousand prisoners but theres so many Lies got up in camp that I dont beleive any of these roumers untill I see it in the news papers but I hope its true about Richmond and I see Corinth is avaquated and there army demorilised.[11] O Jane shurely it cant Last Long now. Why dont they give up Like any other civilised people for its visible to all the world that they are out generaled and out fought at everry point.

That young man that I sent the bible to you with is come back. I thought shurely he would have your Likenesses but no he did not call on you when he Left which I am verry sorry for. It was such a good chance but I hope they are on the way by this time. Jane you must tell [Brother] Peter to Look after the map that I sent with mcnie for you

---

9. On 10 June, the 47th Georgia Infantry attacked and was repulsed by the troops of Brig. Gen. H. G. Wright's division at their camp at Grimball's Plantation on James Island. Union losses were 4 killed and 18 wounded; Confederate losses were much heavier, amounting to between 60 and 70 men, largely due to the deadly fire of nearby Federal gunboats. Union troops had reportedly buried only 14 Confederate dead and taken 6 prisoners, two of whom died from wounds shortly after being captured. O.R., Series 1, vol. 14, 35–38; Patrick Brennan, *Secessionville: Assault on Charleston* (Campbell, Calif.: Savas Publishing Company, 1996), 125–37.

10. From 31 May to 1 June, McClellan's Army of the Potomac and Johnston's Confederate army fought the Battle of Seven Pines (or Fair Oaks), east of Richmond. Confederates suffered higher casualties at Seven Pines than their opponents; among those wounded was General Johnston, who was replaced as commander of the Confederate Army of Northern Virginia on 1 June by Gen. Robert E. Lee. Long, *Civil War Day by Day*, 218–20.

11. On 30 May, General Beauregard pulled his Confederate forces out of Corinth, Mississippi, in the face of Halleck's massive army, which occupied the city shortly thereafter. Ibid., 218.

for he might be apt to forget to deliver it to its owner as Likely things has happened before. I told him to give it to [Brother] Peter and he would give it to you.

I havent much news to night. The regiment is out on picket tonight. Jammie & Matthew is out with it. You know they dont take colors on picket. The camp is verry still on account of them all being out. Its a clear moonlight night and I am writing this all alone and thinking how happy I would bee if I was home. Just as I am writing this the rebels is throwing shells which bursts high in the air. They havent hurt any of our men with them yet. They want to prevent our forces from building earth worke but they cant.[12] I heard tonight that our guns was to be placed in position tonight so that they would open on them by day light in the moarning. Our guns is of farr Longer rang than theres so that we have the advantage.[13]

Now Dear Jane I must come to a close. The other regiments here has sounded Lights out sometime ago so that its getting Late. I am anxious to here from you and Little Jonney & Alexander. I hope there getting on well. I only wish I was home so as I could take them out with you for a walk. That time will soon come please god. You must write when you get this. I hope this will find you all well. We are all quite well. I never was in better helth in my Life.

Now Jane I must finish for want of any more to say. Only good night and I Remain Your Ever Afficonate Husband

Alexander Campbell

Address Jameses Island S.C.

---

12. On 13 June, the 79th New York took its turn on picket duty. One Highlander captured the event: "Our turn on picket duty occurred on that day also, and while at the outposts we were put to work on the batteries designed for heavy guns. In order to protect us, by giving timely warning of the enemy's fire, a man was posted in a tree, who, as soon as he saw the smoke from the Rebel gun, would cry 'Cover!' At this warning we would drop flat on the ground and lie there till the shot passed over; only one of the [Confederate] guns could reach our position, but that was a heavy rifle, and its fire bothered us not a little." Todd, *Highlanders*, 146.

13. By the following day, the Highlanders had mounted four 30–pounder Parrott guns and one 64–pounder James rifle in two small batteries, some 2,000 yards from the Confederate defenses (Tower Battery) at Secessionville. Todd, *Highlanders*, 146–47.

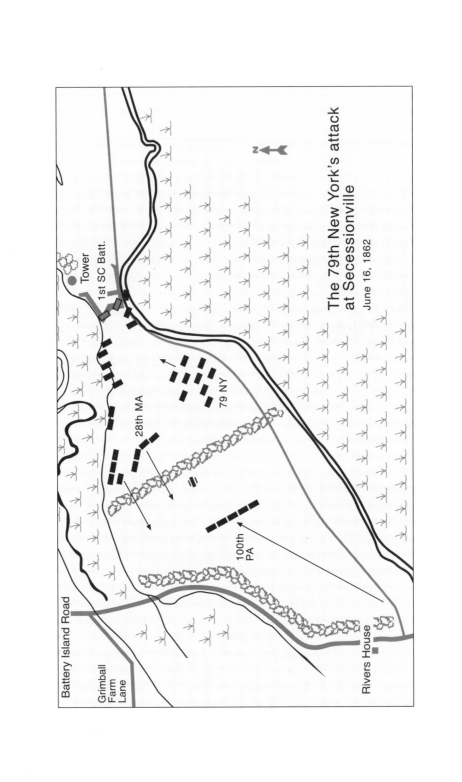

Battery Island Road

Grimball Farm Lane

Tower

1st SC Batt.

28th MA

79 NY

100th PA

Rivers House

The 79th New York's attack at Secessionville

June 16, 1862

N

LETTER 35

James Island S.C.
June 16th 1862

Dear Wife

We have had a fight.[14] I am all right. James & Matthew is all safe. It was a verry severe fight and we have Lost a good many. We had to fall back to our former position. We charged there fort and would have held it if we had been properly supported. Theres only two wounded in the sixth [F] company. One was Left on the field and its thought hes dead and the other is Daniel Larrance him that served his time with Mcmister. You have seen him in our house in 33d st. He has got Badly wounded in the right arm. The ball went through the bone. He acted bravely. He was into the fort when the order was given to retreat and it was then he got wounded. I cant see how Jammie [&] Matthew & me got off with out a scratch. Some of the 79th pulled two or three of the rebels out of the fort by the hair of the head. Our regiment behaved well. The enemy is strongly fortified on this island.

Brother James was in the fort. I asked one of the rebels that was

---

14. The Battle of Secessionville, 16 June 1862. On 15 June, General Benham, commander of the Union forces on James Island, had ordered an attack on Tower Battery, the Confederate position at Secessionville, to begin early in the morning of the 16th. The Union attack was led by the 3,500 troops of General Stevens's two brigades (the 1st Brigade consisting of the 8th Michigan, 7th Connecticut, and 28th Massachusetts, and the 2d Brigade consisting of the 79th New York, the 100th Pennsylvania, and 46th New York). The Union attacking force, under the deadly fire of Confederate artillery and musketry, had approached Tower Battery through a narrow fan-shaped cotton field, bordered on each side by swamps. Two deep drainage ditches, running parallel to the face of the fort, cut across the cotton field, making the Union soldiers' advance increasingly difficult.

Stevens's 1st Brigade had led the attack, and the 8th Michigan, pushing ahead of its supporting forces, reached the parapet of Tower Battery. The Highlanders, realizing that their Michigander comrades were not receiving proper support from the other regiments of the 1st Brigade, advanced and, despite the intensifying fire of the Confederate defenders, joined the 8th Michigan on the parapet. Failing to receive reinforcements, the men of the 8th Michigan and 79th New York, who fought hand-to-hand with their Confederate adversaries at the fort, were soon forced to withdraw. After successive Union attacks met a similar fate, the Federals withdrew orderly under the continuing Confederate fire. Todd, *Highlanders*, 150–63; Brennan, *Secessionville*, 157–267.

wounded and taken prisoner and he told me so. Perhaps he is Killed for our guns shelled them terrebly.[15]

Jane I only write to Let you Know that I am all safe and James & mat is all safe. James is writing beside me. We are verry tired. We Left camp about one oclock this morning and we commenced the fight at day brake and now we are back in camp and its getting Late so I will come to a close hopping to hear from you soon. Good night.

And I remain your afficonate Husband
Alexander Campbell

⟳⟶●⟵⟳

LETTER 36

James Island
June 1862

Dear Brother [Alexander]

I was astonished to hear from the prisoners that you was colour Bearer of the Regmt that assalted the Battrey at this point the other day. When I first heard it I looked over the field for you where I met one of the wounded of your Regt and he told me that he believed you was safe. I was in the Brest work during the whole engagement doing my Best to Beat you but I hope that You and I will never again meet face to face Bitter enemies in the Battle field. But if such should be the case You have but to discharge your deauty to Your caus for I can assure you I will strive to discharge my deauty to my country & My cause.

---

15. The Charleston Battalion, rushed to reinforce Tower Battery, played an instrumental part in the successful repulse of the Union attack. James Campbell's gallant conduct at the engagement was noted by both his military superiors and the local papers. In his report of the day's engagement, a Confederate officer credited James Campbell with "personally repulsing an assaulting party on the left of the battery at Secessionville." The *Charleston Daily Courier* elaborated: "Lieutenant [James] Campbell having no other weapon at first, seized a large log of wood, which, from the rampart, he threw down the side, rolling off several stormers, taking one of their own rifles, and continuing to fight with that."

In the late Battle the killed on your side was verry heavy in propor-
tion to the wounded and for the forses engaged the slaughter terrable.[16]
Most of your wounded is doing well. Col Morison I know nothing of.
He must be killed.[17]
When you write north you will please Let Sister ann know that I
am Still alive and in good health. I am verry anxious to hear from her

---

News of his brother's participation in the battle reached Alexander Campbell by way
of a Confederate prisoner. William Todd, a soldier in the 79th New York and member of
the color guard, reported the incident in a letter home:

There were a great many instances of personal daring shown by our boys—
while in the rampart of the fort and in the field—one man . . . caught a Rebel by the
hair of the head and pulled him out of the fort by man's force. He then took him a
short distance down the field to where we were stationed with the colors and made
the prisoner sit down while he . . . loaded & fired at the enemy in the fort. The prisoner never offered to move but appeared to take matters quite cooly.
If you remember I told you in one of my late letters that one of our Color bearers had a brother in the 42nd Chs Highlanders [the Union Light Infantry] and that
he was on the Island. So Sergt. Campbell (the color bearer) asked this prisoner if he
knew of one Lieut. Campbell about him the prisoner replied that he did and that the
Lieut. was there in the fort. Sergt. Campbell's feelings can better be imagined than
described upon hearing such news. This is truly an unnatural war brother against
brother & Father against son. It happened however that neither of them met during
the day.

The fact that the two brothers did not encounter one another on the battlefield seems
to have eventually disappointed Todd. Roughly twenty-four years after the Battle of Secessionville, Todd, as the regimental historian of the 79th New York Highlanders, wrote that
because the Campbell brothers "did not meet face to face" on the battlefield, "a thrilling
and romantic incident was spoiled." O.R., Series 1, vol. 14, 89, 97; *Charleston Daily
Courier,* 18 June 1862; William Todd to My Dear Parents, 16 June 1862, Todd Box, cour-
tesy of The New-York Historical Society; Todd, *Highlanders,* 160.
16. Of the 3,500 Union troops engaged at Secessionville, 107 were killed, 487
wounded, and 89 captured or missing, a total of 683 casualties. The 79th New York, num-
bering 474 officers and men prior to the engagement, suffered 110 of the 683 casualties (9
killed, 67 wounded, and 34 captured or missing). Confederate losses, significantly lighter
than those incurred by the attacking Federals, totaled 204 (52 killed, 144 wounded, and 8
captured or missing). Of these 204, the Charleston Battalion suffered 42 (10 killed, 30
wounded, and 2 captured or missing). O.R., Series 1, vol. 14, 51, 62–63, 90.
17. Lieutenant Colonel Morrison, while leading the 79th in the attack on Tower Battery, "mounted the walls of the fort and discharged all the barrels of his revolver, in the
very faces of the enemy. Wounded in the head, and unsupported, he was obliged to
retreat." The wound proved superficial and, although temporarily stunned, Morrison was
able retain command and remain with the regiment for the duration of the engagement.
New York Tribune, 28 June 1862; O.R., Series 1, vol. 14, 75.

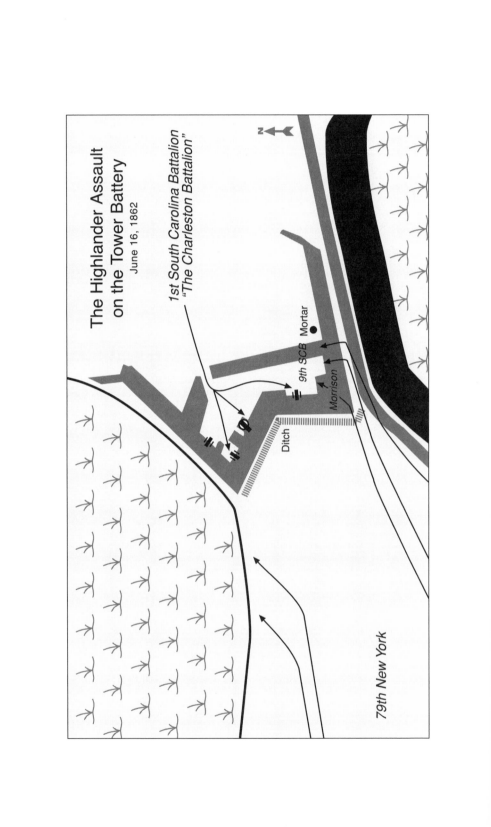

The Highlander Assault
on the Tower Battery
June 16, 1862

1st South Carolina Battalion
"The Charleston Battalion"

9th SCB

Mortar

Morrison

Ditch

79th New York

but surcimstances dos not afford a chance. I will send this (open) by a flag of truce. Give Leut Walker[18] My compliments.

I Am Your Brother
James Campbell

Brother John Left here about Two years ago. I have not hard from him since.

⟹❋⟸

LETTER 37

James Island S.C.
June 25th 1862

Dear Wife

I received your Letter of the 15th in dew time and I was happy to hear that you was all well. You say you have not got a Letter from me in four weeks. I am surprised at that for I have wrote four since we Left Beuafort but I hope you have received them by this time. We got payed the other day and I will send my money to you the first oppertunity. I know you must be in want of money. If we would get payed regular it would not be so bad. In a few days there will be other two mounths dew us but we wont get it. I wish this war was over for I am sick of it. The weather here is getting verry warm but we are all verry healthy so farr. Our wounded has been all sent to Hilton Head. From there they will be sent home as soon a possable. It was an unfortunate affair and I beleive General Benham is under arrest for it. I hope he will be sent home.[19] General steavens the night after the battle cryed Like a child about the Loss of so many brave men.

Jane you will be surprised to hear about me getting a Letter from

18. 2d Lt. Henry Walker of the Charleston Battalion, who had been taken prisoner by the 79th New York on 3 June. Lieutenant Walker was admitted to the U.S. General Hospital on Hilton Head, S.C., on 12 June 1862; he died three weeks later, on the Fourth of July. Compiled Service Record of Henry Walker.

19. General Benham, who had ordered the reconnaissance of Tower Battery over the objections of his subordinate officers, was placed under arrest by General Hunter for disobedience of orders and sent north. Benham's appointment to brigadier general was revoked soon thereafter (7 August) by President Lincoln. Although his rank was later restored, Benham never again commanded combat troops during the war.

Brother James. It came by a flag of truce. There has been a flag of truce sent for to see about our wounded and get there names and it took tow or three days before they could get all our mens names and James had got word about me being in the 79th from our men that was taken prisoners and he wrote me a Letter. I will send you a copy of it and you will see better what he says. I cant send him one for there wont be any more flaggs of truce going over at present. Its rather too bad to think that we should be fighting him on the one side and me on the other for he says he was in the fort during the whole engagement. I hope to god that he and I will get safe through it all and he will have his story to tell about his side and I will have my story to tell about my side.

Dear Jane I have not got much news this time only that James & mat is well and I am in verry good helth myself hopping this will find you all the same. Little Jonney & Alexander I hope will soon have there pappa home to take them out with mamma to walk. Theres something striks me that this warr will be over verry soon and I am shure it cant be too soon for me. Theres a report that our regiment is going away from here comming farther north but theres so many Lies going all the time one cant beleive anything. I will come to a close this time hopping to hear from you soon. So good day and I am Your ever Afficonate Husband

Alexander Campbell

The troops of Stevens's brigades held General Benham in contempt. One Highlander echoed the sentiments of his comrades in a letter written home the day after the Battle of Secessionville: "Let there be no mercy shown to one who shows no mercy. He [General Benham] must be crushed at once, or we are all lost, and even as it is, God only knows whether his folly may not involve us in destruction before any action can be taken. I will not enumerate half the examples of imbecility he has shown, or the wickedness of which he has been guilty. The last act is too real. His folly has culminated in one damning enterprise which must make him eternally infamous." Stevens, *The Life of Isaac Ingalls Stevens*, vol. 2, 399–400, 415; Boatner, *Dictionary*, 58–59; Lusk, *War Letters*, 153–54.

LETTER 38

On Board the Steam Ship Missippia
July 15th 1862

Dear wife

You will be surprised to hear that we are Left South carolina. We have been greatly moved about of Late.[20] You will see by the papers that James Island was avacquated. It was a bad move ever going there at all. We came back to Hilton head and remained there for two or three days and then went up near Beuafort and was putting up our tents when orders came to stop that we were going to Virginia. So nixt moarning [11 July] we got on board the steamer for hilton head and from that got on this steamer for fortress monroe and we are almost in sight of it now. There is another Regt on Board [28th Massachusetts] with us and it makes it verry crowded. Its so crowded that I cant see wheather I am writing on the Line or not and every minute some one comes thump against my arm so you must excuse this writing.

Jane wouldnt it be glorious if we were on our way home. I am weareing for this trouble to be over. We heard before we Left S.C. that Mclellan had been defeated.[21] I hope its not true and if its the case it will prolong the war a Long time.

I sent you a copy of the Letter that I got from [Brother] James. I hope you got it. The night before we Left James Island or rather on the afternoon he came over to our Lines to enquire about me. He thought I had been wounded and he was anxious to know. The first thing he asked was if it was the 79th that was on for picket. I wish it had then I

---

20. By order of the War Department, Union forces were withdrawn from James Island. On 4 July, the Highlanders loaded onto transports first for Hilton Head and then Beaufort, where they arrived on 10 July. The Highlanders then returned to Hilton Head on 11 July, and on 12 July were loaded on the steamship *Mississippi*, which took them back to Fort Monroe, Va. Todd, *Highlanders*, 167–73.

21. The stalemate between the Union and Confederate armies near Richmond was broken on 25 June with the beginning of the Seven Days' Campaign. For the next seven days, Lee's Army of Northern Virginia attacked and pushed McClellan's larger Army of the Potomac away from the Confederate capital. Although the Confederates had suffered greater casualties during their attacks of the Seven Days' Battles (some 20,000 Confederates to 16,000 Federals), McClellan's Peninsular Campaign, for all intents and purposes, had ended in failure. McClellan's failure on the Peninsula coupled with his increasing and open contempt for President Lincoln resulted in his removal as general in chief of all U.S. forces on 11 July. Long, *Civil War Day by Day*, 230–38.

would have seen him. He wanted to see me bad and asked if they would send for me but the officer was afraid to do it. If it had not been so near dark when I heard it I would have asked Leave from the general and nixt moarning we Left the island. It was on the forth of July.[22]

I sent the $20 to you from Hilton Head. It went home on the erricksion. It was in the same pakage with James & mats. We have got payed again and I will [send] it the first chance. We are all well and I hope this will find you all enjoying good helth. I have not time at present. We are in sight of fort monroe and I will try and get this posted there for I dont think we are going to Land there. So good day. I will write soon again.

I Remain your ever Afficonate Husband
Alexander Campbell

P.S. Dear Jane. We have arrived at fort monroe and I have come ashore with the mail. It will Leave tonight for Baltimore and Captian Campbell[23] is coming home and I am sending the money with him $25 and James & mats is in the same Letter $30. I hope you will receive it in dew time.

Your ever
A Campbell

---

22. James Campbell's attempt to find his brother Alexander after the fight at Secessionville left quite an impression on at least one of the soldiers who witnessed the exchange between James and the reluctant Union officer. W. R. Collins, 100th Pennsylvania Infantry, remembered the incident some fifty-five years after the war as follows: "While standing facing the enemies entrenchments a Capt. Campbell, of the 1st S.C., came out with a white flag. He wanted to inquire about his brother, Sandy Campbell, who was color-bearer of the 79th N.Y. He was informed that his brother had gone through the battle alright." *The National Tribune* (Washington, D.C.), 18 January 1917.

23. Capt. Robert Campbell, Co. F, was discharged on 13 July 1862. Phisterer, *New York in the War of the Rebellion*, vol. 4, 2849.

LETTER 39

New Port news Va[24]
July 20th 1862

My Dear wife

I am going to write you a few Lines so as to Let you Know where to write to. I received a Letter from you yeasterday. It came from port royal. It was dated the 7th inst. I was verry happy to hear that you a[nd] the two boys was in good health. We are encamped on the James river banks. Its a nice place and we get plenty of good water a thing we hevent had since we went to South carolina. We have joined what is called the Burnside expidision.[25] It will be some time before it will be ready so that we are Likely to stay here for sometime. We are in a good place to get our mail regular if you send a Letter to day I will get it tomorrow so you can write often now and I will do the same. I hope you got the money I sent from Hilton Head $20 & the $25 I sent with Capt Campbell. He Left here the first night we arrived. James & mats was in the same Letter. You must write and Let me Know if you have got it as soon as this Letter reaches you. I carry our Regts mail to fort monroe every day and bring our other mail up to camp.

---

24. The Highlanders disembarked at Newport News, Va., on 16 July. Todd, *Highlanders,* 174.

25. On 22 July 1862, the recently arrived Union troops of Stevens's division and the returning soldiers of Gen. Ambrose Everett Burnside's expedition to North Carolina were combined to form the IX Corps of the Union Army of the Potomac. The IX Corps, commanded by General Burnside, was initially divided into three divisions, led by generals Stevens, Jesse Lee Reno, and John Grubb Parke, respectively. In truth, Campbell and the Highlanders had been joined with the men of the "Burnside Expedition"; it was not until they were ordered in early August to reinforce the newly formed Union Army of Virginia of Gen. John Pope near Manassas that Burnside and the IX Corps embarked on an expedition of its own.

Formed on 26 June 1862, Pope's Army of Virginia, some 51,000 men strong, was given the task of turning around the North's previously ineffective military efforts in the east through an aggressive campaign in Northern Virginia. The plan was to force the Confederates to pull vital troops from their positions between Richmond and McClellan's lethargic Army of the Potomac on the Peninsula, thereby facilitating the capture of the Confederate capital. Boatner, *Dictionary,* 107, 192, 658–59; Fox, *Regimental Losses,* 81; Todd, *Highlanders,* 176, 179; John J. Hennessy, *Return to Bull Run: The Campaign and Battle of Second Manassas* (New York: Simon & Schuster, 1993), 1–8.

James has not received the box yet that was addressed to Leut gilmore.[26] It has been sent to port royal and it will be some time before it comes here. I expect you have sent me something in it. I hope your Likeness is in it anyhow. That I am most anxious to get. Jane I have not got much news to write this time only that we are all well and wish that our Regt would be sent to do garrison duty till we get recrutied up again. There is a rumer to that effect but we have not got influnce anuph to get a sight Like that. Our Regt can only turn out 400 men for duty and its a shame that full Regts gets doing garrison duty but such is the case. Now Jane i will come to a close this time for its getting near dress parade time. Its sunday and I have felt verry Lonly all day.

Now Jane write soon for I am anxious to hear from you. I hope thes will find you all well. Good night.

> And I Remain Your Ever Affi-
> conate Husband
> Alexander Campbell

⟹➤●◄⟸

LETTER 40

New Port News Va
July 25, 1862

My Dear Jane

I received your noate you sent in Jameses Letter and was sorrow to hear of your mother being sick. I hope she is better by this time. I was glad to hear that you got the money I sent for you must have been in want of some. I see by the news papers that they have commenced paying the familyes of the soldiers again. If its so please Let me Know. If you want a new certificate Lett me no soon I will send one right away.

You want me to come home for a while. I am shure nothing would give me greater pleasure than to get hom to see you all but theres no such a thing as getting a fourlough. They wont Listen to it. I tried. If I could get home on recruting service [I would]. There was only one

---

26. Either 1st Lt. James Gilmore, Co. I, or 1st Lt. Keith Gilmore, Co. E, 79th New York Highlanders. Phisterer, *New York in the War of the Rebellion*, vol. 4, 2851–52.

sent. The sergant is in new york. He was one of the wounded. I would have got home only for that. I wish I could only get home for two weeks to see you and the two boys once more but they only give fourloughs to them that has been wounded and wont be fit for duty for sometime. We are Likely to stay here for a mounth or six weeks yet till all the reinforcements arrives. I think we are to have a verry Large army fitted out here and the nixt fight at Richmond will deside it either one way or the other. I hope we will get a chance to be on the reserve this time. I think we Deserve it now.

New York must be verry stirring again with recruting for more men. Its my opinion they will have to resort to drafting them. In my opinion its the Quickest way to finish the war and it will make a good many come out to fight for what they helped to bring on.[27]

The weather is verry plesant here and good water but our regiment feels much disitisfied about not getting a chance to garrison some place so that they could get fourloughs to see there families. A great part of them is married men and we are verry near the oldest regiment of Vols in the service but such is not our Luck. We will be Highlanders and fight we must. James wrote a Letter yeasterday. Mat & him is quite well. Jane you must write me a few Lines everyday now as Long as we can get them so regular for we might not have this oppertunity Long. I am sorry that the things you sent went south to Beaufort. I am afraid it will be sometime before we get them now. You never told me what Kind of a place you have got in your new house. I hope you are comfortable. Jane when I come home I wont Know how to behave in a house. I wont Know how to Lay in a bed or sit in a chare or eat at a table or in fact any thing Like a civilised being. You will have a har[d]

---

27. On 2 July 1862, President Lincoln had called for 300,000 new three-year volunteers in order to help effect "a speedy and satisfactory conclusion" to the war. In contrast to the massive response of the Northern people to the previous year's call for troops, new recruits responded slowly to Lincoln's latest request. To combat the general lethargy of the Northerners, the government instituted a system of bounties, whereby newly recruited soldiers received in advance a fraction of the $100 bounty normally obtained upon a soldier's honorable discharge (this Federal bounty was often augmented by individual states to help spur enlistment). In addition, on 17 July 1862, Congress enacted the Militia Act, which enabled the president to call state militia into Federal service for up to nine months. As a result, the government ordered the Northern states to produce an additional 300,000 men. In actuality, this call for 9–month militiamen became a "quasi-draft" in places; in states which did not mobilize the required amount of militiamen, the Federal government moved in and did it for them via "militia drafts." By the end of 1862, these policies had produced 421,000 three–year volunteers and 88,000 militiamen. McPherson, *Battle Cry of Freedom*, 491–92.

time of it to breake me in again but I suppose you would not care how soon you had the job to commence to [illegible].

Now Jane I will come to a close this time hoping you wont forget to write soon & often and Let me Know how you are getting along. Now good day and I Remain Your ever Afficonate Husband

Alexander Campbell

I wrote [Brother] Peter yeasterday.

━━━➤●◄━━━

LETTER 41

New Port News V.a.
July 29th 1862

My Dear wife

I received your welcom Letter of the 23d inst in dew time and was most happy to hear that you was well and that the two Boys was getting along so well. I would Like verry much to see them now. There must be a great difference since I saw them Last. It will soon bee a year now.

Its two bad that the Likenesses went to port royal for its a chance if ever we get the box at all. I think it would be a good idea to send us the receit you got from the express company and it will be Less trouble for us to get it so being that it is sent back here or to goo to the express offic and ask them to send it back to you for if its not Looked after they wont care how Long it Lays in there hands down there for I Know how it is with them and they have got to send it back to you or pay for it and its right that it should be Looked after.

Jane theres no news of what we are going to be at here. Every thing Looks to us as we were wating for more reinforcements and that is the only way to finish this war is to send such an overwhelming force against them so that there will be no sight for them no how. It could beem finished Long ago if that had been done.

You speek of me comming home if ever I get the chance. I bet I will and if I had got my rights I would have been able to resign but things dont goo by rights in this regiment but I expect I will have the chance before Long. At Lest I got the promise of a Luetenancy but it will Likely be Like the promice I got before in beauefort when I ought to have got it. If I dont get it the nixt promotions I will throw there colors at them and goo back to my company. I wont make a target of myself much Longer. Its called an honorable position but its a verry dangerous one and I can assure you I can call my self verry fortunate escaping so Long and if I am passed over the nixt promotions they will have to get some one else to carry them.

I will now come to a close this time hopping that this will find you all well as it Leaves us. Now good day and I Remain Your ever afficonate Husband

Alexander Campbell

Now write soon.

LETTER 42

New Port News Va
July 31 1862

My Dear Jane

I received your ever welcom Letter Last night and am happy to Know once more that you are all in such good helth. You see I am as good as my word for I have Lost no time in answering your Letter. Its a pleasure to write when you Know that it goes right away. Just think of how it was in Beaufort when I would write one Letter. It would lay in the post office there until I would write perhaps two more and then you would receive them all at once.

Well Jane we are under orders to march again. Where to that we are not supposed to Know but its verry Likely up the river.[28] The order was read on dress parade Last night to have everything in reidiness to go on board a transport at a moments notice and there was verry strick orders about taking as Little in our Knapsacks as we could and there

28. The War Department issued the following order to General Burnside on 1 August 1862: "The troops of General Burnside's command will immediately embark for Aquia Creek, and on reaching that landing will take position near Fredericksburg; the movement to be made as rapidly as possible, and the destination to be concealed." O.R., Series 1, vol. 12, 3:524.

was to be no company chests or boxes taken at all so you see we are to be shift again. They wont Let us Lay Long in one place. Well Jane they say changes is Lightsome but the Lightsomest change they could give us would be to take us to New York for a change. That will come some time Jane and may god spare us all to see it. Jammey thinks it strange why he dont get a Letter and he say he has wrote 4 since we came here.

Theres not much news here only that we are all expecting to get the order any moment to strike tents but we might not go soo soon. We have been for weeks under the same orders before but I think we will be off soon this time. Its my opinion that we are only going up the river and Land at the places where the rebels fires at our transports going up & down the river and to prevent them from making battries but you Know I am only supposing that myself. You will be surprised to hear that william mitchell[29] and 4 more deserted from here sometime ago and there was word came to the colnel Last night that they were taken. They were in a small boat and a ravenue cutter captured them and fetched them back to fort monroe. Its too bad for it will go verry hard with them.

Now Jane I will come to a close this time. We are all well and hope this will fiend you all the same. Please Let [Brother] Peter & [Sister] Ann [know] that Brother John is well. I heard through the young man thats fathers place is near his. He got a Letter from his father and he menthions that Brother [John] came over to show him the Letter that I gott from [Brother] James in the scottich american. You Know I wrote to him when I was in beaufort but I dont Know whether he got it or not. He never answered it any how. But this man sent word to his father to ask Brother [John] if he got my Letter or not. He has got a splended farm of 50 acers and its in a fine healthy place. He is allright. Now Jane I will come to a close this time and you must write when ever you get this. Now good day and I Remain your ever Afficonate Husband

---

29. William Mitchell, Co. D, 79th New York Highlanders. On 13 May 1861, Mitchell, then 25, had enlisted at New York City to serve for three years and was mustered in as private, Co. D, on 27 May. Mitchell is listed as deserting at Newport News, Va., on 24 July 1862; there appears to be no record of his return to the regiment. *Report of the Adjutant-General*, 974.

Alex Campbell

When you write address
   Burnside expidition
   New Port News
   or elsewhere

LETTER 43

On Board the Steam Ship Atlantic
Potomac river
August 5th 1862

My Dear Jane

I am going to write you a few Lines to Let you Know that we ar on the move again.[30] We are going to reinforce general pope thats what we hear and we expect to Land at alexanderia Va a Little below washington. All Burnsides army is going. They are afraid stone wall Jaxson will make a dash on washington.[31] I wish they may Let us stay to garrison some of the forts there but that would be too good a thing for the 79th to get. We will verry Likely be sent to the front as it has always been.

Jane this is a beautiful river with rising ground for its banks. We expect to get to our destination to day and I will try to get this posted the first thing. There is two regiments and four companies of a third on this ship but theres good accomidation for its a verry Large vessel. We

---

30. On 3 August, after receiving orders to reinforce Pope's Army of Virginia, the IX Corps proceeded to Fredericksburg, Va. The 79th New York, 100th Pennsylvania, and two companies of the 46th New York embarked on the steamship *Atlantic* and sailed toward Aquia Creek, where they disembarked on 5 August and marched toward Fredericksburg. Todd, *Highlanders,* 179.

31. By August 1862, Major General Jackson had become the Confederate whom Northerners feared most in the East. From May to June 1862, Jackson had conducted his brilliant Shenandoah Valley Campaign, during which his extremely mobile forces outmaneuvered larger Union commands down and up the Valley. In so occupying his Federal adversaries in the Valley, Jackson prevented Union reinforcements from being sent to General McClellan on the Virginia Peninsula. From the time of Pope's accession to command of the Army of Virginia on 26 June, the Northern press (and Pope himself) boasted that the new commander would "bag" Stonewall Jackson and his army. Boatner, *Dictionary,* 739–743; Hennessy, *Return to Bull Run,* 6.

Left fort monroe yeasterday afternoon. There was no chance to get ashore at the fort or I would have sent you a few Lines from there. All the flags was at half mast at the fort as we went past and a gun was fired every half hour. We could not fiend out what it was for I suppose some big egg ha[s] croked (as Jammie would say).[32]

You must excuse this dirty paper. Its the best I can get. Its all grease from being in my haversack amngst my salt horse and its so close below decks that the sweat is droping off me on the paper as I am writing. I havent got much news worth menthionion only that James & mat is in good helth and spirits. Thats one way we console our selves. When we Leave one place we think we are going where we will be better. Its best to Live in good hopes. Our hopes that the war would soon be over has been greatly blighted since Mclellan could not take Richmond and if the north dont draft men god only knows when it will be finished. The goverment at washington ought to take a Lesson from the one at Richmond and if it dont they may give it up.[33]

Jane I will come to a close hopping to hear from you soon. I am in good helth and hope this will find you all the same. I Remain Your ever Afficonate Husband

Alexander Campbell

———>○<———

LETTER 44

Fredericksburgh Va
August 10th 1862

My Dear wife

I am going to write you a few Lines to Let you Know that I am well and hope that this will fiend you the same. We Left new port news

---

32. Although possibly not the reason for the military respects being paid on 4 August at Fort Monroe, former president Martin Van Buren, age 79, died in New York on 24 July 1862. Long, *Civil War Day by Day*, 243.

33. On 16 April 1862, the Congress of the Confederate States of America enacted the first ever conscription law in American history. All able-bodied men between the ages of eighteen and thirty-five were eligible for the draft, which was an immensely unpopular act among the people of the South. In truth, the Confederate government had instituted the draft in hopes that such a measure would spur the enlistment of men who wished to avoid

a week ago to day and we are under orders to march again. We are going in Light marching order. We are Likely to have Long marching to doe. We are getting our knapsacks all stowed away. We thought we were going to get staying a while here for General Steavens is appointed militry governer of this place but we are going to joine Pope and there is Likely to bee hard fighting. All the tro[cut out] was here when we came he[re from Hilton] head and we are to follow. Jane [cut out] is a hot bed of ~~sesessh~~ [cut out]. [Th]ey expect stone wal[l Jackson] here some time soon and [cut out] [s]ay its the only place we [cut out] stayed they always runn [cut out]. [T]here was a great many of the r[es]t of them went away.

We are in camped on the west side on high ground and can Look right down on the city.[34] It seemed much Like home when we hear the town clock striking the time of day and this being sunday the church bells was wrung. But we are not going to get Long to enjoy these things. I wish they would send out more troops and not get out numbered as it was a[t] Richmond.

I received your Letter of the 2d inst in dew time and was glad to hear you was all in good helth and I got the receipt for the box and if we could get staying here for a few days I think it would be sent on here. I would only care for the Likenesses for to see you and Jonney & Alexander once more. Jane as I am writing this the wagons is taking away all our knapsacks and I suppose we will soon be going to. I have not much to write about. James says he will write in a day or two. Him & mat is first rate. Tell [Brother] Peter I fell in with an old scotch man here from innerpefry. He has a farm not a hundered yards from our camp. I had a Long talk with him Last night. His name is Brice and he has been in this country this thirty years. He thinks the south will gain its independence yet.

Now Jane I will come to a close tonight for its Late. I will write

---

the stigma of being involuntarily conscripted. As an extra incentive, those who 'volunteered' in the face of the draft could join new regiments and elect their own officers, whereas conscripts were attached to already existing units. As a result of the Confederate conscription law, the total number of men in Southern armies increased from approximately 325,000 to 450,000. McPherson, *Battle Cry of Freedom*, 430–33.

34. Campbell and the Highlanders were encamped west of Fredericksburg on Marye's Heights. In just 4 months, Marye's Heights would be the sight of mindless slaughter and destruction; during the 13 December 1862 Battle of Fredericksburg, where 12,700 Federals and 5,300 Confederates were killed or wounded, Union forces were repeatedly ordered up the slope of Marye's Heights, only to be mowed down by its entrenched Rebel defenders. Todd, *Highlanders*, 179; Boatner, *Dictionary*, 310–13.

soon again. I will expect to hear from you soon again so good night and I Remain your ever Afficonate Husband

Alexander Campbell

Address Fredericksburgh Virginia or elsewhere.

Write soon.

A.C.

⇒►●◄⇐

LETTER 45

Emory Hostpital
Washington DC
Sept 4th 1862

My Dear wife

You will not be surprised to hear that I am wounded after such severe fighting as we were in.[35] I am only slightly wounded in the calf of the Leg. The ball went through. It wont amount to much. I got it on monday evening [1 September] in the fight that general Steavens was

---

35. After playing a peripheral role in the Second Battle of Manassas (29–30 August), where the combined Confederate forces of Lee and Jackson dealt a crushing blow to Pope's larger Army of Virginia on the old battlefield of First Bull Run, the 79th New York took part in the Federal rear guard action at Chantilly, Va., on 1 September. Looking for an opportunity to cut off the Federal line of retreat, Jackson's army cautiously followed Pope's withdrawing army toward Washington. In response, the vanquished Union commander detached two divisions of the IX Corps, led by General Stevens, to march back and confront the threatening Rebels.

About 4 P.M., Stevens's Federals encountered Jackson's Confederates near Ox Hill; the Rebels had halted to wait for reinforcements from General James Longstreet. Quickly, Stevens deployed his 3d Brigade, led by the 79th New York, which pushed the lead element of the Confederate force back. In a windswept, drenching rain, the Union and Confederate forces near Ox Hill battled fiercely until nightfall. The successful Federal stance at Chantilly had ended Lee's and Jackson's hopes of cutting off Pope's retreat toward Washington. However, Union 'victory' had not come without its costs: generals Isaac Stevens and Philip Kearny (regarded at the time as two of the more promising officers in the Union army) had been killed, while the Federals had incurred an additional 677 casualties (136 killed, 472 wounded, and 69 captured). Hennessy, *Return to Bull Run*, 90–91, 243–44, 322, 446–50; Robert Ross Smith, "Ox Hill: The Most Neglected Battle of the Civil War, 1 September 1862," in *Fairfax County and the War Between the States*, Fairfax County Civil War Centennial Commission (Vienna: Fairfax County Civil War Centennial Commission, 1961), 26–64; John G. Moore, "The Battle of Chantilly." *Military Affairs* 28 (Summer 1964): 56–63.

Killed in. I got wounded and was comming off the field the same time his son was.[36] Jammie & matthew is I think all safe. James brown said he seen them and they were all safe then. There was five companies sent out skirmishing and theres was one of them so that they fell back when they found out where the enemy was and they Lost the five companys Lost the regiment so James brown says when he saw them and he was with them they were all right. I got wounded early in the fight and I mangaged to get off in time to get in to a baggage waggen that was going to farfax so I got on to alexandria nixt morning and from there in a steamer to washington. I think that we will be sent to new york soon to make room for more here. They are sending them all farther north so I hope they will send us north soon.

Jane I could not begin to tell you what we have came through since Leaving fredricksburgh. We have been marching night and day and I am shure we cant have marched Less than two hundered miles. Jane I have done my Last soldiring. I am tired of it. Any how it cant Last much Longer. The one or the other has got to be beat before another mounth. The rebels is bound to try to get into maryland and if they get there its all up with the north.[37] The south is desprate and are driving

---

36. With the 79th New York in the lead, the troops of General Stevens's 1st Division pressed forward through a grassy field during the initial phase of the battle, and received a volley from Confederate soldiers concealed in the woods to their front. Capt. and Assistant Adj. Gen. Hazard Stevens was severely wounded in this initial blast. His troops wavering under the intense fire of the Confederates, General Stevens rushed to the front to personally rally his men. By the time he reached the position of the 79th New York, five successive color-bearers, including Alexander Campbell, had fallen. A special correspondent to the *New York Tribune* recorded the scene: "Having made his dispositions, he [General Stevens] led the attack on foot at the head of the 79th (Highlanders). Soon meeting a withering fire, and the Color Sergeant, Sandy Campbell, a grizzled old Scotchman, being wounded, they faltered. One of the color guard took up the flag, when the General snatched it from him. The wounded Highlander at his feet cried, 'For God's sake, General, don't *you* take the colors; they'll shoot you if you do!' The answer was, 'Give me the colors! If they don't follow now, they never will;' and he sprang forward, crying, 'We are all Highlanders; follow Highlanders; forward *my* Highlanders!' The Highlanders did follow their Scottish chief, but while sweeping forward a ball struck him on his right temple. He died instantly. An hour afterward, when taken up, his hands were still clenched around the flag-staff." The *Scottish American Journal* elaborated upon Alexander Campbell's role in the engagement: "Color-Sergeant Campbell distinguished himself. In the [initial] charge Colonel [Addison] Farnsworth tried to get the colors, but the sergeant would not resign them for a moment." Smith, "Ox Hill," 48–51; *New York Tribune,* 8 September 1861; *Scottish American Journal,* 11 September 1862.

37. Campbell's instincts proved to be correct. Flush with victory after the Second Battle of Bull Run, General Lee, on 4 September 1862, launched his first invasion of the North, which ended in the 17 September Battle of Antietam, Md. The Battle of Antietam, regarded as "the bloodiest single day of the war," resulted in an estimated 12,410 Union and 13,724 Confederate casualties. Boatner, *Dictionary,* 17–21.

our troops before them all over. I dont care how it goes now. Our generals dont seem to care and its not Likely the men will. The south is fighing desperatly. I am shure they must be drugged or they never could stand it and the Killed and wounded thats Left on the field in there canteens theres whisky and *gunpowder* in them.[38]

I have nothing more to say only that I am well in helth and my Leg is getting on first rate and if I could only get home to my own house I would fell much better but I expect to get sent to new york as soon as the nixt batch goes and I think that will be soon. Now Jane I will come to a close this time hopping this will find you all well. You must write as soon as you get this for I might be sent north soon. So good day and I am your ever Afficonate Husband

Alexander Campbell

Address
A Campbell
Ward D. Emory Hospital
Washington D.C.
Tell [Brother] Peter to send some papers. Write soon.

LETTER 46[39]

Emory Hospital
September 9th 1862

[Dear Jane]

I received your welcome letter of the 8th just now and am happy

---

38. Throughout the course of his exhaustive research on Union soldiers, eminent Civil War historian Bell Wiley discovered that "when disparagers of Southern bravery were confronted by a dashing performance which utterly contradicted their generalizations, they usually had a ready answer: The Rebels were crazy drunk on whisky and gunpowder. This claim, which interestingly enough was also used by Rebels to explain Yankee gallantry, was found in many soldier letters." Not surprisingly, civilians made similar claims in their letters and diaries. Shortly after the Battle of Secessionville, renowned Southern diarist Mary Boykin Chesnut penned the following lines regarding the conduct of the hard-fighting 79th New York Highlanders: "Scotchmen—for the regiment of Federals at Secessionville were Scotch. And madly intoxicated. They had poured out whiskey for them like water." Wiley, *Billy Yank*, 349; C. Van Woodward, ed., *Mary Chesnut's Civil War* (New Haven: Yale University Press, 1981), 390.

39. The following transcription is from a copy located in the Campbell Family Papers. The original letter apparently did not survive.

to hear that you are all in such good health. I received two letters from you and one from [Brother] Peter the other day. Yours were dated the 8h and 13h and [Brother] Peters the 19th of August. You know we got no mail since we left Frederickberg untill we came here.

Matt came with my letters. He told me the regiment was at the old camp where we were last year the time of the mutiny But he expected they would move soon.[40] They were going to Harpers Ferry. I have since heard that they have gone. The 79th has a poor show now. The Col was wounded in Saturdays fight and the Major on Monday. Let Col Morrison is the only field officer left.[41]

[Brother] Peter tells me in his letter that he has a notion of joining the 79th. Jane tell him from me not to do anything of the kind. They cant draft no man that [is] the only support of his family. I wish I was only clear of it. What man that had any idea of how the war should be conducted has heart any longer to fight under such generals as we have. They seem to want to get men slaughtered and all to no purpose whatever.

I some times think that this war will last as long as our general can get men to fight with them And that the men on both side will giv up in cours of time and it will dwindle down till it stops altogether for the Southeran soldiers are just as sick of it as the northern.

I expect we are to be sent away from here perhaps to morrow. We expected to go to day for they took the names of all fit to be removed and I was one of them. We dont know where they are going to send us but I think somehow it is to N.Y. I hope so I may. I am getting along first rate. My leg dont require much doctoring Only I would rather be home in my own hous than in a hospital. I will come to a close this time hoping to see you soon. You need not write until I do for I will likely be away if going at all.

[Alexander Campbell]

---

40. On 4 September, the 79th New York encamped on Meridian Hill, the place of the Highlanders' mutiny of the previous year. Todd, *Highlanders, 225.*

41. A roll call taken on 3 September revealed that the 79th New York, which had lost 9 killed, 79 wounded, and 17 captured or missing from the fighting between 16 August and 2 September 1862, could only muster 1 field officer (Lt. Col. David Morrison), 7 line officers, and 200 men for duty. Colonel Farnsworth had received a disabling wound in the leg during the Second Battle of Bull Run, while Maj. William St. George Elliott was seriously wounded during the Battle of Chantilly. Lieutenant Colonel Morrison took command of both the 79th regiment and the 3d Brigade, 2d Division, IX Corps, in Farnsworth's absence. O.R., Series 1, vol. 12, 261; Todd, *Highlanders, 203, 225.*

Chapter Five

"IT WONT BE LONG TILL I BE HOME"

15 January 1863 through 29 April 1863

On 10 September 1862, Alexander Campbell was moved from Emory General Hospital in Washington, D.C., where he had spent six days, to Bellevue Hospital in New York City, where he was admitted two days later. Campbell remained in New York City, where he must have seen much of Jane and their two children, until his discharge from Bellevue on 2 January 1863, when he departed for the camp of the 79th New York in Fredericksburg, Virginia.[1]

During Campbell's convalescence in New York, the 79th High-landers took part in the repulse of Lee's first invasion of the North. At the Battles of South Mountain (14 September 1862) and Antietam (17 September 1862), engagements in which both James and Matthew Ralston participated, the 79th New York, as part of the 1st Division of the IX Corps of the Army of the Potomac, lost eight men killed and 38 wounded. To the relief of the Highlanders, their brigade (reorganized

---

1. Carded Medical Records Volunteers, Mexican and Civil Wars 1846–1865, Entry 534 (78 New York Kirsh, A. To 79 New York Cox, J.), Box 2205, Records of the Adjutant General's Office, Record Group 94, National Archives, Washington, D.C.

after Antietam to consist of the 2d, 8th, 18th, and 20th Michigan and the 79th New York) remained in reserve during the Army of the Potomac's slaughterous defeat at the 13 December 1862 Battle of Fredericksburg.[2]
Alexander Campbell rejoined the 79th New York on 15 January 1863 as second lieutenant of Company G, having been promoted to that position on 16 October 1862.[3] James and Matthew Ralston, who remained in Company F, had also risen in rank during the period of Alexander Campbell's hospitalization in New York City; James Ralston was promoted to sergeant on 30 September 1862, while Matthew Ralston was promoted to corporal at approximately the same time.[4]
Although Alexander Campbell had seen his last fighting the previous September at the Battle of Chantilly, he would remain with the 79th for an additional, though hardly uneventful, four months. During this period, Campbell's healing leg proved less painful than his renewed separation from Jane and their two young children. Pressure from home would prove to be an integral factor in his decision to leave the army; as his letters reveal, Jane urged him to resign his commission, informing him that she was pregnant and contemplating an abortion. Fearing this and continuing to suffer from his wound, Alexander Campbell became increasingly committed to leave the Highlanders with honor and return to New York City.

LETTER 47

Camp oppisite Fredricksburg Va.
January 15th 1863

Dear Wife

You will think it rather n[e]glectful of me not writing sooner. The fact of it is I have not been much off my feet since I arrived here. There is not much accomidation here for any more officeres. There was just room made for them that was here at the time. I have got a sort of a plac[e] made out at Last. We was delayed a good on the way com-

---

2. Bilby, "Blue Bonnets Over the Border," 10; Compiled Service Record of James Ralston; Compiled Service Record of Matthew Ralston.
3. Compiled Service Record of Alexander Campbell.
4. Compiled Service Record of James Ralston; Compiled Service Record of Matthew Ralston.

ming out. The only recruit I had Skedaddled from me in Philadelphia. He was an old hand at the business.[5] I Stayed two nights in John Sewarts in washington. They are verry Kind. I Left the box for Billey[6] there so that he can get it when he comes over.

Jane I was verry Lucky this time in getting here at the time I did for they Pay master came down from washington in the same boat that I came in and we have all got payed now only for four mounths. If we had got Six mounths I could have sent you home a good deal of mouney. As it is I only got 15 days Lieuts pay.[7] My appointment as Lieut dates from the 16th day of october and we are only payed to the end of october. Well it cant be helpet. There will be more to draw nixt time. The money I got this time amounted to $112 so that I will send as much as I can home soon.

I dont Know how it will be with me yet in reguard to me being marked absant without [leave]. Collnel Morrison wrote on to washington his statement along with my one and I wont Know how it will be till he received word back.[8] I dont care much how it will be. They cant Discharde me without paying me anyhow.

My Leg is getting on verry well. I get it dressed every morning. I

---

5. By the terms of the July 1862 Militia Act, which allowed Lincoln to call for and, if necessary, draft 300,000 nine–month militiamen, a conscript could hire a substitute to take his place. Many of these substitutes deserted at their first opportunity and then hired themselves out to yet another reluctant draftee. There were also bounty jumpers, men who enlisted in the army to obtain any financial incentives offered from the Federal government and/or the state, deserted, and then repeated the process. An old hand at either business could look forward to making a good sum of money. J. Matthew Gallman, *The North Fights the Civil War: The Home Front* (Chicago: Ivan R. Dee, 1994), 60–62.

6. William ("Billy") Ralston, younger brother of Jane Ralston Campbell. On 29 August 1862, William Ralston enlisted at New York City as a private in Company B, 2d Regiment New York Heavy Artillery. In January 1863, Ralston's regiment was assigned to the defenses of the capital; as a result, he was in a position to pick up the box Alexander Campbell left for him at the residence of John Stewart in Washington, D.C. The remainder of Ralston's wartime service was far from distinguished. In August 1863, he was found to be absent without leave for two days and was sentenced to fifteen days hard labor and fined $10. After being wounded in action at Petersburg, Va., on 17 June 1864, Ralston was again found to be absent without leave and was sentenced to hard labor on public works for six months and fined $30. On 31 May 1865, William Ralston was discharged from the service. Compiled Service Record of William Ralston; O.R., Series 1, vol. 25, 2:30.

7. As a second lieutenant, Campbell was to receive $45 per month. War Department, *Revised Regulations*, 351.

8. Alexander Campbell had been listed as absent without leave since 1 December 1862. On 15 January 1863, Lieutenant Colonel Morrison wrote a letter to the assistant adjutant general in Washington, in which he described Campbell as "an efficient officer"

cant ware my boot now. It blistered all my heel comming out that it made me Quite Lame. The Dr told Col Morrison that it would be two or three weeks before I would be able to do duty and its my opinion that it will be a great deal more than that. Jammey & Matthew Looks first rate and feels well. Jammey would Like verry well to get home for a few days but its verry hard to get that. Colnel Farnsworth came out yeasterday. I have not seen him yet. I beleive he is walking on a crutch yet I think he wont stay Long.[9]

There is some talk of a mouve to be made her[e] soon. They are getting the poontoon bridges ready again but it may not signify anything. Jane you will have to excuse me not writing more this time. The wind is blowing so hard into the tent that I cant write. I will write more nixt time. I heard since I came out that our Regtms time is up in may that we came out before the three years act was past and they cant Keep us Longer than two years and that would make our time up on the 13th day of may.[10]

---

and strongly recommended his restoration to rank. Included with Morrison's letter was an explanatory note from Campbell which reads as follows:

Camp 79 Regt. N.Y. Volunteers
Opposite Fredericksburg Va.
Jan[uar]y 12/[18]63
Colonel [Morrison]
    I have the honor to make the following statement in explanation of my absence from my Regiment.
    On the 1st September last as you are aware I was severely wounded at the Battle of Chantilly. I was sent to the Emery Hospital [in] Washington on the 2nd Sept. and in some ten days there after I was sent to New York to the Bellevue Hospital where I arrived on the 12th Sept. I remained a patient there till my wounds were sufficiently well to enable me to report for duty which I did on the 2d January as [evidenced by the] accompanying pass.
    I am Colonel Very Respectfully Your Obed. S[ervan]t
    Alexander Campbell
    Lieut. Co. G. 79 NYV

Although no specific date is provided in his compiled service record, Campbell was restored to rank sometime in late January or early February 1862. Compiled Service Record of Alexander Campbell.
    9. The wounds Farnsworth received at Second Bull Run never healed sufficiently to permit him to return to active duty. Farnsworth resigned from the 79th New York and was discharged on 17 February 1863. Morrison was promoted to the colonelcy of the regiment in his place. Phisterer, *New York in the War of the Rebellion*, vol. 4, 2851, 2856; Todd, *Highlanders*, 272.
    10. The regiment's time was up in May 1864, not May 1863 as Campbell had heard. See note 5, chapter one, for a discussion of the possible origins of this misunderstanding.

No more this time only tell Little Jonney & alexander that pappa will soon be home again. I Remain ever afficonate Husband

Alex Campbell
Address Lieut A. Campbell Co G 79th
N.Y. Vols ninth army corps Va

LETTER 48

Camp oppisite Fredricksburg Va
January 25th 1863

Dear wife

I received your Letter Last night and was most happy to hear that you and the boys was well and that you got the money I Sent you all right. As you said it will help to clear some of our detts but you must not run your self out of money too soon for it might bee sometime before I get payed again and you will better Leave the card that [Brother] Peter has till I get payed nixt time then I will be able to send you plenty to clear up every thing. They oww us near three mounths now and we may get two mounths soon but you must not rely on that.

I suppose you would think that fiting had been going on here. The army was in motion.[11] All Franklins[12] grand Division moved and that

---

11. On the morning of 20 January 1863, General Burnside began to move his Army of the Potomac across the Rappahannock River at Banks' Ford, roughly five miles north of Fredericksburg, in order to attack Lee's forces on Marye's Heights in the flank and rear. That night, a two-day rainstorm began, which turned the roads into impassable quagmires; those Union soldiers already en route to Banks' Ford were literally stuck in the mud, unable to move artillery or wagons without Herculean effort. Luckily for the Highlanders, the 79th New York had been ordered back and was able to return to the shelter of its camp soon after the storm began, thus avoiding the fate of the lead element of the army. Burnside's failed offensive, which quickly became known as the "Mud March," further demoralized his army and affected his removal as commander of the Army of the Potomac. Todd, *Highlanders*, 268.

12. Maj. Gen. William Buel Franklin. General Franklin commanded the Left Grand Division at the Battle of Fredericksburg and was blamed by General Burnside and the Committee on the Conduct of the War for the Union loss. Franklin was relieved by Burnside on 23 January 1863; he later was assigned to command the XIX Corps during the Red River Campaign (20 August 1863 to 2 May 1864). Boatner, *Dictionary,* 304.

night it came on rain and continued for three days and they had to come back and the artilrey stuck in the mud and it took the duble Quantity of horses to pull them and the men when they were comming back they were the most Disorginised Looking army I beleive ever was seen. The fact of it is this army is demorlisied and the men wont fight. They are deserting all the time. There is Quite a number Leaft our regiment since we got payed. I think we are to stay here for the winter. The best thing that can be done to give this army confidence is to reinstate Mclellan again.[13] They all have confidence in him.

The rebels on the other side is getting tierd of the ware. They tell our men so. They send our men richmond papers and want to get the herald verry bad and they tell our men that there officers cant stop them from speaking to us and say to our men that it is a shame that one nation should be fighting amongst themselves.

I was perfectly astonished when I read in your Letter the Dr.s bill. I never amiganed it would be so Little as that. He has been verry Liberal. I will write to him soon. I ought to have wrote before this time.

Jane I have no news to write about only that I am in good helth. My Leg is getting on verry well. I wont be fit for duty for sometime yet. James & mat is well. You want to Know if I had plenty in my heversack. I had plenty. I was not verry hungry comming out and I was surprised when I was Looking for a cloth for my Leg when I saw the Little flask and of corse I new there was something in it. I have not drank it yet. I did not get any writing paper from [Brother] Peter. I think he must have forgot all about it. I am furnished with writing paper now by the goverment. It is not noat paper. It will do well enouph. I have bought a Likeness of General Steavens. I will send it hom in this Letter.

George Gillie must have been blowing when he was down. I said nothing of the Kind about being bad about if they would not take me back. I dont Know how it will be yet. Col Morrison has not received any answer to the Letter he sent to washington but I dont care how it will be. If I am discharged they will have to give me a phention but I am not the Least afraid of getting discharged.

---

13. Although McClellan was still a favorite among many soldiers in the Army of the Potomac, he would never again command them. On 26 January 1863, command of the Army of the Potomac passed from Burnside to Gen. Joseph Hooker, who had previously led the Center Grand Division (consisting of the II and III Corps) of that force. Boatner, *Dictionary*, 409.

I wont say any more this time hopping to hear from you Soon and that this will fiend you all well. I remain Your ever afficonate Husband

A. Campbell

Lieut Co G
79th Highlanders
We are going to celebrate the anaversary of Burnses[14] birth day to night.

A.C.

━━━━━➤●⊱━━━━━

LETTER 49

Head Quarters 79th Highlanders
Camp Oppisite Fredricksburg
January 31st 1863

Dear Wife

I recieved your Letter of the 25 in dew time. You seem to have been in verry bad spirits when you wrote it. You must not think I can get home so easy because I am an officer. They wont except of an officers resignation at all without a Dr cirtficate and I dont beleive I could get that. There was a chaplan tendered his resignation belongs to a regiment in this division and he got a disonorable discharge for resigning in front of the enemy. You would not have me do that I am shure. Any how we are comming home in may as a regiment. We had a meeting the other day and all the officers sygned a pition and sent it to the govener of the state to call us home on or befor the 13 day of may and there is some of the men received Letters from there friends that Simeon Draper[15] told them the 79th was comming home either in april

---

14. On 25 January, Scots in the 79th New York joined Scottish Americans throughout the states in celebration of the anniversary of the birth of Scottish poet Robert Burns (1759–1796). With customary enthusiasm, celebrators toasted the accomplishments of Burns, a man whose success, according to the head of the Burns Club of the City of New York, "has been appreciated by all who have within their bosoms a spark of national pride." *Scottish American Journal,* 5, 12 February 1863.

15. Simeon Draper, who served as provost-marshall-general of the War Department from September 1862 until April 1863, was chairman of the Executive Committee of the Union Defence Committee of the City of New York. O.R., Series 3, vol. 2, 625, vol. 3, 169–70; Stevens, *Union Defence Committee,* 70.

or may. So I am shure Jane you would rather see me comming home with the regiment and it comming home so soon and I will promise that if it dont come home then (I will).

I hear that we are going back to washington that this army is to be broken up and part sent out west. There is one thing certain they cant march through Virginia in winter. They tryed it and had to give it up.

You Say you are going to move on the first of the mounth. I think you are verry comfortable where you are but I wont interfeer in that. You Know best yourself.

When I wrote you before I told you we were going to celebrate Burns birth day. Well we had a great time. You will see about it in the Scottish American. Theres been a verry severe snow storm here Lately. Its verry near all gon now but the ground is in a horable condition. James & Mat is well. They have just come in off picket. My Leg in getting better fast. I am not on duty yet.

I have to go before a Bord of officers to inquire what reasons I had for being absent without Leave. Its mearly a form thats got to be gon through. Now Jane I will come to a close this time hopping this will fiend you & the twa Barnes[16] will. You will write soon an Let me Know where you move to. I am Your Ever Afficonate Husband

Alex Campbell

I send this Dollar to you to treat you to an oyster stew and the two Boys to what ever you think best for them to sever. A.C.

LETTER 50

Camp Near Fredricksburg Virginia
Febuary 11th 1863

Dear Wife

I received your Letter in dew time and was happy to hear that you was all well. I would wrote sooner but we were expecting to move and I was not going to wait till after we had moved but we have not moved

---

16. Scottish for two children. In the Scottish language, 'twa' is "a small number, two or three, a few, several;" 'bairn' is "a child, male or female; offspring of any age." Grant, *Scottish National Dictionary*, vol. 9, 451, vol. 1, 23.

yet and I thought I would write you a few Lines. We are all packed up wating every moment expecting to get the order to fall in. We ar ordered to fort monroe to report to general Dix.[17] What comes after we cant tell but its verry Likely we are going on some other expidition again. Its only the ninth army corps thats going. I ame not sorry to get out of virginia. Its a horrable place in winter time. Nothing but mud.

I received your Letter two days ago and your Likeness in it. Its a great Looking Likeness. One of the Sides of your face is Quite Black. No mater. I have a better one here. I dont Let any one see the Last one for its not as good Looking as you. I will send you mine the first chance. I am not on duty yet. My Leg is getting better but I wont be able to march as far as I ust to. I wrote to [Brother] Peter that time I wrote you. He has not sent me any papers yet. I would Like verry much to get some weekly papers. We get the herald every day. We pay 10cts for it.

Febuary 13th

Jane

I stoped writing on accoint of the Divison head Quarters having moved there was no place to post the Letters and on the same accoint we have not got any mail this Last tow nights and we have been all packed up for sometime expecting every order that came that we would go the nixt one shure and since I commenced writing this part theres word that we are going to morrow morning at 5 1/2 oclock so I will post this at aquia creek to morrow or when I get there. I heard since I commenced the first of this Letter that we are going with Burnside and he is to superseed general Dix at fort monroe. We might be sent to norflok or sume of these places around there. Any how I will Let you Know where as soon as we get to our detination.

You will be wearing for a Letter but I could not help it and I will write and send you word from fort monroe if there will be a chance to get ashore. You need not write till I write again so as you will Know whare to write to. I am glad to get out of this part of this country. You must Let me Know how you Like your new apartments and how you

---

17. The IX Corps, including the 441-man-strong 79th New York, was to depart on 14 February for Suffolk, Va., an area believed to be threatened by Confederate troops under General Longstreet, and report to Gen. John Adams Dix, commander of the Federal Department of Virginia. Todd, *Highlanders*, 272–74; Bilby, "Blue Bonnets Over the Border," 10.

get on with the Doctor. I had a verry strange Dream Last night. I dreamed that Jonney was dead and the baby was dying too but it would not doe of one was to beleive dreams to be true. I hope that one of mines is not true. I wont say any more this time. I will write soon again.

> I remain Your afficonate Husband
> A. Campbell

When you write Let me Know where Quackenbush Lives not where works but his number and street. You can ask [Brother] Peter. Dont Let [Brother] Peter Know that I want to K[n]ow. Its for a man that K[n]ows Qucenbush and he wants to K[n]ow where he Lives he K[n]ows where he works.

LETTER 51

> Camp near newport news Va
> Febuary 19th 1863

Dear Wife

We arrived here on the 16th. I would wrote you sooner but had no chance. It has been raining this two days back and we have been fixing our tents for to make them as comfortable as possable so that I have had no oppertunity sooner. We are camped near the old place that we were before. The whole ninth army corps is in camped in a Line along the banks of the James River the Left resting at newport news ant we are the extream right which makes us about 3 miles farther up the River. I think we are here for to reorginise and prepare for another expidition. I hope they will Let us stay here till may but I am afraid not.

The men is hard at work getting Logs to rais there tents. They have got new ones.[18] This is much more comfortable a place than where we

---

18. The men of the 79th received new A tents upon their arrival at Newport News. A simple wedge tent, the A tent was often stockaded, or raised above walls of logs, to provide its inhabitants with more room and comfort. Todd, *Highlanders*, 272–73; Billings, *Hard Tack and Coffee*, 49, 66.

Left. Theres not so much mud here. Theres going to be a great deal of Drilling here 4 times a day.[19]

There going to grant fourloughs to the men two to each company. There will be some of them that wont come back and if the Regiment dont get home in may the most of the old hands will Leave anyhow.

I sent a Letter in Jameses one to you from aquia Creek as we came through. I had no stamp to post on it. I wish you would send me a few in your nixt Letter. I had a Letter fron John Stewart and he says that Billy was there and got his box. When you write Let me Know how you Like your new house.

Capt montgomry[20] got a Letter that day we arrived or rather a telegraph Despatch that his youngest Boy was dead and the Wife was verry sick. I happened to ask him when he was reading it if his folks was all well and that was the answer that his boy was dead and his wife verry sick. He felt verry bad and I was verry sorry for him. He ought to have got the Despatch 3 days ago but this moving Kept it Back.

Jane I will come to a close this time hopping this will find you and the boys well. You must write soon. I am getting along verry well. Mat & James is well. Good Day and I Remain Your ever Afficonate Husband

Alex Campbell

Adress Ninth army corps Newport news Virginia

P.S. Tell [Brother] Peter to send me some weekly papers. I have not got any from him yet. I cant think why he has not sent me some before. I would Like if I could get the rest of these thistle bottons all thats on the Jacket too. I will Let you Know when theres any chance to send them. Please Let me Know how many theres of them in your nixt Letter.

A Campbell

---

19. The men of the 79th New York were put through the following daily routine during their stay at Newport News: "Reveille, 6 A.M.; police, 6:30 A.M.; breakfast, 7 A.M.; guard-mounting, 8 A.M.; drill (company) manual of arms, 8:30 A.M. to 9 A.M.; drill (battalion) 10:30 A.M. to 11:30 A.M.; dinner 12 A.M.; drill (company), skirmishing, 1 P.M. to 2 P.M.; drill (battalion) 3 P.M. to 4 P.M.; dress parade (retreat) 5 P.M.; brigade drill (twice a week) from 1 to 4 P.M." In the words of one Highlander, this was "quite a tidy day's work, and sufficient to keep all hands occupied." *Scottish American Journal*, 5 March 1863.

20. Capt. William S. Montgomery, Co. F, 79th New York Highlanders.

LETTER 52

Camp near newport news Va
Febuary 28th 1863

Dear wife

I am almost out of pations wating to hear from you. I wrote you
since I came here and its time that I should have an answer to it now. I
am verry anxious to Know how you ar all in helth. I am on duty now.
I feel Quite well. My Leg is getting on well. Its almost all Skined over.
We have had two men died since we came here one with typhoid feaver
and another with taking the rong midisine. He was one of the Hospital
attendants and it happened when we were all out on revue so there was
no docter present to attend to him or he might have been saved. It was
rather a melincolly affair. He took the poison himself instead of something else.[21]

We have had some verry stormy weather since we come here heavy
snow but it dont Lay Long and when the sun comes out its quite
warm. This is a verry good place but I am afraid we wont be long here
to enjoy it. Its too good to Last Long. I dont Know what to think
about the war now. Its beyond my comprehension.

I hear we are going to get payed soon again. They owed us four
mounths now they will only pay two. I want to get some things when I
get payed but I will let you Know what when I do get payed. James
and matthew is is good helth. There is not much to write you about
hear. You must excuse me if I dont write a Long Letter this time. I
hope you and Jonney and Alexander is well and that you Like your
place that you moved to and I hope to be at home the nixt time you
move. I hope the midisine you took wont do you any harm.

Now Jane I will bid you good day and I hope to hear from you
soon and oblige your ever afficonate Husband

Alex Campbell

---

21. Campbell is referring here to the death of Pvt. William Watt, Company C, 79th
New York Highlanders. During a review of the regiment, Watt, a hospital aid, "com-
plained of indisposition, and took a dose of what he thought was a preparation of rhubarb,
but which turned out to be a solution of aconite, a very deadly drug. He died in the course
of about fifteen minutes after swallowing the fatal stuff." Although a doctor arrived on the
scene before Watt died, "all attempts at resuscitation were futile." *Scottish American Journal*, 19 March 1863.

P.S. If you could send the bottons with Colnel morrison when he comes back. He is home at present. Send (13). You can call at his house yourself and he will bring them when he comes. Remember (13) thistle and if you woold make me another vest Like the one I have I would Like.

A.C.

━━━━➤✦◀━━━━

LETTER 53

Camp near newport news Va
March 4 1863

Dear Wife

Your Letter of the 26th came in dew time. I was sorry to hear of the boys being sick. Little alex must have been verry bad. His arm must be all marked where he was vaxinated. Poor Little fellow. He must have suffered verry bad. I hope he is all right now. What does Jonney say I am gon to now? I suppose he will have forgotten me now almost. I hope you will not think on taking anything to destroy your helth. You have seen enouph of what follows. I suppose you are trying a race the three of you to see who will be first. Never mind. Jane you must Let nature take its way. It wont doe to try to prevent it.

I have got two parcles of papers from [Brother] peter since I wrote you Last. I suppose he will so[o]n move down town again. I wrote a Letter to Brother James and sent it. I went to general Wilcox[22] and gave it to him. He said he would send it to general Dix to be forwarded. Its got to be Left open. I think it will be all right. Theres Letters sent south that way. Our chaplan[23] sent one to his father in tenesee and sent him a Letter from here. I wont Know whether he got it or not for some time. I expect to get an answer to it through time.[24]

Jane I scarsley have time to write now we are drilled so much so

---

22. Brig. Gen. Orlando Bolivar Willcox commanded the 1st Division of the IX Corps, to which the 79th New York belonged. Boatner, *Dictionary*, 926.

23. James C. Wyatt, Jr. Wyatt, the third chaplain to serve with the 79th, held that position from 18 March 1862 until his death on 10 July 1863 at Memphis, Tenn. Phisterer, *New York in the War of the Rebellion*, vol. 4, 2843, 2859.

24. No response to this letter survives with the Campbell Family Papers.

you must not think strang of me not writing you sooner. I am writing this to night after being out mostly all day. I commenced it this morning but could not get it finished to send away with the mail this afternoon so it will have to stay here till tomorrow afternoon. I mentioned in my Last Letter for you to make me another vest. I would Like to get pants made too but I will have to wait till nixt pay. You can make the vest as soon as you can and send it out the first chance. This is a verry good place to get any thing that way. My Leg is getting on verry well. Its not altogether heald up yet. I wont say any more this time hopping this will fiend you all well as it Leaves me at present and I Remain Your ever Afficonate Husband

Alex Campbell

Write soon.

—————⟫•⟪—————

LETTER 54

Head Quarters 79th N.Y. Vols
near newport news
March 8th 1863

Dear wife

This being Sunday and no Drilling to doe I thought I would write you a few Lines to Let you Know I was well. I was out on picket the night before Last. Its the first picket I have been on in some time. Its Quite plesant on picket here. No danger of the enemy surprising you and the weather is verry plesant here now. James was on with me. Its Quite dull in camp to day. I have been thinking about home all day. All wise when I feel wearied (and thats often) I think of home. I hope the boys is well again.

Since I commenced writing this I received t[w]o parcles of papers from [Brother] Peter. He sends a great many and I am shure theres non of them goes astray. I get them everry day. Jane I scarcely no what to say. Theres nothing but camp Life to talk about and thats not enteresting to you I Know but so Long as they Keep us here we are all right. I hear that Morrison is verry sick. Theres all sorts of roumers going round in the regiment that he wont come back but its hard to tell. I guss he is about tierd of souldering.[25]

You will I hope not think of trying to put away any thing. Its a verry dangerious operation to tryphle with. I was just reading of an instance where a young girl got a Dr to take a baby away and it resulted in her Death. But you have read enouph about such things yourself and ought to Know better.[26] You will just have to take better care the nixt time. You I suppose will put all the blame on me. You said you would Like a Little girl. You Know you must not show this Letter to any one. I need not tell you for I Know you wont.

This is a beuiteful day and as [I] am sitting in my tent I hear the chaplan of the nixt Regt to us preashing to his regiment under the canopy of heaven. Winter is all over here now at Least one would think so its so warm to night. I have a stove in the tent but dont require any fire in it now except sometimes in the morning. Jane you must write soon and often and I will try and doe the same. I am your ever Afficonate Husband

Alexander Campbell

LETTER 55

Head Quarters 79th N.Y. Vols
newport news Va
March 13th 1863

Dear Wife

I write you a few Lines to Let you Know that I sent my commish-ion home. You will please Let me Know when you receive it. I sent it

---

25. Lieutenant Colonel Morrison departed for New York on 21 February 1863; he returned to the 79th New York as its colonel on 20 March. Todd, *Highlanders*, 273–75.

26. Abortion was prevalent during the Civil War. Northern women had numerous options, many of which were neither effective nor safe. Women could seek advice about abortion from various medical publications and brochures, as well as purchase so-called home remedies which were frequently advertised in the daily papers. In addition, women looking to end their pregnancies could solicit the aid of physicians at a wide variety of well-advertised abortion clinics. Many of the proscribed methods were ineffective (such as horseback riding and jumping) while others were dangerous (at least one physician used

away yeasterday. You must take good care of it but I Know you will. I am anxious to hear from you. You must write oftener. I have nothing to write about only I am well James & mat also. I hope this will fiend you & the boys in good helth. I will have to come to a close this time for we have to go on Drill. I have just come in off target practise this morning. We are to have it every morning instead of company Drill. Its much better. You will please write when you get this.

Your husband
Alex Campbell

P.S. This is rather a short Letter but I have not got time to write any more to day. I will write more nixt time. Writ soon. A. Campbell

---

LETTER 56

Head Quarters 79th Highlanders
newport newes
march 18th 1863

Dear Wife

I Received you Letter of the 12 & 15 in dew time and was happy to hear from you once more and that you and the boys is well. We have just received orders to bee ready to march tomorrow morning at 8 oclock. Its Late to night and I have get ready so I wont have time to write much. Its not nowing where we are going. Sume thinks its across the river to norfolk or sufolk and it might be farther south.[27] I will write as soon as I Know where we are going and Let you Know.

---

electrodes to administer electric shocks to the abdomens and lower backs of his patients). News of botched abortions and of physicians being prosecuted for them were frequently reported in newspapers, alerting women and their husbands to the possible dangers of the process. Thomas P. Lowry, *The Story the Soldiers Wouldn't Tell: Sex in the Civil War* (Mechanicsburg: Stackpole Books, 1994), 95–98.

27. On 16 March 1863, Major General Burnside was ordered to assume command of the Army and Department of the Ohio (the latter which consisted of Illinois, Indiana, Ohio, Michigan, and Kentucky east of the Tennessee River). Burnside was to be joined on his new assignment by the 1st and 2d Divisions from his former command, the IX Corps. Unbeknownst to the Highlanders, their ultimate destination was Kentucky. Todd, *Highlanders*, 275–77; O.R., Series 1, vol. 23, 147; Boatner, *Dictionary*, 606.

You seem to bee down hearted by your Letters. You must Keep up and not Let your spirits down. I will be home soon if I can get away honorable. You Know what I menthioned in a Letter befor that they would not give an honorable Discharge to officers without a Drs cirtificate. We I whink wont be in any fight for sume time yet so you need not feel bad about us moving this time. I dont want to see any more fighting. We might get some fort to garrison or some such job as that and it would be too bad if I did not stay and get my pay for a few mounths more.

Jane I will come to a close this time. Its after 11 oclock and I must get a Little sleep for we will have plenty to doo tomorrow. I will write the first chanc again so good night.

I am your ever afficonate Husband
Alex Campbell

That was a verry narrow escape you had from being burned out. I hope you will have no more till I am home at any rate. A.C.

LETTER 57

Head Quarters 79th Regt N.Y. Vols
Lebanon Ky
March 31st 1863

Dear Wife

You will think it strange of me not writing you sooner but if you beleive me this is the first chance I have had since I sent you these few Lines from parkersburg Va and you could not call that a chance. We have had hard time of it since we Left newport news and I am perfectly sick of soldering. We have been kicked about rather too much.[28]

---

28. On 19 March, the 79th New York boarded the steamship *John Rice* (at which time they were rejoined by Colonel Morrison) and headed for Baltimore, where they arrived on 22 March. From there, the Highlanders were crowded onto rail cars and traveled westward along the Baltimore and Ohio Railroad. The slow-moving train reached Parkersburg on 24 March, where the men left the rail cars and loaded onto the steamer *Majestic*, a flat-bottomed river boat, on which they continued the journey along the Ohio River. Finally, on 26 March, the 79th New York landed and disembarked at Louisville, Ky. Todd, *Highlanders*, 275–80.

Jane I am comming home as soon as I can get squared up. I have not got my pay yet on accoint of not being mustered into the service as a Lieut. There is a good many more of them in the same fix. There getting too pirticular all at once and I am afraid its two Late and as soon I get mustered and get payed I am going to resign and I hope they will except of it.

We are away out here guarding the railroad.[29] Tis only a branch and it dont go any farther than this. We are about 75 miles from Louisville Ky thats where we Landed off the boat and the most of the regiment stayed there that is they have Deserted and they entend not to be brought back either. James is behind too. I dont Know if he intends to Leave or not for he neaver said any thing about it to me. Matthew is here. He thinks James wont Come back. Them thats behind is mostly all the oldest hands in the regiment. The regiment got on one of the greatest sprees ever they were on before when they were payed. There was men drunk that I beleive never was so in there Lives before. They are so mad to think they cant get home in may it makes t[h]em reguardless of what they doe.[30] This town we are camped at is read hot sessesh and they will help all our men to get away that wants to.

Jane I cant write to day its verry cold in this tent and I have got a verry severe cold. I never had such a sore throat before. I can scarsely speak but I think its a Little easier to day. The weather has been verry cold since we came here.

Now Jane I will come to a close this time hopping this will fiend you all better that it Leaves me and I expect to hear from you soon.

---

29. On 29 March, the 79th New York, along with the 8th Michigan, was shipped to Lebanon, Ky., to join Union forces already active in the protection of the town and its surrounding rail lines from the seemingly omnipresent Confederate guerrillas commanded by Gen. John Hunt Morgan. Todd, *Highlanders,* 277, 282–83.

30. On 27 March, the paymaster visited the 79th New York and distributed four months' back pay to the Highlanders. A majority of the suddenly wealthy Highlanders, lured by both the "scarlet women" and liquor to be had in Louisville, made their way into town despite their officers' attempts to keep them within the confines of camp. For the next several days, members of the 79th New York drove themselves to excess until their money all but vanished. In reference to the soldiers' behavior, the regimental historian stated: "It would be merciful, perhaps, to draw the curtain over this, a most unfortunate episode in the career of the Highlanders."

Many of the soldiers involved in this "episode" initially failed to report back to duty. Among those Highlanders absent without leave was James Ralston, who, along with 30–40 other members of the 79th, rejoined the regiment in Lebanon the following week. Todd, *Highlanders,* 281–82, 284; Compiled Service Record of James Ralston.

I am Your ever Afficonate Husband
Alex Campbell

address
Lebanon Kentucky

LETTER 58

Head Quarters 79th Regiment N.Y
Lebanon Kintucky
April 10th 1863

Dear Wife

I write this few Lines to Let you Know how I am. I am getting a Little better of my cold but I dont Like this part of the country at all and as I said in my Last letter I wrote you from here that I was comming home as soon as I got mustered and payed. I still adhear to it and every day seems as Long as two now that I have made up my mind to goo and I hope that my resignation will be excepted of. I am verry anxious to hear from you. We have got no mail since we have come here. I would Like verry much to get a Letter from you now but I hope you and the boys is well. Tell them there papa will soon be home at Least expects to. There is a good many of the officers going to resign. Jane two years is Long enough to be away from home. James came back from Louisville.[31] Him and matthew is well. I have nothing farther to write only I earnestly hope this will find you all well and that I will soon be home for good. It will be a strange war that will get me to Leave home again. Now I will say no more hopping to hear from you soon.

I Remain you ever Afficonate Husband
Alexander Campbell

---

31. James Ralston officially returned to the 79th New York on 3 April 1863. Compiled Service Record of James Ralston.

LETTER 59

Head Quarters 79th Highlanders
Lebanon Ky
April 13th 1863

Dear Wife

I received your welcom Letter to day and was most happy to hear
from home away so far away from it. The farther away one goes from
home they think the more of it.

I see by the tone of your Letter that some one has been writing
Lies. I hope you will Let me Know whou it was that told you and how
they heard of it or whou wrote from here. I would Like to fiend out. If
things is got up for a joke here they wont be considered as such when
wrote of to new york. The fact of it is there was a joke got up on the
boat about me throwing my sword over board. It was not so. You see I
was put under arrest when that we got aboard the boat. The reason
was that I took possession of a berth and it seems another officer had
secured it before me but he was not in it when we went into it (there
was another with me at the time and he was put under arrest too).
Well we had possesion when the others came in to go to bead and they
of corse wanted us to Leave that it was there state rooms. We of corse
did not Like to Leave and was not going to either and they went and
reported us to the colnel and we had to Leave the births and of corse
spoke pretty sharp about it and the result was we was both put under
arrest. I was Kept in arrest for some time but the other one went and
got himself relievied. I was in no hurry but Leterly got relievied without
giving in one insh. Colnel Morrison did not want to put me in arrest at
all but Lieut Col More[32] took it upon himself to do so. I will bet I will

---

32. Lt. Col. John More, 79th New York Highlanders. In May 1861, More, age 38,
enrolled at New York City to serve for three years and was mustered in as first lieutenant,
Company D. Promoted to the captaincy of Company D on 28 October 1861, More was
wounded and captured at the Second Battle of Bull Run on 30 August 1862. More eventually rejoined the regiment and was promoted to major on 26 November 1862. On 17
February 1863 he replaced David Morrison as lieutenant colonel upon Morrison's appointment to the colonelcy of the regiment. More would serve as lieutenant colonel of the 79th
New York until mustered out on 31 May 1864. After Morrison's promotion to command
of the 1st Brigade, 1st Division, IX Corps in April 1863, Lieutenant Colonel More was
given direct command of the 79th New York. Phisterer, *New York in the War of the Rebellion*, vol. 4, 2856; Todd, *Highlanders*, 285.

get Square with him yet. There verry few in the regiment Likes him and he is ruining it. He wont have many men to command after the 13th of may just one mounth to day. Never mind.

It wont be Long till I be home anyhow just as soon as I get mustered so that I can get my pay. You can rest assured Jane that I Lost no money for I had non to Lose. A verry good reason is it not? Them that told that Lie I am verry anxious to Know. I can take care of myself and my money and I would Look after them too if I Knew whou they are. There has been some promotions since we came here. They have passed over me. I had a right to a first Lieutenantsey but did not get it. I dont want it anyhow but it shows the fair play thats going in this regiment.

I am all right of my cold now. The weather is getting Quite warm. We had a revue Last week. The folks never saw anything of the Kind here before and was verry much taken with it. James and matthew is both well. I wrote you that James had got back before. I am glad to hear that tread is so brisk at home.

Theres a number of the old officers resigning.[33] There is too much politics getting into it. You menthioned in one of your Letters about a Mrs Simpson that hir husband was a captain in the 79th. He the said simpson is Major now he that ust to ring 32nd st bell.[34] He is a political hunbog. He cant drill a corporals guard. These are the men that gets all the high positions in the Federal army. It can never be succesful and I think the sooner I am out of it the better.

Jane its getting rather Late and I have nothing farther that I can think of only I hope this will fiend you and the Bairns well as it Leaves me and Beleive me to be your ever afficonate Husband

Alexander Campbell

Write soon.

---

33. In all, six officers of the 79th New York resigned their commissions and were discharged during April 1863. Phisterer, *New York in the War of the Rebellion,* vol. 4, 2847–59.

34. William Simpson, major, 79th New York Highlanders. At the age of 39, Simpson had, on 13 May 1861, enrolled at New York City to serve for three years and was mustered in on 27 May as a private in Company C, 79th New York. Simpson steadily rose in rank while with Company C, attaining the rank of captain on 2 January 1863. On 7 March 1863, Simpson was elevated to major of the 79th New York, a position he held until he was mustered out of the service on 31 May 1864. Phisterer, *New York in the War of the Rebellion,* vol. 4, 2858.

LETTER 60

Head Quarters 79th N.Y. Vols
Lebanon Ky
April 20th 63

Dear Wife

I send you this few Lines with Capt Gilmore[35] he that came to see me with Charles sanderson one night. He resigned and it has been excepted. There is another been excepted and the rest came back to be reconsidered. They wont except so many all at once. I have not been mustered yet. I have to be discharged as an in Listed man first and it will take a Little time before I can send my resignation in. I will send it as soon as I can after getting mustered. I wish I had some money to send you but it cant be healped. Its all good when the time comes.

Jane theres verry Little thats worth writing about here. The weather is getting quite warm here. I have got all well of my cold and all thats wrong with me now is I am Longing to get home.

Matthew & James is well. If the old members of the regiment dont get home on the 13th of may the most of them will goo anyhow. There will be a grand burst up nixt mounth or I am cheated.

Now Jane I wont say any more this time hopping to hear from you soon. I hope this will find you & the Boys well. I hope soon to be able to take them out on sunday for a walk.

I am your Husband
Alex Campbell

---

35. Keith Gilmore, captain, Co. I, 79th New York Highlanders. Gilmore, age 30, had enlisted at New York City in 1861 to serve for three years and was mustered in as first sergeant, Co. G, on 28 May 1861. Promoted to the captaincy of Co. I on 19 February 1863, Gilmore resigned his commission and was discharged from the service on 15 April 1863. Phisterer, *New York in the War of the Rebellion*, vol. 4, 2852.

LETTER 61[36]

Headquarters Co "G." 79th Regt.
N.Y. Vols.
Green River Ky.
April 29th 1863

Sir

I have the honor to tender you my resignation as 2nd Lieutenant of Co. "G." 79th Regt. New York State Vols.

I have been connected with the Regiment since May 13th 1861 being wounded in the leg at the Battle of Chantilly Va. Sept. 1st 1862. I experience great inconvenience during a march caused by said wound. Further in consequence of sickness in my family I am compelled to adopt this course. There are also business matters which require my presence in New York City in the want of my failure to give them my personal supervision it would result in serious pecuniary loss to myself and family.

On these considerations I would urgently request that it be accepted immediately.

I remain Very Respectfully
Your most ob[edian]t Servt.
Alexander Campbell
2nd Lt. Co. "G."
79th Regt. N.Y.S. Vols.

LETTER 62

Head Quarters 79th N.Y. Vols
Green river Ky
april 29th 63

Dear Wife

I received your ever wilcom Letter Last night and was glad to hear

---

36. The following letter is contained in the Compiled Service Record of Alexander Campbell.

from you once more. I hope you wont require to write me many more times before I get home. I have sent my resignation in and I am almost shure it will be excepted for I gave good reasons for it. It has got to goo to Lexington in this state to be excepted of and as soon as it comes back I Leave for home that is if it is approved of and I am almost shure it will. I dont expect to get payed till then. Then I will it all in a Lump so you must doe the best you can till then.

We Left Lebanon on monday 27th and arrived here on the 28th yeasterday. Its 28 miles from Lebanon. Its away far into the state. We marched all the way. There is no ralway near here. I Kept up all they way but I would not be able to continue the march any farther my Leg is too weak. We are not Likely to stay Long here.[37]

There must have been a great time abou that Lie that was got up one me. I would Like to Know whou sent such Lies to new York. I will fiend out yet. You must not expect me hom too soon. You Know it might be some time before I get word back. They sometimes dont hurry themselves. I mearly menthion this so as you wont expect me home too soon and thinking the time too Long. Some times they take Longer to go through than others. I will Lose no time in getting home after I get it excepted of than I can help. James got a Letter Last night two. He & Matthew is well.[38]

I won write any more to night only I am well hopping this will fiend you and the boys well and I expect to be with you soon and not to goo for a soldier again. And I Remain Your Long Absent but soon to be present Husband

Alexander Campbell

P.S. Dont write till I write you again.

---

37. On 27 April, the 79th left Lebanon and, in heavy marching order, moved south to the Green River. On 28 April, the Highlanders arrived to find the Green River Bridge destroyed; for the rest of their stay at Green River, which lasted until 11 May, the Highlanders were kept busy with, among other tasks, repairing the destroyed bridge. Todd, *Highlanders*, 286–87.

38. James Ralston did not remain with the 79th New York much longer; on 6 June 1863 he deserted at Louisville, Ky., with "rifle, bayonet and full set of equipment," and never returned. Matthew Ralston, on the other hand, not only served out the remaining year of his three-year enlistment with the 79th New York (mustered out in New York City on 31 May 1864), but reenlisted and served for the rest of the war in a New York artillery unit. See Appendix B for a letter written by Matthew to Alexander Campbell during his service in the artillery. Compiled Service Record of James Ralston; Compiled Service Record of Matthew Ralston; Matthew Ralston to Alexander Campbell, 10 October 1864, CFP-SCDAH.

Chapter Six

"I REMAIN YOUR BROTHER"

9 November 1863 through 5 May 1865

Alexander Campbell's resignation was approved by his superiors in the 79th New York and forwarded to the Headquarters of the Department of the Ohio in Cincinnati, where, on 6 May 1863, Special Order No. 162 was issued accepting Campbell's resignation to take effect the following day. On 13 May, Alexander Campbell was honorably discharged from the service for wounds received at the Battle of Chantilly and returned home to his family in New York City.[1] In October 1863, five months after Alexander's discharge from the army, his wife Jane gave birth to their third son. They named him James, for Alexander's Confederate brother.

Although the war was over for Alexander Campbell by July 1863, the war was, in many respects, just beginning for his brother James. 2d Lt. James Campbell, Company F, Charleston Battalion, not only had survived the previous year's fierce fighting on James Island, but had distinguished himself in the process. Yet the next (and final) two years of

---

1. Compiled Service Record of Alexander Campbell.

142

the Civil War would prove to be the most trying of his wartime service, if not his entire life.

After their costly and humiliating defeat at the Battle of Secessionville in June 1862, Union forces in South Carolina continued to pressure the Confederate defenses of Charleston with little success. On 12 June 1863, Brig. Gen. Quincy A. Gillmore assumed command of the Federal Department of the South and quickly created a new plan to effect the surrender of the prized Rebel city. Gillmore designed a campaign to take Charleston via Morris Island, which lay on the south side of the mouth of Charleston Harbor. The odds were overwhelmingly tipped in the Federals' favor; Gillmore had some 11,500 soldiers and 98 pieces of artillery with which to take the island, while his Confederate adversaries, as of 10 July, could muster only 927 troops.[2]

Having deployed 4,000 troops to James Island as a diversionary force, General Gillmore landed the lead element of his main army on 10 July 1863, establishing a foothold on the southern end of Morris Island. The severely outnumbered Rebel forces gave way and retreated to the relative safety of Battery Wagner, the southernmost of two Confederate fortifications on Morris Island, which lay across the full width of the island's narrowest point.[3] Battery Wagner, as described by one of its Confederate defenders, was "an inclosed earth-work, measuring within the interior slopes, from east to west, six hundred and thirty feet; and from north to south, two hundred and seventy-five feet. The sea-face contained a bomb-proof magazine, forming a heavy traverse to protect the three guns north of it from land fire. Behind this sea-face was a bomb-proof which could not accommodate more than nine hundred men standing elbow to elbow; and this capacity was further reduced by cutting off one third for the hospital. The land-face was irregular, with re-entering angles, and with chambers for five guns, to sweep the land approach. The front was protected by a ditch filled with water at high tide."[4] As General Gillmore soon discovered, the construction and location of Battery Wagner made it a formidable obstacle to any Union attempt to take Morris Island from the south.

---

2. Morris Island, which runs northeast to southwest, is approximately 6500 yards long and 2500 yards wide at its widest point. Burton, *Siege of Charleston*, 151–54; Paul Hamilton Hayne, "The Defense of Fort Wagner." *Southern Bivouac* 1 (1885/86): 600.

3. John Johnson, *The Defense of Charleston Harbor, Including Fort Sumter and the Adjacent Islands, 1863–1865* (Charleston: Walker, Evans & Cogswell Co., Publishers, 1890; reprint, Germantown, Tenn.: Guild Bindery Press, 1994), 22, 88–92.

4. Hayne, "Defense of Fort Wagner," 601.

After an unsuccessful assault on Battery Wagner on 11 July, Gill-more regrouped for a second attack. Meanwhile, the outnumbered and exhausted Confederate defenders of the fort were relieved by fresh troops between 11 and 17 July, and their numbers were augmented to approximately 1,300 men. Among the reinforcements were Lt. James Campbell and the Charleston Battalion.[5] The Charleston Battalion had been on provost duty in Charleston since shortly after the Battle of Seces-sionville, where they were held "in readiness to be sent to any point in the vicinity which was to be attacked."[6]

On the morning of 18 July, General Gillmore renewed his attack on Battery Wagner with a severe land and naval bombardment that lasted approximately eleven hours. Gillmore hoped to soften, if not destroy, the Confederate defenses and defenders of the fort, thereby laying the groundwork for a successful infantry attack that evening. Unfortunately for Gillmore and his Federals, the Confederates within Battery Wagner sat out the massive bombardment in the bombproof shelters (except for the men of the Charleston Battalion, who, with the bombproof shelters full, sought the protection of the parapets); by the time the Union guns quieted toward nightfall, the Confederates within the fort had suffered only twenty-eight casualties and their artillery batteries remained largely unscathed.[7]

At sundown, Gillmore sent the first of his three infantry brigades to attack the fort. The Confederates, sufficiently alerted and virtually unharmed by the day-long bombardment, were ready for the attack. The assaulting troops of the first brigade, ordered to rely upon the bayonet and not the bullet, were beaten and repulsed by artillery and musketry fire, requiring Gillmore to send his second brigade forward. Hindered by the darkness, the unrelenting fire of the Confederates, and the confusion caused by the dead, wounded, and retreating men of the first wave of the

---

5. The garrison of Battery Wagner now consisted of the Charleston Battalion (com-manded by Lt. Col. P. C. Gaillard), the 31st and 51st North Carolina, and various artillery companies from the 1st South Carolina Infantry, 1st South Carolina Artillery, and 63d Georgia. During the battle on 18 July, these Confederates would be reinforced by the arrival of the 32d Georgia. Hayne, "Defense of Fort Wagner," 603; Johnson, *Defense of Charleston Harbor*, 100–101, 106.

6. *Charleston News and Courier*, 12 November 1899.

7. F. Edgeworth Eve, Charles C. Jones, Jr., and H. D. D. Twiggs, *Defence of Battery Wagner, July 18th, 1863: Addresses Delivered Before the Confederate Survivors' Associa-tion in Augusta, Georgia, on the Occasion of its Fourteenth Annual Reunion on Memor-ial Day, April 26th, 1892* (Augusta: Chronicle Publishing Company, 1892), 16; Johnson, *Defense of Charleston Harbor*, 101–3.

assault, approximately 100 men from the second brigade nevertheless succeeded in penetrating the defenses of Battery Wagner. They established a foothold in the southeastern salient of the fort, where the Confederates had been weakened by the absence of the 31st North Carolina, whose men refused to leave the protection of the bombproof and take their positions.[8]

The Confederates within Battery Wagner moved quickly to repulse the infiltrating Federals. Volunteers were requested to counterattack the now isolated handful of Union soldiers inhabiting the southeastern salient; approximately forty men from two companies of the Charleston Battalion, including James Campbell's company, the Union Light Infantry, responded. With the assistance of the 51st North Carolina and the newly arrived troops of the 32d Georgia, these men were able to dislodge their Federal adversaries, effectively bringing an end to the night's fighting. After the Union's second brigade was repulsed, General Gillmore refused to send his third and final brigade forward. His men had been badly beaten. Union casualties for the night's fighting were estimated between 1,500 and 2,000 killed, wounded, or missing; Confederate losses amounted to only 174.[9]

Although the 18 July 1863 engagement at Battery Wagner was a resounding Confederate victory, it was a personal defeat for James Campbell, who that evening began his grueling two-year experience as a prisoner of war. Shortly after the Federal breakthrough at the southeastern salient of Battery Wagner, Confederate general William Booth Taliaferro, anxious to discover the size and disposition of the intruding force, called for someone to investigate the Federals' position. James Campbell volunteered for the mission and made his way toward the threatened sector of the fort.[10] The local papers reported what happened next:

> *The Lieutenant had sprung upon the parapet to reconnoitre, when seeing a large number of men before him he inquired their regiments, and was answered by members of the 6th Connecticut, 76th Pennsylvania, and others. He called upon them to surrender.*

8. Johnson, *Defense of Charleston Harbor*, 105; *Charleston Daily Courier*, 20 July 1863; O.R., Series 1, vol. 28, 76–77.

9. *Charleston Daily Courier*, 21 July 1863; Johnson, *Defense of Charleston Harbor*, 106–7.

10. Stephen R. Wise, *Gate of Hell: Campaign for Charleston Harbor, 1863* (Columbia: University of South Carolina Press, 1994), 109.

Two of them immediately charged, intending to strike him, but missed and crossed bayonets. Lieut. Campbell, with great presence of mind, and with his usual well known activity, pushed them off the parapet, both falling, it is said, on their own bayonets. He was then siezed by the leg, drawn off the works and hurried to the enemy's rear.[11]

Shortly after his capture, Campbell was sent to Hilton Head, South Carolina, where he reportedly rejected his captors' offer to take the oath of allegiance "with the utmost scorn and contempt."[12]

    James Campbell remained a prisoner at Hilton Head until October 1863, when he was transported to Fort Columbus in New York Harbor; shortly thereafter, Campbell was again moved, this time to the prison for Confederate officers at Johnson's Island, Ohio, where he arrived on 10 October.[13] The prison on Johnson's Island, a 300-acre landmass located in the Sandusky Bay of Lake Erie, had received its first Rebel captives in April 1862 and was, by the time of Lieutenant James Campbell's arrival, home to approximately 2,452 Confederate prisoners of war.[14]

    During his two year confinement in Northern prisons, James wrote 14 letters to his brother Alexander, the first one on 9 November 1863.

LETTER 63

Johnsons Island Sandusky OH
Nov 9th 1863

My Dear Brother

    I rote to Brother John immediatelly on my arivel here and Brother Peter about ten days ago. Strange to say I have not heard from either of them in answer to my Letters. I cannot think that [Brother] John got my Letter or I think he would of answered it under the sircumstances. It may be that I have the rong address. I hope you will write me as

---

11. *Charleston Daily Courier*, 25 July 1863.
12. Ibid.
13. Compiled Service Record of James Campbell; Roger Long, Port Clinton, Ohio, to Terry A. Johnston, Jr., Clemson, S.C., 30 January 1995, transcript in the hand of Terry A. Johnston, Jr., Clemson, S.C..
14. Charles E. Frohman, *Rebels on Lake Erie: The Piracy, The Conspiracy, Prison Life* (Columbus: The Ohio Historical Society, 1965), 1–5, 7, 39.

soon as you get this and ask Mr Jones to write me. I dont know his address or I would write him first. Let me know how [Brother] Peter got along with the Express Co[15] in regard to the money he sent me which I never got.[16] When you answer this I will give you a long account of our situation here and the ruels of the prison.[17]

Hoping to here from you soon. I remain Your Brother

James Campbell

Address
Lt James Campbell
Prisoner of War
Johnsons Island
Sandusky Ohio

---

15. The Adams Express Company. During the time James Campbell was at Johnson's Island, it was possible for prisoners to receive express packages and money through the Adams Express Company. Incoming parcels were, however, inspected for contraband by Federal officials and were not delivered to prisoners until all forbidden materials (e.g., liquor, banned books, propaganda, weapons, etc.) were removed. Roger Long, "Johnson's Island Prison," *Blue & Gray Magazine* 4 (February-March 1987): 18; Roger Long, Port Clinton, Ohio, to Terry A. Johnston, Jr., Clemson, S.C., 22 February 1995, transcript in the hand of Terry A. Johnston, Jr., Clemson, S.C.

16. Prison officials at Johnson's Island strictly regulated the captive Confederates' access to money. Upon arrival, each prisoner was ordered to turn over all his United States money (Confederate notes were deemed worthless by Federal officials) to the authorities, and that money was placed in the soldier's sutler account. Each prisoner could then purchase items at the sutler store, the value of which was subtracted from his sutler account funds by a Federal clerk who recorded all transactions.

James Campbell's sutler account reveals that he arrived at Johnson's Island with $23 (as a second lieutenant in the Confederate army, Campbell was to have received $80 Confederate dollars per month). During his imprisonment there, Campbell received sums of $14 and $3, most likely from his brothers Peter and/or Alexander. When, on 10 February 1864, James Campbell was transferred from Johnson's Island to Point Lookout, Md., he had but $2 left to take with him. Roger Long, "Johnson's Island Prison," 6; Roger Long, Port Clinton, Ohio, to Terry A. Johnston, Jr., Clemson, S.C., 22 March 1995, transcript in the hand of Terry A. Johnston, Jr., Clemson, S.C.; Confederate States of America War Department, *Regulations for the Army of the Confederate States, 1863* (Richmond: J. W. Randolph, 1863; reprint, Harrisburg, Pa.: The National Historical Society, 1980), 176; Sutler account of Lt. James Campbell, Ledger volume 5, p. 136, Johnson's Island Military Prison Records (MS 22), Center for Archival Collections, Bowling Green State University (CAC-BGSU; hereafter cited as Sutler Account of James Campbell).

17. James's letters to Alexander from Johnson's Island were not very informative about prison life, a fact which is not surprising, given that Federal officials regularly censored their prisoners' correspondence. Letters could not be longer than twenty-eight lines, and passages detailing prison conditions were routinely removed. Roger Long to Terry A. Johnston, Jr., 22 February 1995.

LETTER 64

U.S. Prison Johnsons Island
January 17th 1864

Dear Brother

Your Letter to the commanding officer of this Post[18] has just been received. I was surprised that you did not answer my Letters. I now see that you have not received all the Letters I sent you. The last one I wrote was to [Brother] Peter asking him to send me a news paper occasionally. I received two papers but no reply. I wish you would give me his residence so that I can open a correspondance with his wife as I have come to the conclusion that he is either too loving a husband to weast his time writing me or too indelant and cant weast his hours of ease. I am sorry to inform you that capt Macbeth[19] has been confined to the Hospital for the last two months suffering from dropsey. I think he is getting better.[20]

18. Col. William Seward Pierson. On 18 January 1864, the day after James Campbell wrote this letter, Pierson's tenure as commander of Johnson's Island prison ended. He was replaced by Brig. Gen. Alexander Shaler. Frohman, *Rebels On Lake Erie*, 6–7; Roger Long to Terry A. Johnston, Jr., 22 March 1995.

19. Capt. John Ravenel Macbeth, Co. E, 1st South Carolina Artillery. During a 10 July 1863 engagement on Morris Island, S.C., Captain Macbeth, whose father, Charles, was the mayor of Charleston, was slightly wounded in the head and taken prisoner by the opposing Federals. Macbeth, who had on 24 May 1861 enlisted in Co. E of the 1st South Carolina Artillery (in which he was, by order of the governor of the state, "to hold the commission of his pleasure," second lieutenant), was sent to the prison at Johnson's Island, where he remained until 8 October 1864, when he was sent to Fortress Monroe for exchange. After Macbeth was officially exchanged on 12 October 1864, he returned to his old unit and fought with them until the war's end, losing an arm at the 19 March 1865 Battle of Bentonville, N.C. Compiled Service Record of John Ravenel Macbeth, 1st South Carolina Artillery, Compiled Service Records of Confederate Soldiers Who Served in Organizations from the State of South Carolina, War Department Collection of Confederate Records, Record Group 109, National Archives, Washington, D.C., National Archives Publication M-267, Roll 62; O.R., Series 1, vol. 28, 370, 527, Series 2, vol. 7, 927; Edward Young McMorries, *History of the First Regiment Alabama Volunteer Infantry, C.S.A.* (Montgomery: The Brown Printing Co., 1904), 134–35; *Charleston Daily Courier*, 13 July 1863; Sifakis, *Compendium*, 5–6.

20. Captain Macbeth's near-fatal illness was well known among the prisoners at Johnson's Island. Writing of Macbeth's condition, Col. I. G. W. Steedman, a captured Confederate officer from Alabama and the chief surgeon of the prison hospital which cared for the sickly Confederate, stated: "While an inmate of the prison he [Macbeth] was dangerously ill, and was nursed to health in the prison hospital. He was so grateful for this service, that he became a nurse in the hospital for many months. Later he was made hospital

I have no news to give you. The monoteny of Prison Life is getting burdensom and still there is no prospects of exchange. There was a rumer here some days ago that we was all to be sent to Point look Out but that seems to have died out. This post has been reignforsed by a Brigade from Meeds Army as several of the prisoners had broken out of here. Some mead their escape others was recaptured.[21]

I dont think I ever suffered as much from cold as I did the first week in January. I liked to of freesed and so did most of the prisoners here.

So if you please send me some news papers. If [Brother] Peter has been sending them I never got but two. You can guide yourself by what he says whether to send me any more or not. Please write me soon as you get this. Give my compliments to ann and Your Wife.

> Your Brother
> James Campbell

LETTER 65

> Johnsons Island
> Feby 6th 1864

Dear Brother

I wrote you a Letter about two weeks ago in answer to yours enquiring of the commanding officer of this post if I was Still here [and] if not here to inform you of my whereabouts. I hope you received it. Since that time I have received several news papers the last one a

steward." According to Col. Steedman, J. Ravenel Macbeth, besides having a wealthy father, "had large funds in New York and Liverpool as a stockholder in a blockade running company" and "donated twenty-two thousand dollars for the relief of his fellow-prisoners, besides lending money to many others." It appears that James Campbell was among those who benefited from Macbeth's willingness to lend money; Campbell's sutler account shows that on 5 January 1864 he had $9.50 transferred to Macbeth's account, most likely as reimbursement for a previous loan. McMorries, *Alabama Volunteer Infantry*, 134; Sutler Account of James Campbell.

21. Several escape attempts were made during the first week of January 1864; a few prisoners did make it to Canada and freedom. In response, Shaler's brigade, Army of the Potomac, was sent as reinforcements to Johnson's Island. Frohman, *Rebels on Lake Erie*, 55–57; Roger Long to Terry A. Johnston, Jr., 22 February 1995.

herald. It was Post Marked Cleveland Ohio. I am not fameliour with the handwriting that directed them and am at quite a loss to know to whom I am indepted for these kiend favioours. Perhaps you can give me some light on the subgect.

I am going to ask you a special faviour. If you will but grant it I assure you I will feal ever greatful. One of my men is a prisoner at Point Lookout Md. I had a Letter from him two days ago in which he informs me that he has been sick for two months and is suffering for want of some little necessaries that had he means to precure them would aid greatly to his comfort. What I want is that you will send him Five Dollars by what every way you think safest. When you write him ask him to ackowledge the recept of the money. Had I any money of my own I would not tax your generosity to assist one you never heard of before. I intend recompencing you for any thing you may do to assist me in making the days of my protracted captivity as lightsom as possable.

When you send the money direct to

M OBrian[22]
Co K 4 Division
Prison camp
Point Lookout
Md

Rummers is rife that we are to leave here soon for some other Prison. For myself I dont care how soon. I never hear a word from [Brother] Peter. He must be mad with me for some cause or other. With repects to all

I Remain Your Brother
James Campbell

---

22. Mortimer OBrian, private, Co. F, 1st South Carolina (Charleston) Battalion. OBrian, age 21, enlisted in the Charleston Battalion on 15 March 1862 for a term of twelve months. His military service record lists him as "one of the men captured by the enemy's barges on the night of the evacuation of Morris Island, S.C., Sept. 6, 1863." Compiled Service Record of Mortimer OBrian.

LETTER 66

Point Lookout Md[23]
Feby 29 1864

Dear Brother

Tomorrow Two Hundred officer leaves here to be offered on Exchange. I am included in that number. We are uncertain whether our commissioner will except of us unless the terms of a general exchange is agread on. Should I have to come back I will write you immediatelly on my return.

I wrote you a Letter a few days after my arrive here in which I begged you to send Five Dollars to one of my men who is a prisoner here. I have not heard from you and am fearful that you did not receive it. If you have not sent it you will do me a great faviour to do so as early as possable. His address is M OBrian Co K 4 Division Point Lokout Md. I have been verry anxious to know whether [Brother] Peter got the money he sent me to Hilten Head but he never wrote on line on the subject. Should I be exchanged which you will know by me not writing you in two weeks you can send me a Letter by flag of truce. The limit for you will be one Page with 10¢ inclosed directed to me the out side invelope directed to the commanding officer at Fort Monroe for flag of Truce.

So for a while I bid you All farwell. Yes it may be for ever.

Your Brother
James Campbell

---

23. Rumors of exchange were widespread when Campbell wrote his last letter. The prison at Johnson's Island had become crowded, and prison officials feared further escapes across the frozen ice of Sandusky Bay. On 9 February, a steamboat managed to break through the ice and reach the prison, where it was loaded with 400 prisoners, presumably to be taken away for exchange. Instead, they were put on trains for the prison camp at Point Lookout, Md., where James Campbell and the other prisoners from Johnson's Island arrived on 14 February. Roger Long to Terry A. Johnston, Jr., 22 February 1995; Compiled Service Record of James Campbell.

LETTER 67

Point Lookout Md
June 18th 1864

Dear Brother

I have not heard from you in Such a long time that I am allmost persuaded to think that you have forgotten me. I have sent you several Letters since I heard from you. I hope you got them. I get Letters regular from Peters Wife. I can hear of you and your family through her but would like to hear from you personally at times. By the by I saw in some paper the arrival home and reception of the 79 Regt. How many of the original Regt came home with them from the hard servace they have seen? I would not think many of them was left.[24]

I have finally come to the conclusion that there will not be a general exchange of Prisoners while the war lasts. If I do get off before that time it will be mear chance. I have been Eleven months Prisoner to day and the probability is that I will be such for Eleven months to come.

I have been verry sick for some time back but have rallied wounderfully in the last few days. I am gathering strength faster then I thought it was possable for man to do. In a few days under present aspects I will have quite recovered. I have heard from my Regt. It is with Lee.[25]

---

24. On the morning of 18 May 1864, the 324-man-strong 79th New York returned to New York City, where they "were received by the New York Caledonian Club, and escorted up Broadway by the Sixty-Ninth regiment." The 79th New York had gone on after Alexander Campbell's discharge to take part in several engagements, including Fort Sanders, Tenn. (29 November 1863) and Spotsylvania, Va. (9 May 1864). On 31 May, the remaining original members of the regiment, approximately one hundred men, having completed their 3-year term of service, were formally mustered out. The remaining 224 Highlanders whose term of service had not yet expired were organized into a two-company battalion and sent back to Virginia where they were assigned guard duty before being reattached to the IX Corps. Todd, *Highlanders,* 472–73; Bilby, "Blue Bonnets Over the Border," 14; *Scottish American Journal,* 28 May 1864; *New York Times,* 17, 19 May 1864.

25. In September 1863, James Campbell's unit, the Charleston Battalion, was merged with the 1st South Carolina Battalion Sharpshooters to form the 27th South Carolina Infantry Regiment. The 27th South Carolina, attached to Gen. Johnson Hagood's brigade, was transferred to Virginia in May 1864 and saw action in the Battles of Drewry's Bluff (4–16 May 1864) and Cold Harbor (31 May-12 June 1864) before serving in the trenches around Petersburg. Sifakis, *Compendium,* 104–5.

Please write me soon and let me know the result of your mission to Washington.

Your Brother
James Campbell

━━━━►➤●◄━━━━

LETTER 68

Fort Delaware[26]
July 10th 1864

Dear Brother

Your Letter of the 28 came to hand on the 8 ulto. I am sorry I did not get the Letter you wrote me. You do not mention having received two Letter of mine Still unanswered. There is at times a great amount of irregularity in the mails of Prisoners. It can be accounted for in no other way.

Capt Macbeth has not been exchanged. He is still on Johnsons Island. Only two of the officers who came from Hilton Head with me has been exchanged. I can apreciate your meaning when you say that I

---

26. On 23 June 1864, James Campbell was transferred from Point Lookout to Fort Delaware, where he arrived two days later. Fort Delaware, located on Pea Patch Island in the Delaware River, had been used as a prison for captured Confederates since April 1862. One captured Virginian Rebel, also sent to Fort Delaware in June 1864, remembered the prison as follows: "We reached the fort . . . and were assigned to quarters in the thirty-three board structures, already partially occupied by previous prisoners of war. These structures, called divisions, occupied three sides of a square, and each accommodated about a hundred and twenty-five persons. Tiers of three shelves seven feet wide served for sleeping quarters in these structures, which had small diamond shaped openings in the outer wall to serve for observation by sentinels." The fort itself had 32-foot-high granite walls and was surrounded by a 30-foot-wide moat. During his imprisonment in Fort Delaware, James Campbell was located in Division 22. Compiled Service Record of James Campbell; W. Emerson Wilson, *Fort Delaware*, Institute of Delaware History and Culture Pamphlet Series, vol. 4 (Newark, Del.: University of Delaware Press, 1957), 3–13; James H. Wood, *The War: "Stonewall" Jackson, His Campaigns and Battles, the Regiment as I Saw Them* (Cumberland, Md.: The Eddy Press Corporation, 1910), 171–72; Record of James Campbell, 2d Lieutenant, 27th South Carolina, Record Group 109, War Department Collection of Confederate Records, M-598, Selected Records of the War Department Relating to Confederate Prisoners of War, 1861–1865, Roll 45, Fort Delaware Microfilm, Volume 117–151 of Registers of Prisoners in Prison Divisions, numbers 22–39, National Archives, Washington, D.C. (hereafter cited as James Campbell Fort Delaware Record).

am safer where I am then if I was with Lee [and] that my Regiment will tell me that they never saw Fighting untill they got with him. You dont know what I have indured in the last twelve months or in other words If I had my choice I would take my chance in twenty Battles rather then stay another twelve months in Prison. Prudence commands halt. I wish I had a chance to talk with you. I could tell you lots.

I wrote [Brother] Peters wife yesterday and beg her to send me a small Box of Eatables. If she sends it ask her to Poot a coarse towel, a Pocket handkercheif, a Piece of soap, some Letter Paper & Envalopes in the Box. I dont wish any clothing as I expect some from another quarter. If you know any thing about Mr Pauls or his friends (the man who took you for me on Broadway) tell them that Geo Gailling[27] from the Isle of man was killed in one of the late Battles Near Petersburg. I think they stay at McDonald & Co drygoods store.

Hoping to hear from you as soon as convenant. My space being limited I can go no farther.

Your Brother
James Campbell

By the By if you see any of the 79[th New York] that I know, please give them my regards.

LETTER 69

Fort Delaware
July 26th 1864

Dear Brother

Your faviour is to hand. I have not heard from [Brother] Peters wife since I wrote her about the Box. Should you fiend Mr Pauls friends ask them to write me as I have got more news for them.

I have written [Brother] John since I got your last Letter and begged him to send for [Sister] Ann and as you desired mead no men-

---

27. 2d Lt. George Brown Gelling, Co. C, 27th South Carolina Infantry. Gelling was killed in action on 16 June 1864 at Petersburg, Va. *Roll of the Dead: South Carolina Troops in Confederate States Service* (Columbia: South Carolina Department of Archives and History, 1995), n.p.

tion of the other matter. I should like to get and out line of his cortship. Of corse you can know nothing about it. Should you hear from him do let me know how he is satisfied and how he likes a farmers life.

I hade a Letter from home lately the first from that quarter since my capture. I think I told you that I owned stock in some steam ship companies. They have been verry succesful and I have mead a heap of money.[28] You could not of got the Letter I sent you from Johnsons Isld in answer to one I got from you containing a slip from the Herald with an account of the capture of the Margrett & Jessy.[29] I owned stock in her but dont think I lost much as she mead several succesful trips before her captu[r]e.

I have nothing of Interest to write about. There is daily wied rummers aflot in the prison faviourable and unfaviourable. As we dont get the papers parties get up all kinds of scandles sensation rummers for their own amusement.

Your Brother
Ja[me]s Campbell

My complements to your wife.

---

28. At least seven different incorporated blockade running companies formed in South Carolina during the course of the war. James Campbell owned stock in at least one of these, The Charleston Importing and Exporting Company, which was incorporated on 17 December 1863 and owned the blockade runners *Margaret and Jessie* and *Syren*. Company stockholders profited from their investments; during the war, approximately four or five dividend payments were made (the second and third of which paid a combined $2,000 Confederate per share); at the end of the war, the Company possessed 30,000 pounds sterling in Liverpool, which was converted into gold dollars, sent to Charleston in late 1865, and distributed to its stockholders at $100 per share. Marcus W. Price, "Blockade Running as a Business in South Carolina during the War between the States, 1861–1865," *American Neptune* 9 (January 1949): 44–46; Stephen R. Wise, *Lifeline of the Confederacy: Blockade Running during the Civil War* (Columbia: University of South Carolina Press, 1988), 225.

29. On 5 November 1863, the Confederate blockade runner *Margaret and Jessie* was captured by two Federal gunboats at New Inlet, a channel entrance to the port of Wilmington, N.C. The *Margaret and Jessie* (205' x 26' x 14' with wooden hull), formerly known as the *Douglas*, was a paddle steamer of great speed and had been, from June 1862, the property of The Charleston Importing and Exporting Company. Before her capture, the *Margaret and Jessie*, which carried a crew of 46 men, had successfully made eighteen of twenty runs through the Federal blockade in 1863; on one of those runs, she carried a shipment of 836 bales of cotton out of Charleston valued at $173,345. After her capture, the *Margaret and Jessie* was purchased as a prize by the Union Navy and converted to the gunboat *Gettysburg*, and, ironically, sent back to the Carolina coast to capture other blockade runners for the remainder of the war. Wise, *Lifeline of the Confederacy*, 138–39, 311; Marcus W. Price, "Ships that Tested the Blockade of the Carolina Ports, 1861–1865," *American Neptune* 8 (April 1948): 204–5, 229.

LETTER 70

U.S. Prison Fort Delaware
18th Aug 64

Dear Brother

Your faviour of the 14th Inst has been received. I was fearful that you had not received my last Letter and enquired of Annie a feaw days ago whether or not you received it. I am anxious to know who it was that told [Brother] Peter of Capt Macbeth. If you fiend out who he was pleas inform me in your next. I am not aware that we are to be sent their. Six Hundred Officers leaves here in a few days for Hilten Head S.C. I am not of that number.[30]

The Box [Brother] Peter sent me arrived all right. I am pleased that you did [not] send the Bitters for I would not be allowed to receive them. Liquers of all kiends is strickelly prohibated.

I have nothing of intrest to write about nor have I any way of hearing news. When you hear from [Brother] John please inform me. I wrote him but like yourself have not got an answer. I have come to the conclusion that unless we strike him in an extroardenarry good humar he will not pay any attention to our Letters.

With regards to all I am your
Brother
James Campbell

---

30. On 20 August 1864, 600 Confederate prisoners from Fort Delaware, who came to be known as "The Immortal Six Hundred," were relocated to Morris Island. In retaliation for the alleged use of Union prisoners in Charleston as human shields (i.e., prisoners placed in areas normally targeted by the fire of their own forces), Federal officials positioned these 600 Confederate prisoners in similarly exposed areas on Morris Island. "The Immortal Six Hundred," who were later relocated to Fort Pulaski, Ga., spent six months down South before being sent back to Fort Delaware, where they were reunited on 12 March 1865 with many of their former prisonmates. Wilson, *Fort Delaware*, 20; J. Ogden Murray, *The Immortal Six Hundred: A Story of Cruelty to Confederate Prisoners of War* (Roanoke, Va.: The Stone Printing and Manufacturing Co., 1911), 59–95.

LETTER 71

Fort Delaware
Sep 17th 1864

Dear Brother

Yours to hand. I have not heard from [Brother] John yet. You know he never was a great hand at writing. I am limited to Ten Lines and that only to Sister or Brother.

The capt of the 79th whom you saw misinformed you about my Regt. 3 officers was captured and are here. All the news he tolold you is news to them for they never heard it before. He told them among other things that I had taken the oath and was living with you so he has misrepresented matters all round. Let us drop him. I have heard from my Regt as late as the middle of August. My permotion had not been published up to that time.

I hate to beg but my situaiton is such that it will excuse me. Will you be kiend enugh to send me ($10) Ten Dollars. If you will oblige me so much send a check or draft on some house in Philadelphia so that no one can draw it without my signature and oblige

Your Brother
James Campbell

＝⟫●⟨＝

LETTER 72

Fort Delaware
Oct 5th 1864

My Dear Brother

Your faviour of the 28th Ulto came safe to hand with the money you enclosed. If you will send me such amounts from time to time it will relieve me greatly. There can be no chance of bribing any one with money. We dont get the money sent us. Checks on the Suttler is issued in lue of our money. These checks is valualess to any one other then a prisoner as the Suttler receives them from no one but us. Watches and all other valuables was taken from us and we are only allowed to have one sute of clothes with a change of Under clothing.

I have not heard from Brother John yet and dispare of hearing from him at this late hour. I did not think when we last parted that he would treat me so unkiend. Perhaps the widow you mentioned occuapies all his spare time. I am much pleased with the news of his intentions as a good wife will be a great comfort to him especially now as he has settled down in life. I hope you will persue a regular correspondance with him. When you write give him my kiend reguards.

There is a rummer here that a general exchange will soon commence. God grant that it may be so. I hardly credit the report. I have been so often dissapointed by such rummers. With many thanks for your last faviour and kiend love to all

I Remain Your Brother
James Campbell

(the 10 Line restriction has been removed)

LETTER 73

Fort Delaware
Oct 18th 1864

Dear Brother

Your faviour of the 14th Just is to hand. You all thinking me exchanged accounts for Annies long Silance. I wrote her a few days ago and blew her Sky high for her neglect.

There is none being exchanged except crippels and such as are unfit for service. I have settled down to the conviction that there will be no general exchange during the war your Gov[ernment] refusing to Exchange the prisoners whoes term of service have expired during their captivity. That is a chearing veiw to take of the question after 16 months imprisonment.

We are not allowed any clothing from the Gov but I will be better provided for then I was last winter. I have been a long time without a coat. A friend of mine died recently and I fell Aire to his. It is too light for winter but better then none. I am pretty well supplied with under clothing so upon the whole I am not so bad off in that line at present. One of my comrads have sent to N.Y. for clothes for himself and me. Should they come I will be O.K. in that line.

I have heard nothing from [Brother] John yet and at this late houre dont expect to hear. I am anxious to know how he is getting along with the widow. Perhaps she has kicked him. If so that accounts for him not writing us. Such a lick would scatter his sensas as well as his calcelations and make a divel of a Stink.

Your Brother
James Campbell

Postage stamps is hard to get here. Please enclose a few in your next.

———⇒❯●❮⇐———

LETTER 74

Fort Delaware
Nov 4 64

Dear Brother

I have got such a treacharious memory that I am at a loss to know whether or not I answered your Letter of the 27th Uto in which you was so kiend as to enclose me two Dollars. If I have this will be to you another proof of my weakenesss as one of Gods unworthy images which he is sparing from day to day to fulfil some tradgy of his own creation. Thanks to his kiendness for leaving me ignorant on that score.

I have not got a thing to write about. Every thing is dull all around me. Be good enugh to kiendly remember me to your wife and family. Tho I never saw her nor herd from her directly I carry her in my pocket every Day. By the way talking about family matters how is my name son? You told me when I last saw you that you named your youngest Boy after me.[31] Let me know how he is progressing when you write me again.

Your Brother
James Campbell

---

31. James Campbell, third child of Alexander and Jane Campbell, was born in early October 1863.

159

LETTER 75

Fort Delaware Del
Jany 9th 1865

Dear Brother

Not hearing from you is some time I fear that you did not get my last Letter. [Brother] Peters Wife informes me that Mr Livingston took my Picture about which I wrote him. I am glad that it is gon for I promised sister [Ann] some years ago that I would send it to her. I am anxious to know whether or not Mr Livingston got the Letter I wrote him. Please inform me.

Should you heare from Scotland I would be glad to heare the news as it is more then Likely they will write you on recept of the word you sent by your friend. I have no news to write that would interest you. We are getting along in the usual way without any thing occuring to better our position.

When you write again please send me a few stamps.

Your Brother
Ja[me]s Campbell

P.S. By the By do you ever hear from [Brother] John? If so what is he doing and how is he getting along and what progress is he making with the Widow?

J.C.

Alex Campbell
54 Gavsavort St
New York
Received January 12th 1865 A.C.

———◄●►———

LETTER 76

Fort Delaware Del
May 5 1865

Dear Brother

Not hearing from you in some time I fear that you have not been getting my Letters. Since the surrender of Lee & Johnsons armies we see no hope for the confedersy.[32] Her downfall is but the queston of days. Most of us here has signified our intenention of taking the Oath of allegiance to the U.S. Govt. There is no other way by which we can be relieced.[33]

I want to get some of your influencial friends to apply to the authorities at Washington for my immediate release and have the Papers sent on here as early as possable. Write me at once and let me know what is my prospect of getting out of here. I am more then tierd of this life. I hope you will go about this matter at once and let me know what I am to expect. [Brother] Peter or yourself ought to know some one whoes influence can assist you with the authorities.

Your Brother
Ja[me]s Campbell

Mr Alex Campbell
54 Gansevoort St
New York

---

32. Lee surrendered the Army of Northern Virginia to Grant on 9 April 1865 at Appomattox, Va.; seventeen days later, on 26 April, Johnston surrendered the Confederate Army of Tennessee to Sherman.

33. After Lee's surrender at Appomattox, the spirits of the Confederate captives at Fort Delaware, according to one prisoner, "were broken indeed." Shortly thereafter, Federal officials polled the prisoners to ascertain how many would, in the words of the Rebels, "swallow the yaller dog," or take the oath of allegiance; only 700 out of a total of 1,500 replied that they would. One prisoner described the nature of their resistance: "We who refused to take the oath held an indignation meeting, protesting against the insult offered us by asking us to take the oath . . . but it did no good in stemming the desire of our men to get home. They were worn out by prison cruelty, and General Lee had no army. . . . In a few days the roll was again called. At this call but two hundred of us were left who refused to take the oath, and at the third call there were but three of us left, out of the whole number, who declined to take the oath upon any condition." The oath of allegiance that James Campbell and other Confederate prisoners had to sign before receiving their release from Fort Delaware reads as follows:

I, [name] of the [county and state of residence] do solemnly swear, in presence of Almighty God, that I will henceforth faithfully support, protect, and defend the Constitution of the United States, and the Union of the States thereunder; and that I will, in like manner, abide by and faithfully support all laws and proclamations which have been made during the existing rebellion with reference to the emancipation of slaves: So help me God.

Wilson, *Fort Delaware*, 26; Murray, *Immortal Six Hundred*, 193–94; Collections of the Fort Delaware Society, Delaware City, Del.

EPILOGUE

The war finally came to a close for James Campbell on 12 June 1865, when he was released from the prison for Confederates at Fort Delaware, thereby ending his nearly two-year ordeal as a prisoner of war. James chose to return to his adopted hometown of Charleston, South Carolina, a city severely damaged during the final stages of the war, where he resettled and began to rebuild his life.[1]

On 1 November 1865, James Campbell reestablished correspondence with his brother Alexander when he penned the following letter from Charleston:

Dear Brother

I hope you will not think I have entirely forgotten you owing to my not writing you Persionelly. Your many acts of kiendness to me in the last Two years I will ever remember apart from any other tie that might biend us.

I have not been able to see the surgen who had charge of the Mart Hospital in which Mc Millan of your Regt Died in order that I might designate his grave but will persavear in the matter.

There is verry Little business doing here at present. The entire community is completely Bankrupt and still there is a great many goods comming into the market. I expect to see a regular smash up

---

1. James Campbell Fort Delaware Record.

of a number of stores here who has got large stock of goods but no sales. Roy is still here after the surrender of Johnsons Army. He went to Union Dist in this State and lived with Mr Grant.

Give my regards to Jane & [Sister] Ann [& Brother] Peter and [his wife] Annie. Hoping to hear from you occasionelly.

I am Your Brother[2]

James Campbell soon found employment as manager of Charles T. Lowndes's Oakland plantation, located on the Combahee River. Oakland, which had been badly damaged during the June 1863 Union raid of Confederate property on the Combahee, was occupied for a time after the war by Federal soldiers and was the center of Freedmen's Bureau activities in the area.[3] By the time James arrived there, the plantation was run according to the sharecropping system, in which ex-slaves were afforded the opportunity to labor for a portion of the crop they produced. James described the situation at Oakland, as well as the nature of his job there, in a 5 March 1866 letter to Alexander:

I am planting on the Cumbhee River on shares of the crop. The owner pays all the expences of supplying the Plantation and I get a 5th of the crop for managing. It is a large cotton and Rice Plantation and I think I will do well. I have been here since January organising labour. The negrowes stuck out and would not contract under the impression that the Lands belonged to them. Starvation compelled them to contract. I give them $100 per year and Rations [and] Houses and fuel with 2 acers of land to each man. . . .

I am hard pushed at present preparing My lands for a crop. I have had a late Start. All the lands have been abandoned for three years and is almost a wilderness. . . .[4]

James's stay at Oakland plantation was, however, brief; sometime in

---

2. James Campbell to Alexander Campbell, 1 November 1865, CFP-SCDAH.

3. *Charleston News and Courier*, 4 March 1907; Daniel E. Huger Smith, Alice R. Huger Smith, and Arney R. Childs, eds., *Mason Smith Family Letters, 1860–1868* (Columbia: University of South Carolina Press, 1950), xx, 7, 44–47; D. E. Huger Smith, *A Charlestonian's Recollections, 1846–1913* (Charleston: Carolina Art Association, 1950), 117–22; Suzanne Cameron Linder, *Historical Atlas of the Rice Plantations of the ACE River Basin—1860* (Columbia: South Carolina Department of Archives and History, 1995), 400.

4. James Campbell to Alexander Campbell, 5 March 1866, CFP-SCDAH.

1867, he moved to and rented the nearby Smithfield plantation, which he "kept . . . for two years at a trifling rent."[5]

By 1870, James Campbell had purchased a plantation of his own in Lowndes Township, Colleton County, South Carolina. James's plantation, nearly 1,500 acres located on the Ashepoo River, proved a very lucrative investment, producing thousands of pounds of rice per year.[6] James continued to buy land along the Ashepoo over the next 20 years, concentrating on an area near the Chessey and Horseshoe Creeks; at the time of his death in 1907, James's Ashepoo River plantation had grown to just over 2,300 acres.[7]

By 1882, James Campbell, now a wealthy and successful rice planter, had reestablished his primary residence in the city of Charleston at 1 Laurel Street, where he lived with a servant; in 1902, he relocated to 1 Ashe Street.[8] For the rest of his years, James planted his land and actively participated in both the Union Light Infantry Charitable Association and the St. Andrew's Society of Charleston, which he joined in June 1884.[9]

James Campbell, who never married, died at his Ashe Street residence on 2 March 1907 at the age of 74. Eulogized as a "gallant son of Scotland, who proved a valiant defender of his adopted Southland," James Campbell was laid to rest at Magnolia Cemetery, "where so many who worthily wore the grey are buried."[10] In his will, which was drafted two weeks before his death, James left each of his siblings the sum of $50 and named Mary A. Miller, a niece who had nursed him during his final illness, sole recipient of the remainder of his substantial estate.[11]

---

5. Smith, *A Charlestonian's Recollections*, 126.

6. *Charleston News and Courier*, 4 March 1907; 1870 Federal Census, Agricultural Schedules, Colleton County, Lowndes Township, South Carolina, pp. 11–12, line 31.

7. Colleton County Deed Book 28, pp. 154–55, South Carolina Department of Archives and History, Columbia, S.C. Campbell also sold parcels of land from 1873 to 1904, including Cockfield Plantation, located on the Combahee River some two miles north of Smithfield Plantation. Linder, *Historical Atlas*, 144.

8. James Campbell's servant was Rebecca Deas, a literate black widow who was born in South Carolina. 1900 Federal Census for Charleston County, South Carolina, Enumeration District 110, sheet no. 21, line 73–74; W. H. Walsh, ed., *Walsh's Charleston, S.C., City Directory, 1903* (Charleston: The W. H. Walsh Directory Company, Publishers, 1903), 270.

9. *Charleston News and Courier*, 4 March 1907; Membership Register, St. Andrew's Society of Charleston.

10. *Charleston News and Courier*, 4 March 1907.

11. At the time of his death, James Campbell's estate was valued at $49,745.30. Will of James Campbell, Box 470, Will Book W, p. 266, 5 March 1907, Probate Court of Charleston County, South Carolina; *Charleston News and Courier*, 4 March 1907; War-

By the end of the Civil War, Alexander Campbell, still a young man at age twenty-eight, had resumed his life with Jane and their three sons in New York City. After a failed attempt in September 1864 to join the Veteran Reserve Corps, in which disabled Union veterans unfit for field service could serve in noncombat positions, Campbell continued his pre-war work as a stonecutter.[12] On 26 January 1865, Alexander Campbell was granted a four-dollar-per-month invalid pension for the wound he had received at the Battle of Chantilly.[13] Campbell's injured left leg never completely healed—frequent swelling, numbness, and stiffness of his calf and ankle plagued him for the rest of his life.

Tragedy struck the Campbell family during the winter of 1865. On 19 November, the eldest and the youngest of Alexander and Jane's three sons, John and James, died from illness. Alexander, Jr., the Campbell's only surviving child, died three weeks later.[14] Upon learning of the deaths

---

rant of Appraisment for Executor, In Re Estate of James Campbell, Book M, p. 574, 20 June 1907, Probate Court of Charleston County, South Carolina.

12. The board of five officers who decided against Campbell's admission into the Veteran Reserve Corps issued the following report: "The Board having carefully examined Alexander Campbell Late 2d Lieut. 79th New York Vols. upon General Education, Intelligence, Knowledge of Tactics, Regulations, Articles of War, Discipline and Service Finds him deficient in Knowledge of Tactics, and after mature deliberation, Decides not to recommend him for a commission in the Veteran Reserve Corps, but believing that he possesses merit and capacity, the Board recommends him to correct his deficiencies and apply for a second examination." No evidence survives to indicate that Campbell ever took the Board's advice. Office of the Board of Examination of Officers of the Veteran Reserve Corps, Report of the Examination of Alexander Campbell, in Compiled Service Record of Alexander Campbell; H. Wilson, *Wilson's New York Commercial Register for the Year Ending May 1, 1864* (New York: John F. Trow, 1864), 141.

13. The amount which Alexander Campbell received each month as a pensioner increased from $4 to $6 on 13 February 1878, to $12 on 6 February 1907, and to $15 on 26 November 1907. After Alexander Campbell's death, Jane Ralston Campbell continued to receive his pension; on 8 September 1916, the rate was increased to $20 per month. Pension Case File of Alexander Campbell.

14. Accompanying the death notice of John and James Campbell in the *Scottish American Journal* was the following poem:

> No more with their little prattle
> Shall they greet their father's return.
> No more with their little tattle
> Shall they lighten the hearts that mourn.
> But God is the Heavenly Father
> Who foldeth his arms of Love
> Round little ones whom He doth gather
> To the innocent's home above.

Scottish American Journal, 2 December 1865. No notice for Alexander, Jr., ran in the *Scottish American Journal* following his death three weeks later.

of his nephews, James Campbell wrote the following lines in a letter to Alexander: "I can sumpathy with you in your loss of your 3 nice Boys. Johney I was perticularly Struck with. He had the sagasetty of matured age and a cool manly bearing which is rarely found in one of his years."[15]

In 1866, Alexander and Jane moved from New York City to Hartford, Connecticut. On 1 September 1866 (four years to the day after Alexander's wounding at the Battle of Chantilly), Jane gave birth to a boy, whom they named in memory of their eldest son, John (2d). In 1867, the Campbell family moved again, relocating this time to Middletown, Connecticut, where they would spend the next thirty-five years.

Soon after their arrival in Middletown, Alexander Campbell found employment as a partner in a local stoneworking business, where he worked for nearly three years. In 1870, he and his brother-in-law James Ralston established their own business, the short-lived Campbell & Ralston stone yard, opposite the Hartford and New Haven Railroad Depot.[16] Campbell & Ralston became even more of a family business with the addition of Campbell's brothers-in-law William Ralston and David Mathie (husband of Jane Ralston's sister Jeannette), who, with James Ralston, shared a house with Alexander and Jane Campbell and their children in downtown Middletown.[17]

The Campbell and Ralston partnership had ended by 1872, at which time Alexander Campbell went into business for himself. For the next thirty-four years, Alexander's stoneworking business, of which he remained the sole proprietor, proved very successful—the products of Campbell's work, done in a variety of American and foreign stones, were "seen on every hand" in Middletown. Not only did he assist in the construction of many prominent business, residential, and educational buildings in Middletown and other nearby cities, but his "finely executed monumental and cemetery work" was amply displayed in a number of local and neighboring cemeteries.[18]

In addition to his prolific work as a stonecutter, Alexander Campbell found time to join and participate in Middletown's Post 53 of the veterans organization of the Union army, the Grand Army of the Republic (G.A.R.), and to maintain his connection with the 79th New York Highlanders through membership in the regimental veterans' associa-

---

15. James Campbell to Alexander Campbell, 6 March 1866, CFP-SCDAH.
16. Bigelow, *The Middletown Tribune, Souvenir Edition*, 29; *Middletown Directory for 1871–1872* (Hartford: Geo. L. Coburn Steam Print, 1871), 16.
17. 1870 Federal Population Census for Middletown, Conn., p. 159, Dwelling 833.
18. Bigelow, *The Middletown Tribune, Souvenir Edition*, 29.

tion.[19] He and Jane also added two more children to their family: their first daughter, Jennie M., was born on 21 August 1868; Clementine M. was born on 24 February 1871. In 1906, Alexander Campbell left Middletown and moved his family back to New York City.[20]

Alexander Campbell lived with Jane and their two oldest children at their residence on W. 128th Street for three years, until, on 2 February 1909, he died of pneumonia at the age of seventy-one; he was buried two days later in the family plot at a New York City cemetery.[21] Jane Ralston Campbell continued to live at their New York City home for another ten years, until her death on 4 November 1919, at age seventy-six.[22]

Jane's brother James Ralston relocated to Chicago sometime after his business partnership with Alexander Campbell came to an end. James married but had no children; he died on 5 August 1905.[23] Her other brother Matthew returned to Scotland after the Civil War, married twice, and had two children. He died sometime before his brother James.[24]

The last surviving letter between the Campbell brothers was written by James on 20 October 1886. In it he discusses a recent earthquake in Charleston, the status of his plantation, "trouble" with their sister Ann, and a proposal previously made by Alexander to erect a monument over their parents' graves. James was particularly enthusiastic about his brother's idea for the monument and urged Alexander to "see to it & have it don." As for the funds to pay for its construction, James wrote that he believed their brother John, although elusive and aloof as always, would assist them. Their brother Peter was dead, and, as James pointed out to Alexander, "Of corse Peters widow cant assist [us] she being too poor." The inability of others in the family to contribute significantly to the monument should not impede the project, urged James, because he was "in a position if necessary to pay the whole bill."[25]

James concluded by discussing Alexander's recent "enquirery about

19. Alexander Campbell Pension Case File; "Veteran Association 79th Regt. Highlanders, N.Y. Vols., November, 1890," Harris Collection, Brown University Library.
20. Alexander Campbell Pension Case File; *Middletown and Portland Directory, 1906* (New Haven: The Price & Lee Company, 1906), 37.
21. *Penny Press* (Middletown, Conn.), 6 February 1909.
22. Alexander Campbell Pension Case File.
23. Probate File of James Ralston, Box 3, file 8294, docket 86, p. 244, Probate Court of Cook County, Illinois (hereafter cited as James Ralston Probate File).
24. James Ralston Probate File; General Index of Marriages for Scotland (1873–1874, 1878–1881), New Register House, Edinburgh, Scotland.
25. James Campbell to Alexander Campbell, 20 October 1886, CFP-SCDAH.

stone cutting" in Charleston. "You propose coming here this winter," responded James. "I would be glad to see you," he continued, "but If you come Ex[p]e[c]ting Stone cutting I fear you will be disopointed."[26] Although the Campbell brothers almost certainly remained in contact for the rest of their lives, it is unknown whether Alexander traveled down to Charleston that winter or ever saw his brother James again.

What is most intriguing about this last letter between the Campbell brothers is, as was the case with all of their previous Civil War correspondence, that which is conspicuously absent from its pages. No hint of residual bitterness or resentment stemming from their past participation on opposing sides during the Civil War is communicated. For those who have read their Civil War letters, this should come as no surprise. In truth, no such ill feelings ever existed between James and Alexander, who, in the springtime of their lives, had performed what they perceived to be their duty to their respective adopted countries and causes, and, most importantly, never resented each other for doing so.

"I hope to god that he and I will get safe through it all," wrote Alexander Campbell to his wife shortly after his near encounter with his brother James at the Battle of Secessionville, "and he will have his story to tell about his side and I will have my story to tell about my side."[27] Thankfully, their story will continue to be told in their own words, indefinitely preserved through their surviving Civil War correspondence.

---

26. Ibid.
27. Alexander Campbell to Jane Campbell, 25 June 1862, CFP-SCDAH.

APPENDIX A

Chronological Listing of Letters

Key to terms: AC=Alexander Campbell; Jane=Jane Ralston Campbell;
JC=James Campbell; PC=Peter Campbell; HQ=Headquarters.

CHAPTER ONE:

1. 4 June 1861	AC to Jane	Georgetown College, D.C.
2. 12 June 1861	AC to Jane	Georgetown College
3. 22 June 1861	AC to Jane	Georgetown College
4. 29 June 1861	AC to Jane	Georgetown College
5. 5 July 1861	AC to Jane	Camp Lochiel, Va.
6. 11 July 1861	AC to Jane	Virginia (Camp Weed)
7. 26 July 1861	AC to Jane	Washington, D.C.
8. 28 July 1861	AC to Jane	Washington, D.C.

CHAPTER TWO:

9. [3 September 1861]	AC to Jane	[Washington, D.C.]
10. 6/8 September 1861	AC to Jane	Chain Bridge
11. 9 September 1861	AC to Jane	Camp Advance, Va.
12. 13 September 1861	AC to Jane	Camp Advance
13. 21 September 1861	AC to Jane	Camp Advance
14. 26 September 1861	AC to Jane	Camp Advance
15. 4 October 1861	AC to Jane	Camp Advance
16. 7 October 1861	AC to Jane	Camp Advance
17. 10 October 1861	AC to Jane	Camp Advance
18. 13 October 1861	AC to Jane	Camp Big Chestnut, Va.
19. 16 October 1861	AC to Jane	Camp Big Chestnut
20. 18 October 1861	AC to Jane	Camp Big Chestnut

CHAPTER THREE:

21. 23 October 1861	AC to Jane	Steamship *Vanderbilt*
22. 13 November 1861	AC to Jane	Off Port Royal, S.C.
23. 4 December 1861	AC to Jane	Bay Point, S.C.
24. 16 December 1861	AC to Jane	Port Royal Ferry, S.C.
25. 21 December 1861	AC to Jane	Port Royal Ferry
26. 31 December 1861	AC to Jane	Port Royal Ferry
27. 5 January 1862	AC to Jane	Beaufort, S.C.
28. 10 March 1862	AC to Jane	Beaufort
29. 2 April 1862	AC to Jane	Beaufort
30. 12 May 1862	AC to Jane	Beaufort
31. 22 May 1862	AC to PC	Beaufort
32. 31 May 1862	AC to Jane	Beaufort

CHAPTER FOUR:

33. 10 June 1862	AC to Jane	James Island, S.C.
34. 13 June 1862	AC to Jane	James Island
35. 16 June 1862	AC to Jane	James Island
36. June 1862	JC to AC	James Island
37. 25 June 1862	AC to Jane	James Island
38. 15 July 1862	AC to Jane	Steamship *Mississippi*
39. 20 July 1862	AC to Jane	Newport News, Va.
40. 25 July 1862	AC to Jane	Newport News
41. 29 July 1862	AC to Jane	Newport News
42. 31 July 1862	AC to Jane	Newport News
43. 5 August 1862	AC to Jane	Steamship *Atlantic*
44. 10 August 1862	AC to Jane	Fredericksburg, Va.
45. 4 September 1862	AC to Jane	Emory Hospital, D.C.
46. 9 September 1862	AC to Jane	Emory Hospital

CHAPTER FIVE:

47. 15 January 1863	AC to Jane	Fredericksburg, Va.
48. 25 January 1863	AC to Jane	Fredericksburg
49. 31 January 1863	AC to Jane	Fredericksburg
50. 11/13 February 1863	AC to Jane	Fredericksburg
51. 19 February 1863	AC to Jane	Newport News, Va.
52. 28 February 1863	AC to Jane	Newport News

53. 4 March 1863	AC to Jane	Newport News
54. 8 March 1863	AC to Jane	Newport News
55. 13 March 1863	AC to Jane	Newport News
56. 18 March 1863	AC to Jane	Newport News
57. 31 March 1863	AC to Jane	Lebanon, Ky.
58. 10 April 1863	AC to Jane	Lebanon
59. 13 April 1863	AC to Jane	Lebanon
60. 20 April 1863	AC to Jane	Lebanon
61. 29 April 1863	AC to HQ	Green River, Ky.
62. 29 April 1863	AC to Jane	Green River

CHAPTER SIX:

63. 9 November 1863	JC to AC	Johnson's Island, Ohio
64. 17 January 1864	JC to AC	Johnson's Island
65. 6 February 1864	JC to AC	Johnson's Island
66. 29 February 1864	JC to AC	Point Lookout, Md.
67. 18 June 1864	JC to AC	Point Lookout
68. 10 July 1864	JC to AC	Fort Delaware, Del.
69. 26 July 1864	JC to AC	Fort Delaware
70. 18 August 1864	JC to AC	Fort Delaware
71. 17 September 1864	JC to AC	Fort Delaware
72. 5 October 1864	JC to AC	Fort Delaware
73. 18 October 1864	JC to AC	Fort Delaware
74. 4 November 1864	JC to AC	Fort Delaware
75. 9 January 1865	JC to AC	Fort Delaware
76. 5 May 1865	JC to AC	Fort Delaware

Appendix B

LETTER FROM MATTHEW RALSTON TO ALEXANDER CAMPBELL

The following is from a copy of the original letter found with the Campbell Family Papers, SCDAH.

In front of Richmond
Oct. 21st 1864

[Alexander Campbell]

Well Sandy, as I have not much to do this afternoon I guess I may as well write a few lines to you, and let you know how I am getting along.

We had a nice little fight one day last week, and I ratherly think we came off second best. Our Battery was engaged about two hours and I tell you we did plow through the Johnies for a while, but our infantry had to fall back, and so had we. We had to do the same old job covering the retreat, and we made the Rebels jump I tell you, but we got all safe into camp and we have lay here ever since—but then we do not know the moment that we have to get up and go on the double quick, for they are eternally on the run here.

Man Sandy! I like the Artillery first rate, there is no knapsacks to carry here, and it is mighty seldom that we are in among the little bullets. It is nice to be about a mile and a half from where they are fighting, and you going in like Sixty; this Battery has been out for three years, and they have only lost two men yet. We were laying in the breast works but we were taken out to go on that humbug of a fight that took place, and we have been laying back in the rear ever since. They are a fine lot of fellows in the Battery. They have been very good to me since I came here. The Orderly Sergeant that was on James Island is Captain now, and a good fellow he is too.

I am getting along very quick with my drill. We have very hard times just now, mounted drill for one hour and a half in the morning, and when we come in, one hour of standing gun drill and in the afternoon we have one hours gun drill again, but it is nice fun. I am a great favorite with the men. There is no rum sucking here Sandy. There is the greatest difference in the World between this Battery and the 79th Regiment. The men have to show some respect for their Superior Officers here, which I am sure the men of the 79th had not for their Officers. Everything goes on here as nice as anything.

Sandy, do you ever see Harry Hutchinson? For if you do, you can get that ten Dollars from him, which I lent to him, the day that I got my bounty, and if you do get it, you can give it to my Mother. Harry will give it to you if he has it.

Now Sandy, perhaps you will be saying that I was a damned fool for enlisting again, but I dont think I was. If I had worked to the day of Judgement I never could have made five or six hundred dollars, and what is more of it, I like soldiering any how, and I like it better now than ever I did.

There was a salute fired last night in honour of that Victory of Sheridan's in Shenandoah Valley and I tell you there was some firing for about an hour out of all the guns, along the whole line from the Jame[s] River to Petersburgh. I dont know exactly how far that is, but I think it is all of fifteen miles of earth work. There was some fun. The Rebs' did not fire a single shot.

I think the war will soon be over, for they are getting hammered every place they are, and if we could only close them in Richmond the way we did at Vicksburgh, then the war would be over.

You can tell my father that I got his letter with the receipt of the box in it, but the box has not come yet. There is a crowd of them coming every day. Sandy, you must not think of enlisting again. There is enough here when I am here, but I think that I will soon be home again, for the war will soon be over.

Give my respects to Henry and Matty, and all the rest of them. I think that I can say no more at present, only you must write soon and let me know how you are getting along.

"Matt Ralston"

1st Light Battery C. V.
Light Artillery Brigade
10th Army Corps
Fortress Monroe V. A.

You must write soon and send me a couple of stamps, for you can not get any here. Tell Mother that I am first-rate, fifty times better than if I was at home.

"Matthew"

Appendix C

Agricultural Holdings of James Campbell

From the 1870 Federal Census, Agricultural Schedules, Colleton County, Lowndes Township, South Carolina, pp. 11–12, line 31, SCDAH.

Acres of Land:

      1. Improved.......380
      2. Woodland.......500
      3. Other Unimproved.......600

Present Cash Value:

      1. Of Farm.......$5,000
      2. Of Farming Implements and Machinery.......$26
      3. Total Amount of Wages Paid During The Year, Including Value of Board.......$5,000
      4. Livestock:
      Horses (2)
      Mules and Asses (12)
      Milk Cows (3)
      Other Cattle (23)
      Swine (3)
      Total Value of Livestock.......$1,420
      5. Produce (during the year ending 1 June 1870):
      Bushels of Indian Corn (1000)
      Bushels of Sweet Potatoes (25)
      Pounds of Rice (330,000)
      Total Value of All Farm Production.......$10,358

BIBLIOGRAPHY

PRIMARY SOURCES

Manuscripts and Government Documents:
Brown University Library
    Harris Collection
Center for Archival Collections, Bowling Green State University (CAC-BGSU)
    Johnson's Island Military Prison Records (MS 22)
Confederate States of America War Department. *Regulations for the Army of the Confederate States, 1863.* Richmond: J. W. Randolph, 1863; reprint, Harrisburg, Pa.: The National Historical Society, 1980.
Fort Delaware Society
    Fort Delaware Prison Records
New Register House (Edinburgh, Scotland)
    General Index of Marriages for Scotland
    Old Parish Registers
    Census Records
National Archives
    Record Group 15. Records of the Veterans Administration
        Pension Case Files
    Record Group 94. Records of the Adjutant General's Office
        Compiled Military Service Records
        Carded Medical Records
    Record Group 109. War Department Collection of Confederate Records
        Compiled Military Service Records
        Selected Records of the War Department Relating to Confederate Prisoners of War
New-York Historical Society
    Todd Box
New York State Adjutant General's Office, *Annual Report of the Adjutant-General of the State of New York for the Year 1861.* Albany: C. Van Benthuysen, Printer, 1862.

176

————. *Annual Report of the Adjutant-General of the State of New York for the Year 1901.* Serial No. 29. Albany: J. B. Lyon Company, State Printers, 1902.

Official Records of the Union and Confederate Navies in the War of the Rebellion. 31 volumes. Washington: Government Printing Office, 1894–1922.

Probate Court of Charleston County, South Carolina
  Will of James Campbell
  Warrant of Appraisement for Executor, Estate of James Campbell

Probate Court of Cook County, Illinois
  File of James Ralston

Roll of the Dead: South Carolina Troops in Confederate States Service. Columbia: South Carolina Department of Archives and History, 1995.

South Carolina Department of Archives and History
  Campbell Family Papers and Photographs 1860–1886
  Colleton County Deed Books

South Carolina Historical Society
  Wilmot G. DeSaussure Collection

St. Andrew's Society of Charleston, South Carolina
  Membership Register

Thomas, John P. "The Raising of Troops in South Carolina for State and Confederate Service." *Reports and Resolutions of the General Assembly of the State of South Carolina* 1 (1900): 7–89.

United States Census
  1860 Federal Population Census for New York City
  1860 Federal Population Census for City of Charleston, South Carolina
  1870 Federal Agricultural Census for Colleton County, South Carolina
  1900 Federal Population Census for Charleston County, South Carolina
  1900 Federal Population Census for Middlesex County, Connecticut

United States War Department. *Revised Regulations for the Army of the United States, 1861.* Philadelphia: J. B. Lippincott & Co., Publishers, 1862.

War of the Rebellion: A Compilation of the Official Records of the Union and Confederate Armies. 129 volumes. Washington: Government Printing Office, 1880–1901.

Newspapers:

Charleston Daily Courier
Charleston News and Courier
Military Gazette (New York)
National Tribune (Washington, D.C.)
New York Herald
New York Times
New York Tribune

Bibliography

Penny Press (Middletown, Conn.)
Scottish American Journal (New York)

Memoirs, Regimental Histories, Letters, Diaries and Other Sources:

Billings, John D. *Hardtack and Coffee, or The Unwritten Story of Army Life.* Boston: George M. Smith and Co., 1887.

Blackburn, George M., ed. "The Negro as Viewed by a Michigan Civil War Soldier: Letters of John C. Buchanan." *Michigan History* 47 (March 1963): 75–84.

Buel, Clarence Clough, and Robert Underwood Johnson. *Battles and Leaders of the Civil War.* 4 volumes. New York: The Century Co., 1888; reprint, Harrisburg, Pa.: The Archive Society, 1991.

Casey, Silas. *School of the Soldier and Company.* Vol. 1, *Infantry Tactics for the Instruction, Exercise, and Manoeuvres of the Soldier, a Company, Line of Skirmishers, Battalion, Brigade, or Corps d'Armée.* New York: D. Van Nostrand, 1865.

Corcoran, Michael. *The Captivity of General Corcoran.* Philadelphia: Barclay & Co., 1865.

Crawford, Samuel Wylie. *The Genesis of the Civil War: The Story of Sumter, 1860–1861.* New York: Charles L. Webster & Company, 1887.

Donlan, H. F., ed. *The Middletown Tribune, Souvenir Edition: An Illustrated and Descriptive Exposition of Middletown, Portland, Cromwell, East Berlin, and Higganum.* Middletown, Conn.: E. F. Bigelow, 1896.

Eve, F. Edgeworth, Charles C. Jones, Jr., and H. D. D. Twiggs. *Defence of Battery Wagner, July 18th, 1863: Addresses Delivered Before the Confederate Survivors' Association in Augusta, Georgia, on the Occasion of Its Fourteenth Annual Reunion on Memorial Day, April 26th, 1892.* Augusta: Chronicle Publishing Company, 1892.

Everson, Guy R. and Edward W. Simpson, Jr., eds. *Far, Far from Home: The Wartime Letters of Dick and Tally Simpson, Third South Carolina Volunteers.* New York: Oxford University Press, 1994.

Hayne, Paul Hamilton. "The Defense of Fort Wagner." *Southern Bivouac* 1 (1885/86): 599–608.

Heller, J. Roderick III and Carolynn Ayres Heller, eds. *The Confederacy Is on Her Way up the Spout: Letters to South Carolina, 1861–1864.* Athens: The University of Georgia Press, 1992.

Lusk, William C., ed. *War Letters of William Thompson Lusk.* New York: William Crittenden Lusk, 1911.

McClellan, George B. *McClellan's Own Story.* New York: Charles L. Webster and Company, 1887.

McMorries, Edward Young. *History of the First Regiment Alabama Volunteer Infantry, C.S.A.* Montgomery: The Brown Printing Co., 1904.

Middletown and Portland Directory, 1890–91. New Haven: Price, Lee & Co., Publishers, 1890.

Middletown and Portland Directory, 1906. New Haven: The Price & Lee Company, 1906.

Middletown Directory for 1871–1872. Hartford: Geo. L. Coburn Steam Print, 1871.

Murray, J. Ogden. *The Immortal Six Hundred: A Story of Cruelty to Confederate Prisoners of War*. Roanoke, Va.: The Stone Printing and Manufacturing Co., 1911.

Priest, John Michael, ed. *From New Bern to Fredericksburg: Captain James Wren's Diary*. Shippensburg: White Mane Publishing Co., 1990.

Rhodes, Robert Hunt, ed. *All for the Union: The Civil War Diary and Letters of Elisha Hunt Rhodes*. New York: Orion Books, 1985.

Rivers, William James. *Rivers' Account of the Raising of Troops in South Carolina for State and Confederate Service, 1861–1865*. Columbia: The Bryan Printing Co., State Printers, 1899.

Sherman, William Tecumseh. *Memoirs of General William T. Sherman*. New York: D. Appleton & Company, 1875; reprint, Bloomington: Indiana University Press, 1957.

Smith, D. E. Huger. *A Charlestonian's Recollections, 1846–1913*. Charleston: Carolina Art Association, 1950.

Smith, Daniel E. Huger, Alice R. Huger Smith, and Arney R. Childs, eds. *Mason Smith Family Letters, 1860–1868*. Columbia: University of South Carolina Press, 1950.

Stevens, Hazard. *The Life of Isaac Ingalls Stevens*. 2 volumes. Boston and New York: Houghton, Mifflin and Company, 1900.

Stevens, John Austin, ed. *The Union Defence Committee of the City of New York: Minutes, Reports, and Correspondence*. New York: The Union Defence Committee, 1885.

Todd, William. *The Seventy-Ninth Highlanders: New York Volunteers in the War of Rebellion, 1861–1865*. Albany: Press of Brandow, Barton and Co., 1886.

Walsh, W. H., ed. *Walsh's Charleston, S.C., City Directory, 1903*. Charleston: The W. H. Walsh Directory Company, Publishers, 1903.

Wilson, H. *Trow's New York City Directory for the Year Ending May 1, 1859*. New York: John F. Trow, 1859.

———. *Wilson's New York Commercial Register for the Year Ending May 1, 1864*. New York: John F. Trow, 1864.

Wood, James H. *The War: "Stonewall" Jackson, His Campaigns and Battles, the Regiment as I Saw Them*. Cumberland, Md.: The Eddy Press Corporation, 1910.

Woodward, C. Vann, ed. *Mary Chesnut's Civil War*. New Haven: Yale University Press, 1981.

SECONDARY SOURCES

Books, Articles and Pamphlets:

Adams, James Trunslow, ed. *Dictionary of American History.* 6 volumes. New York: Charles Scribner's Sons, 1940.

Beard, William Arley, III. *History of the 79th New York Cameron Highlanders, 1859–1876, With a Treatise on the Uniform and Equipment.* Strawberry Plains, Tenn.: Strawberry Plains Press, 1996.

Berlin, Ira, and Herbert G. Gutman. "Natives and Immigrants, Free Men and Slaves: Urban Workingmen in the Antebellum American South." *The American Historical Review* 88 (December 1983): 1175–1200.

Bilby, Joseph G. "Blue Bonnets Over the Border: The 79th New York Highlanders in the Civil War." *Military Images Magazine* 3 (July-August 1984): 5–14.

Boatner, Mark M., III. *The Civil War Dictionary.* New York: David McKay Company, Inc., 1959.

Brennan, Patrick. *Secessionville: Assault on Charleston.* Campbell, Calif.: Savas Publishing Company, 1996.

Burton, E. Milby. *The Siege of Charleston, 1861–1865.* Columbia: University of South Carolina Press, 1970.

Cooling, Benjamin Franklin, III, and Walton H. Owen II. *Mr. Lincoln's Forts: A Guide to the Civil War Defenses of Washington.* Shippensburg, Pa.: White Mane Publishing Company, 1988.

Davis, William C. *Battle at Bull Run: A History of the First Major Campaign of the Civil War.* Baton Rouge: Louisiana State University Press, 1977.

Department of the Navy, Naval History Division. *Civil War Naval Chronology, 1861–1865.* Washington: U.S. Government Printing Office, 1971.

Easterby, J. H. *History of the St. Andrew's Society of Charleston, South Carolina, 1729–1929.* Charleston: Walker, Evans & Cogswell Company, 1929.

Ernst, Robert. *Immigrant Life in New York City, 1825–1863.* New York: King's Crown Press, 1949.

Faust, Patricia L., ed. *Historical Times Illustrated Encyclopedia of the Civil War.* New York: Harper and Row, Publishers, 1986.

Fowler, William M., Jr. *Under Two Flags: The American Navy in the Civil War.* New York: Avon Books, 1990.

Fox, William F. *Regimental Losses in the American Civil War, 1861–1865.* Dayton: Morningside Bookshop, 1974.

Frohman, Charles E. *Rebels on Lake Erie: The Piracy, The Conspiracy, Prison Life.* Columbus: The Ohio Historical Society, 1965.

Gallman, J. Matthew. *The North Fights the Civil War: The Home Front.* Chicago: Ivan R. Dee, 1994.

Grant, William, ed. *The Scottish National Dictionary.* 10 volumes. Edinburgh: Riverside Press Limited, 1941–1976.

Hennessy, John J. *The First Battle of Manassas: An End to Innocence, July 18–21, 1861.* Lynchburg: H. E. Howard, Inc., 1989.

———. *Return to Bull Run: The Campaign and Battle of Second Manassas.* New York: Simon & Schuster, 1993.

Jackson, Kenneth T., ed. *The Encyclopedia of New York City.* New Haven: Yale University Press, 1995.

Jeffrey, William H. *Richmond Prisons, 1861–1862.* St. Johnsbury, Vt.: The Republican Press, 1893.

Johnson, John. *The Defense of Charleston Harbor, Including Fort Sumter and the Adjacent Islands, 1863–1865.* Charleston: Walker, Evans & Cogswell Co., Publishers, 1890; reprint, Germantown, Tenn.: Guild Bindery Press, 1994.

Linder, Suzanne Cameron. *Historical Atlas of the Rice Plantations of the ACE River Basin—1860.* Columbia: South Carolina Department of Archives and History, 1995.

Linderman, Gerald. *Embattled Courage: The Experience of Combat in the American Civil War.* New York: The Free Press, 1987.

Long, E. B. *The Civil War Day by Day: An Almanac, 1861–1865.* New York: Da Capo Press, Inc., 1971.

Long, Roger. "Johnson's Island Prison." *Blue & Gray Magazine* 4 (February–March 1987): 6–31; 44–61.

Lonn, Ella. *Foreigners in the Confederacy.* Chapel Hill: The University of North Carolina Press, 1940.

———. *Foreigners in the Union Army and Navy.* Baton Rouge: Louisiana State University Press, 1951.

Lowry, Thomas P. *The Story the Soldiers Wouldn't Tell: Sex in the Civil War.* Mechanicsburg, Pa.: Stackpole Books, 1994.

McAfee, Michael J. "79th Regiment, New York State Militia." *Military Images Magazine* 11 (September–October 1989): 28–29.

McPherson, James M. *Battle Cry of Freedom: The Civil War Era.* New York: Oxford University Press, 1988.

———. *For Cause and Comrades: Why Men Fought in the Civil War.* New York: Oxford University Press, 1997.

———. "A War That Never Goes Away." *American Heritage* 41 (March 1990): 41–49.

Miller, Randall M. "The Enemy Within: Some Effects of Foreign Immigrants on Antebellum Southern Cities." *Southern Studies* 29 (Spring 1985): 30–53.

———. "Immigrants in the Old South." In *Dictionary of American Immigration History,* ed. Francesco Cordasco, 365–70. Metuchen, N.J.: The Scarecrow Press, Inc., 1990.

Mitchell, Reid. *The Vacant Chair: The Northern Soldier Leaves Home.* New York: Oxford University Press, 1993.

Bibliography

———. *Civil War Soldiers: Their Expectations and Their Experiences.* New York: Viking, 1988.

Monaghan, Jay. *Diplomat in Carpet Slippers: Abraham Lincoln Deals with Foreign Affairs.* New York: The Bobbs-Merrill Company, Inc., 1945.

Moore, John G. "The Battle of Chantilly." *Military Affairs* 28 (Summer 1964): 49–63.

Nevins, Allan. *The War for the Union.* 4 volumes. New York: Charles Scribner's Sons, 1957– 1971.

Newman, Edgar Leon, ed. *Historical Dictionary of France from the 1815 Restoration to the Second Empire.* New York: Greenwood Press, Inc., 1987.

Phisterer, Frederick. *New York in the War of the Rebellion, 1861 to 1865.* 3d edition, 6 volumes. Albany: J.B. Lyon Company, state printers, 1912.

Porteous, Alexander. *The History of Crieff, from the Earliest Times to the Dawn of the Twentieth Century.* Edinburgh and London: Oliphant, Anderson & Ferrier, 1912.

Price, Marcus W. "Ships that Tested the Blockade of the Carolina Ports, 1861–1865." *American Neptune* 8 (April 1948): 196–241.

———. "Blockade Running as a Business in South Carolina during the War between the States, 1861–1865." *American Neptune* 9 (January 1949): 31–62.

Robertson, James I., Jr. *Soldiers Blue and Gray.* Columbia: University of South Carolina Press, 1988.

Rose, Willie Lee. *Rehearsal for Reconstruction: The Port Royal Experiment.* New York: Oxford University Press, 1964.

Severin, John P. and Frederick P. Todd. "79th Regiment, New York State Militia, 1860–1861." *Military Collector and Historian* 8 (1956): 20.

Shannon, Fred A. *The Organization and Administration of the Union Army, 1861–1865.* 2 volumes. Gloucester, Mass.: Peter Smith, 1965.

Sifakis, Stewart. *Compendium of the Confederate Armies: South Carolina and Georgia.* New York: Facts on File, Inc., 1995.

Silverman, Jason H. "Stars, Bars and Foreigners: The Immigrant and the Making of the Confederacy." *Journal of Confederate History* 1 (Fall 1988): 265–85.

Smith, Robert Ross. "Ox Hill: The Most Neglected Battle of the Civil War, 1 September 1862." In *Fairfax County and the War between the States,* Fairfax County Civil War Centennial Commission. Vienna, Va.: Fairfax County Civil War Centennial Commission, 1961.

Stauffer, Michael E. *South Carolina's Antebellum Militia.* Columbia: South Carolina Department of Archives and History, 1991.

Stockton, Robert P. *Information for Guides of Historic Charleston.* Charleston: Arts and History Commission, 1975.

Wert, Jeffry D. "Mutiny in the Army." *Civil War Times Illustrated* 24 (April 1985): 13–19.

Wiley, Bell I. *The Life of Billy Yank: The Common Soldier of the Union.* Indianapolis: Bobbs-Merrill, 1952.

———. *The Life of Johnny Reb: The Common Soldier of the Confederacy.* Indianapolis: Bobbs-Merrill, 1943.

Wilson, W. Emerson. *Fort Delaware.* Institute of Delaware History and Culture Pamphlet Series. Volume 4. Newark: University of Delaware Press, 1957.

Wise, Stephen R. *Lifeline of the Confederacy: Blockade Running during the Civil War.* Columbia: University of South Carolina Press, 1988.

———. *Gate of Hell: Campaign for Charleston Harbor, 1863.* Columbia: University of South Carolina Press, 1994.

Wood, Edwin O. *History of Genesee County, Michigan: Her People, Industries, and Institutions.* 2 volumes. Indianapolis: Federal Publishing Company, 1916.

INDEX